THE POLITBURO HAS DECIDED THAT YOU ARE UNWELL

John Waters

The Liffey Press

Published by
The Liffey Press
Ashbrook House, 10 Main Street
Raheny, Dublin 5, Ireland
www.theliffeypress.com

A catalogue record of this book is
available from the British Library.

ISBN 1-904148-46-8

The author and publishers are grateful to *The Irish Times* for permission to
reproduce articles previously published in the newspaper.
All articles © *The Irish Times*, except where otherwise stated.

Printed in the Republic of Ireland by ColourBooks Ltd.

CONTENTS

II
Millennial Revisions:
Changes and Contradictions

III

John Waters is Unwell:
Sex, Spuds and Rock 'n' Roll

For my mother, my sisters and my daughter.
With love and gratitude.

THE HEADS OF THE SOCIALIST MURDERERS

T HE PHYSICAL CELLS OF THE BODY are in a state of constant re-
newal and replacement, so that, if I understand things correctly,
the entire body is renewed once every seven years. Yet, in the matter
of opinion, society appears to regard as more virtuous a clinging to
old viewpoints, to what is dubiously termed "consistency", and to
fully paid-up membership of a singular outlook or ideology. I have
never subscribed to any such outlook, although from time to time I
have found myself allied with people who have, and who think me
one of them, and indeed have been criticised by people of a different
viewpoint for holding to a view which, clearly, they imagine to have
some permanent attachment to my being. I tend to hold views firmly
while I hold them, but then, inevitably, in response to life's relentless
torrent of change and suggestion, I move on, sometimes leaving my
erstwhile allies with a sense of betrayal. Since I became a member of
the Irish commentariat, at the beginning of the 1990s, my fluctuations
have occurred in public, and have, from time to time at least, attracted
a perhaps disproportionate degree of notice on that account.

I have always been a bit too conscious of how opinions attach
themselves to me in the first place to be over-surprised when they
prise themselves away again and become replaced by others. What
we think or believe is not us, but the material by which we form our
future selves. It is acquired for all kinds of good and dark reasons,
including circumstance, influence, imitation, emulation, reaction,

1

neurosis, pain, shame, hate and, sometimes, love of someone else.
Sometimes I form my views of things by observing and working out
why other people have arrived at their perspective, and then construct
my own on the basis of whether or not I believe them to be reliable
guides. Sometimes I look at a consensus, be it ever so apparently
axiomatic, and regard with suspicion that so many people find it convenient to believe in the same thing, and then, disliking mobs, I edge
away in the opposite direction.

There is a tendency in our society to assume that the reason people change their opinions is that they become older or more comfortable, i.e. that they acquire a vested interest in maintaining a certain
view of the world — the syndrome perceived as "moving to the right
in middle age". There may be some truth in this, but not as much as is
alleged. What it is, I have found, is a reflection of the discovery in the
individual of his own mortality and of the brevity of his life compared
to how he saw it when young. At twenty, a human being may see the
world as capable of infinite change, and the views he forms are
weapons to assist in this reconstruction. Behind this desire, though it
is often couched in terms of idealism, is a wish to make the world a
better place to live in. This, in common with much we do, think and
say, can be a selfish impulse. At a young age, a package of outlooks
forms in the heart, soul and mind of an individual and becomes his
toolbox for this project. And because time has, to a youthful perception, a quality of relative protraction, many of us acquire in our twenties a sense that the views we hold are settled ones, that they represent
us in some distinctive way, and that to review them as we grow may
be evidence of dilettantism or caprice.

But growth is impossible without change of some form, and, often
after a period of extended adherence to ill-fitting views, we move on.
In middle age, we gradually arrive at a perception of life which is
utterly different to the way we may have seen it at twenty. It seems
shorter, less responsive to our interventions. Our idealism and utopianism tend to come under review. Rather than devoting our energies
to the wholesale renovation of a flawed world, we begin to look

pragmatically at the little things we might do to make things better around us. This happened to me in my forties. Up until then, my views had been a slightly customised version of the standard liberal-left outlook. I believed in the state, the concept of social intervention, but also, without perceiving any contradiction, believed in the freedom of the individual to do more or less as he or she pleased. To the extent that it seemed relevant, I believed in the feminist analysis of human relations. I poked fun at the inconsistencies and weakness of liberalism, but in truth was a liberal myself.

The role of the newspaper columnist is not merely to fill space with entertaining copy. The job also involves a brief to challenge orthodoxies, make new connections and, all the time, to assert the right of life and its logic to dominate the formulation of public thought. This is both an objective and a subjective endeavour: the columnist deals with public facts and events, but he or she does so from a singular perspective, a particular lived life within the society, and brings to everything the personal perspective based on experience that turns technocratic issues of law and policy into a language of human aspiration and desire. A columnist who fails to do this is but a propagandist for the way things are. In my view, many of my colleagues in the commentariat have in recent times taken to repeating the same mantras and messages, implying that they are confronting and challenging established orthodoxies, when in truth the monoliths in question have already been dissolved and replaced by new orthodoxies, which my colleagues actually support and therefore refuse to question. In doing so, they have abnegated their duty to the truth, and so have become part of a new establishment pretending to be in opposition while all the time it is in power.

I have this strong sense that all the things that, as a young man, I yearned for in the public life of my society — leftist thinking, liberal policies, youth-centredness — and which I never really believed would be adopted by a majority, have now been absorbed into the core belief systems of the present. Because I have an instinctual resistance to any form of monolith or consensus, I believe I would have been suspicious of these developments regardless of personal experience. As it happens, my personal experiences have conspired to galvanise me against them and against the new ideologies they have unleashed into the public thoughtstream for their own protection.

In his celebrated essay "The Power of the Powerless", Václav Havel described ideology as "a specious way of relating to the world". Ideology, he argued, from the perspective of one who has spent his life fighting precisely this phenomenon in the white heat of its totalitarian incarnation, is a vital element of a relatively new way of wielding power. Modern forms of dictatorship, Havel maintained, do not require what he termed "a Ugandan bandit" to assert their will over large numbers of people. Power, rather than being vested exclusively in the regime, is in reality a kind of collusion between the regime and those who, by their acquiescence or silence, agree to their own subjugation because they are afraid or because there is something in it for themselves. The weight of power is not uniformly spread, but neither is it confined to a despot or tyranny at the top. It is vested in a multitude of minor interests and compromises, and largely asserts itself through the control of public thought. Ideology forms a bridge between the regime and the people, offering rationalisations for the discrepancies between what the public conversation would claim to be the truth and what life tells in its own voice, a means of creating the illusion that "the system is in harmony with the human order and the order of the universe". Ideology, Havel argued, "offers human beings the illusion of an identity, of dignity, and of morality while making it easier for them to *part* with them", in effect enabling us to conceal the truth of what we are and what we truly know from the evidence of the world and our lived experience of it. The great enemy of culture and human society is not weapons of mass destruction as much as the scleroticisation of public thinking as a result of contamination by ideologies in ways that makes it possible for great wrongs to be justified as right, as reparations or as necessary evils.

The proper role of the commentariat, therefore, is to provide opposition, not so much to the government, or the established church, or even "the system", but to "the regime" in a much more profound sense, in the sense of a power establishment which, though largely invisible, may have acquired control over the most vital levers of society's machine, and, through the promulgation of its ideologies, succeeded in holding them. The role of the columnist is to say No, to refuse to agree, to answer back, to pose a different question, to publicly announce that the emperor, or the empress, is wearing no clothes.

Dissent, dissidence, does not have to take on great subjects or epic themes — the very essence of it belongs to the banal and the everyday, where free speech begins. Unless you have truth and free speech in the minor ways, it is impossible to have these things when you need them in the big ways. But moreover, many of the issues I have tackled in the past decade are in truth the most vital in the intimate relations of men, women and children, and are perforce the most important in the canon of human concerns.

Conventional wisdom has been hijacked to exclude — by rendering unacceptable — notions that are no more nor less than common sense. And there is a clear distinction to be made between conventional wisdom and common sense. The first might be called the state of collective indoctrination, whereas the second is that more profound layer of understanding which in modern societies becomes buried under the ideologies of the day. The role of the columnist, again, is to say those things that many people in their heart of hearts believe but had come to understand were no longer acceptable ways of seeing things. In many things, the views I have articulated, and which are reproduced in this book, are only exceptional because they have been deemed unacceptable by the regime. In a lifetime or so, people will read this book and be amazed that anyone thought its contents remotely controversial.

I reckon that I have had three key moments in my life which changed completely how I viewed the world and how it should be regarded. All were public moments, in a sense, and all were personal, in a deeper sense. I believe, along with the founding feminists, that the personal is political.

The first was a moment I shared with more than half the world, watching the Berlin Wall come down. Up until then, I had, as I say, regarded myself as something of a socialist. In common with many of my generation, I felt the world would be a better place if run on left-wing lines. There were, of course, a number of inconvenient aspects to this belief, not least the reality of actually existing socialism in Eastern Europe, but the failures, and even the abuses of this were readily ascribable to the paranoia of the West and the inhospitality of the Cold War. Even after the wall came down, I continued to imagine that it was possible to separate out the socialism that had failed in reality and the theoretical model that had not yet been tried.

Then, in 1990, I went to Prague to cover the first post-revolutionary Czechoslovakian elections for *The Irish Times*. There, I met a man about my own age, named Ivan, who lived in a beautiful small apartment just around the corner from Narodni Street, where the November 1989 revolution had started when a students' march in memory of a dead hero was attacked by police.

How many people now remember the reports that emerged in the wake of that revolution to the effect that this incident had actually been engineered from Moscow by the KGB, on Mikhail Gorbachev's direct command? It appears that there were fears in the Kremlin that the communist regime in Prague had become so hardline that the inevitable full-blooded revolution would result in the removal of communism and the termination of the link with the USSR. Gorbachev's plan was to infiltrate the Czech student movement so as to bring about a controlled rebellion which would allow the existing regime in Prague to be replaced by a more moderate, reformist administration of the Kremlin's choosing — still socialist, but socialism with a human face.

The scheme was, if anything, too successful. The student demonstration was put down by the police and the word went out that a student had been killed. Within days, the revolution was unstoppable. In fact, the "student" had been a member of the KGB, who had infiltrated the student group, and who lay down and pretended to be dead so as to provoke precisely the situation that resulted. But the plan began to backfire when none of the people Gorbachev wished to put in place were willing to serve, and the result was the removal of the communist regime and its replacement by a fully democratic administration under Václav Havel.

But, in the arcade of a shop on Narodni Street, at the point where the bogus student had fallen, an impromptu altar was created. In accordance with tradition, people came to pay tribute at the altar and to light candles in memory of the fallen hero. Soon, hundreds, perhaps thousands of candles were burning there around the clock. Soon, too, the candle wax became something of a social menace, pouring onto the street and blocking up the drains. My friend Ivan succeeded in having himself placed in charge of the problem, with instructions to clean up the altar every day and remove all the excess candle wax from the sidewalk. Soon, he had quite a store of the stuff. A mixture of every conceivable colour of candle, it had fused together in a shite-coloured brown.

Then Ivan had an idea. He bought himself a number of bronze busts of the communist leaders of Czechoslovakia and the USSR, still readily available in only-just post-communist Prague. From these he made moulds, into which he poured the candle wax, making new candles in the shape of the heads of Lenin, Stalin and the erstwhile Czech tyrant Klement Gottwald. He called his products "Gottwalds" (pronounced "Gottvolds"), and began selling them to the many curious visitors being attracted to Prague at that time.

When I was leaving Prague after the election to return to Dublin, Ivan accompanied me to the airport. On the way out in the taxi, I couldn't help noticing that he was carrying a somewhat conspicuous cardboard box, which he refused to discuss in any serious way. When we reached the airport, he handed me the box, saying: "You must bring to Ireland the heads of the socialist murderers."

It was at this moment that any illusion about socialism melted away from me forever. For what struck me immediately was the banality of my own clinging to an ideology which, for Ivan and his countrymen and women, was an ideology of death. Literal death, certainly, but also other kinds of death, rendering Czechoslovakia "a Biafra of the spirit" in Havel's powerful phrase.

The second moment that changed me was a more elongated one, stretching through much of my forties, amounting to the slow realisation that, in a certain respect, I was a second-class human being. Like many men of my generation, I had subscribed completely to the idea of what was termed women's emancipation. I would rarely have dared to describe myself as a feminist, but I undoubtedly subscribed to a broadly liberal-feminist worldview, and my essential views on relevant matters were pretty much indistinguishable from most of the feminists I knew. I agreed with the feminists that women in history, and right up to the present, had had a pretty bad deal at the hands of men, and that the relationship between the sexes was characterised by a gross imbalance of power and opportunity. For these sins I condemned all men, apart, oddly enough, from myself. I reckoned, I suppose, that my willingness to acknowledge the past wrongs of my sex was sufficient to exonerate me from any responsibility for the, as I would have seen it, continuing injustice towards women. Any feminist acquaintance, seeking to gain support for her condemnations of the evils of patriarchy would have found herself pushing an open door with me. As a journalist I gave voice to these ideas in a fairly consistent manner, and as an editor I was more than willing to provide space to feminists to promulgate their views.

And then I became a father and discovered almost overnight that most of what we were peddling was humbug. Within days or weeks of the birth of my child, it began to dawn on me that, whatever had been happening between the sexes, and however society had formed its arrangements in this regard, the picture was, at the very least, nothing like as one-sided as I had previously accepted. As an unmarried father, I found myself without even the most basic legal entitlement to conduct a worthwhile relationship with my own child. On discovering this, as I have frequently outlined, I immediately headed back to the place where I had last seen my liberal-feminist cohort and urged them to *Come quickly!*, for they would never guess what I had just stumbled upon. What I had stumbled upon, in my own certain view, was a clear instance of the kind of injustice and inhumanity that, as left-liberal-feminists, we had railed against for so long. The only difference was that the victims on this occasion were not women and children, but men and their children, but that didn't matter — did it? — because the principle was what was important after all. A little breathless at my discovery, I poured out my story, whereupon my erstwhile cohort set about trying to kick my head in.

As I began to reflect and read more and more about the subject, it slowly came home to me that the idea, which I had taken for granted all my life, that the world operated on the basis of the oppression of women by men was one of the greatest hoaxes of the twentieth century, an elaborate tissue of Orwellian lies. And so, for several years at the end of the second millennium, I found myself writing publicly about things I could not believe: that in a supposedly modern, civilised society (whatever that is), abuses of fundamental human rights were taking place on a routine basis which, in another context, would be condemned outright by those who now and here sought to defend them. Nothing I have written about has attracted so much opprobrium, but it seemed to me that few things in the world could matter so much, so I couldn't stop. In some way, I believe, I was hoping someone would be able to explain to me that it wasn't true, that I was seeing it all wrong. But, to my dismay as much as to my increasing disbelief, I found that the responses to my observations were based not on factual refutation but on *ad hominem* assault. What was being questioned was not so much the factual basis of what I was saying as my right to say it at all, my state of mind in saying it, my emotions, my motivation, my masculinity, my personal relationships with women, my sex life. Although I was, for perhaps five years, subjected to almost constant splenetic attacks from representatives of the ideology I had identified and begun to question, it has often occurred to me that, without the concept of misogyny, they would have precious little in their armoury. I cannot recall a single deconstruction of my views on these matters that stuck to the facts, systematically deconstructed my arguments and exposed their weaknesses. I have, however, a drawerful of cuttings of personal attacks, snide commentaries and, indeed, a handful of grotesque defamations. One leading feminist writer, whom I had for several years imagined to be a friend, used the knowledge of my personal life she had accumulated in the course of our relationship to portray me as someone who was writing what he was writing because he had been embittered by his personal experiences. In perhaps the ugliest piece of journalism I have ever provoked, this former friend began her sneaky tirade by attacking my use of facts: "Never begin an argument with John Waters unless you have command of the facts to back that argument. And not just the facts but the source of the facts. And not just the source of the facts but the willingness to accept that there are alternative facts and alternative sources for facts which you have either been too intellectually lazy to seek out or too prejudiced to accept." This, you might say, could be used as a workable set of riding instructions for any journalist seeking the truth about anything, but, for this individual, it was the basis of an assault which she clearly imagined would find favour among her chosen audience. I have no doubt she was correct. Having thus dismissed the concept of fact, she then sought out the safer ground of daubing me as someone so "seared" by personal "trauma" as to be an unreliable witness.

A good friend, reading such tirades, remarked that they reminded him of a story he had heard from one of the eastern-bloc countries during the Cold War, about one of the local party members who started to get uppity and make speeches critical of the Kremlin. An envoy was despatched from Moscow who sat the malcontent down, looked him in the eye and declared: "The Politburo has decided that you are unwell."

And so I was, in my early forties, visited by a feeling that has not yet gone away, and probably never will. I would describe that feeling as akin to mourning someone deeply loved, except in this case what was being mourned was the innocence of certain beliefs — in justice, truth, honesty and decency in the public realm. These values, it seemed to me, which I had taken for granted for most of my adult life, were not present in the way I had imagined — unconditionally and indivisibly — and so could not really be said to exist at all. I still feel the same, except that, at another level, I accept that life must go on. I worry sometimes about what I am supposed to teach my child about what she should expect to find in the public domain of the values I once took for granted. I am frequently visited by an almost surreal feeling, for example when speaking about politics or social affairs in a public context, perhaps on radio or television, and find that I have reverted temporarily to my old way of perceiving the world. It is as though the memory of what I have discovered has disappeared, allowing me to talk about politics or democracy or freedom or justice, as though these concepts still had the meaning for me that they once had — and then I recall that, even to this day, the laws and legal system of my own country refuse to recognise one of the most fundamental elements of my own humanity, and I am bereft yet again, sitting or standing right there, with my mouth wide open.

The third episode that changed me, as it changed so many people in the world, was 11 September 2001. Beyond all contest, the column of mine which attracted the most responses appeared two weeks after the devastation of the World Trade Centre, when I wrote about the most heartbreaking image of my life: a photograph in a magazine of a man and woman jumping from one of the towers hand-in-hand. I described their descent, speculated about what had preceded it and shudderingly considered what might have passed between them in the moments before they jumped and just before they hit the ground. A few local pedants wrote to inform me that it was a "simple" matter of the temperature in the building as the fire reached the height of its frenzy. But most people who got in touch had got the point and expressed their sense of identification, grief, horror and, humblingly, gratitude to me for enabling them to comprehend the event at some more personal level. It moved me greatly that many were women, and many were also from the United States. A self-confessed hard-bitten female media colleague from the US wrote: "I hope with all my heart

you are right, that they're laughing at how little they had been prepared to settle for. The idea gives me comfort and I occasionally go
back to your column. I read it for two reasons, the first being, to make
sure it still moves me, because if it doesn't, I know this job has hardened me too much, and the second, to get to the end of it, where I can
find that little piece of hope and hold on to it."

Other readers sent poems, some by other people, some they'd
written themselves.

> We fell like stars
> Through the pain
> Through the memory
> We fell like stars.

Like so many others, I had watched the events as they happened
in the company of someone I loved far more than I am capable of loving a thought, a belief or a political idea, and was overcome by the
thought that, with a slightly different spin of the die, this person
might have been plummeting to the Manhattan pavement. I have no
doubt that this is why it became for me a life-changing moment. As
Camus observed: asked to choose between those we love and even
the most refined and beautiful ideas, we will choose the ones we love.

A couple of weeks later, I revisited the theme to express a view,
based on my new sense of the meaning of things, that Irish neutrality
had reached the end of its relevance. My thinking, if I can summarise it
at all, was that September 11 had made a luxury of objective moralising about international conflict. In the past, I believed, we had properly
reserved our right to stand back from any potential conflict and debate
its merits and our responses on the basis of rights and wrongs. September 11 posed a new and simpler question: whose side are we on?

The response to these ruminations ranks with the most viciously
vituperative and personalised I have received. People I had never
heard of wrote to tell me that I had "disappointed" and "betrayed"
them. Some speculated on how much of a backhander I had taken to
write the column. Others decided that I had written it to fall in with

the editorial and commercial agenda of *The Irish Times*. One reader wrote to diagnose venereal disease.

I don't really know why it is that people react so strongly to the fact that someone else has ceased to agree with them about something. Perhaps it is the ideology's way of protecting itself from attack. Perhaps it is that, deep down, none of us is sure to what extent what we believe about anything is based on much other than prejudice, fear and a desire for the approval of others. Perhaps someone moving to a different perspective has somewhere in it an accusation of our own lack of resolve, or courage, or willingness to face the hardened arteries of our own beliefs.

In any event, the pieces republished here, though not entirely chronologically, are together a representation of a journey that might simultaneously be characterised as a journey from youth to age and from death to life.

The pieces in this book are the bones of my newspaper work over a decade from the mid-1990s to early 2004. Most of them are taken from *The Irish Times*, for which I have written a weekly column since 1990. Most of the pieces are more or less in the form in which they originally appeared, but occasionally, for the purposes of the present collection, I have merged a number of separate articles on the same subject. Here and there, I have reverted to slightly earlier drafts of columns than the one which appeared, undone some of the work of over-zealous sub-editors, or engaged in my own economies in the interests of clarity, accuracy or, very occasionally, taste.

John Waters, February 2004

I

The Notorious Crime:
Men and Fatherhood,
Women and Sisterhood

I

MEN HAVE NO ONE TO BLAME
BUT THEMSELVES

S OMEONE MUST HAVE BEEN telling lies about the average adult
male because, without having done anything wrong, he awoke
one morning to learn that he had been forgiven. What was he to do?
Accept the forgiveness with gratitude and relief that at least he was
not now going to be banished from human society? Or risk opening
the wound again by restating his innocence and demanding a fair
trial? It was a difficult dilemma. Most of his compadres had given up
the fight, and some had even begun to curry favour by giving evidence against their own sex. The chances of unconditional acquittal
were remote, because any attempt to defend himself would have been
regarded as adding to the sins of the past. Much better to plead diminished responsibility and invite some mercy by not wasting the time of
the court.

After four decades of onslaught from feminism, the western male
is a beaten docket. It might not appear so on the surface — in certain
superficial ways, men still appear to be dominant — but the underlying reality is of a rapidly disintegrating male psyche. And so, while
feminists still talk about the glass ceiling and the gains that remain to
be made, men have taken down the flag and slipped quietly into their
shells. Men still appear to have power, but it is the hollow appearance
of control. While the battle was underway, a massive change was happening to the nature of power, which was moving out of the hands of
human beings and into the less tangible command of impersonal

forces. Women who climbed the greasy pole found that it wasn't what they wanted, but by then it was too late because men had found that it wasn't what they wanted either. Nobody seemed to know what to do next. Moreover, because what was laughingly described as a dialogue had become a clash of opposites rather than a genuine effort to achieve harmony and synthesis, the final collapse of the alleged patriarchy's tottering edifice would leave behind nothing but a pyrrhic victory for women and a heap of rubble where the supposedly male-dominated society used to be.

But it was all right. The male could begin to feel good, because after all he had been forgiven. The less strident of the victors were extending the hand of friendship, acknowledging that not all men were brutes, wife-batterers, paedophiles or sadists. A few, it appeared, were not so bad if you kept a close eye on them. Sister Stanislaus Kennedy wrote in *The Irish Times* that women should "embrace those men who are trying to be better". Now that man had been conquered, it was time to accept his surrender, though under certain conditions. These included the condition that each and every man take personal responsibility for each and every rape, abuse and act of violence committed by each and every human being who happened to be a member of the same male sex as himself.

Men have no one to blame but themselves? It is a question. The sins of human beings who happen to be male are indeed manifold. They are the sins of power and its abuse. They are the sins of absolute power corrupting absolutely. Perhaps if the truth be told, they are the sins of mankind rather than the sins of men, but such speculation is not admissible as evidence. They are the wrongs of those with power and responsibility in a frail and sinful world. The statistics are not kind to the male. Often, where there was wrong — violence, incest, rape — he, or one of his fellows, was in the frame. Strangely, or per-haps not, in an age of individualism, in which not only was everyone supposed to be responsible for his own destiny, but the spirit of the age was to deny collective culpability for some of the most heinous atrocities in the history of the world, the male alone among types or peoples found himself lumbered with collective guilt, shouldering the blame and shame for the transgressions of a few who also called themselves men. The circumstantial evidence was overwhelming, as was the power of the supposition that everything might be different if only women were in charge. It would be a brave man, or an even braver woman, who would suggest the possibility that all that would result from a reversal of roles would be an interchange of culprits.

Men have no one to blame but themselves. It is a statement of literal truth. If upwards of four times as many young men take their own lives as do young women, perhaps it is because the adult male has no one to blame. Women accuse, point the finger, lay the blame firmly at the door of some man, men or men in general. (Much of feminism, you might say, simply elevated this syndrome to the condition of politics.) But a man has nowhere to go to pass the buck. And so, in the quiet of the night, he takes a gun, puts it in his mouth and pulls the trigger. What is not so often remarked about male suicides is the often graphic nature of their symbolism: while women tend to favour drug overdoses, men take away their own meaningless lives in ways that have self-accusing meaning, throwing themselves off high-rise buildings or annihilating their brains with humane killers. If you spend some time around a coroner's court, you get to thinking that men would blow their balls off except that this has a low success rate as a means of self-termination.

The language of self-defence is a minefield of political incorrectness. Men had better button their lips except to whisper agreement with the Judases who apologise on behalf of their sex. We had better put out of our minds any thought of pleading Not Guilty, never mind of counter-accusation. There is no word in everyday use for the female equivalent of a misogynist, and to attempt to coin one would itself be an indictable offence of misogyny.

And so, to the question of punishment. It is already in hand. At first, men thought that their punishment was to be a little unsettling confusion. Having been conditioned to behave in a certain way by a society comprising both men and women, they were now being blamed and accused for doing as they had been told. They were told they were powerful when they felt no such thing. Some of them had no power at all, not even the power to buy themselves a packet of fags, because they had no job and no money, but this did not save them from being harangued by women who manifested many of the characteristics with which they labelled men. I must be powerful, they decided, if everyone is telling me I am. They were accused of being rapists and abusers, but had no memory of any of these crimes. But they apologised anyway, just in case. They must have done something, for how else could they explain the torrent of accusation?

They noticed, too, that women were also confused, though for different reasons. They kept meeting these women who said they wanted equality and had no time for traditional notions of how women should behave. Men said okay, be my guest, and if there's anything I can do. And then one day the women turned around and said that what they had really wanted was children and a family and a house to live in, and all the other things which, curiously enough, tradition had ordained, and now it was too late and it as all the man's fault for not knowing what they really meant when they said they wanted equality. The woman threatened to kill herself. The man killed himself.

But that was not to be his punishment at all. That was but the crowning with thorns that preceded the scourging at the pillar and the long walk to Calvary.

His punishment was to be banishment. Banishment from the bosom of the family, yes. But more than that — banishment from the everyday company of his children. Because the war between the sexes had occurred against the backdrop of other "modernising" phenomena, both victors and vanquished awoke on the morning after to an utterly altered reality. The "traditional" family was falling apart, dividing at the seam between mother and father. And because the whole thing was occurring in a culture of recrimination, it was deemed appropriate that the consequences should reflect the appropriate levels of culturally agreed blame. The man found his economic power shrinking, as the economic power of women increased. As it decreased, he found that his entire being was diminished accordingly, for his sense of self had comprised almost nothing besides. And there was no compensatory increase in his rights in other domains, such as, for example, those in which women had traditionally been dominant.

And so, it was ordained that the man, male, father, be banished to a place of solitude, a bedsit perhaps on the edge of town, a place where, traditionally, so to speak, the refuse of the society had been deposited. From here, he had permission to venture forth, at the whim of a male judge, who in all probability had abandoned his own children in all but literal fact, on perhaps the second and fourth Saturdays of every month, to blow the horn of his second-hand car outside the house which he was still working to keep, so as to alert his children to his presence and invite them to spend the afternoon in McDonald's, without soiling the entrance to his erstwhile dwelling with his sin-stained fingers or his guilt-stained shoes.

The voices of a few banished fathers apart, it is generally thought acceptable that throughout much of modern Europe, culture and law conspire to separate fathers from their children and children from their fathers. The standard prejudice that "Men only respond lovingly to children when they're getting something back" — i.e. when the child is able to kick a ball or hold a fishing rod — enables and feeds a conventional wisdom seemingly determined to exclude any prospect of a more fruitful relationship between fathers and children. Society has ordained that the role of men be confined to the supply of spunk and spondulicks.

From time to time it was remarked that the children, too, were being punished, but this was regarded as an unavoidable element of collateral damage, and in mitigation it was pointed out that half of such children would one day be adult males. And they, too, would only have themselves to blame.

(October 1996)

2

THE GREATEST SECRET
IN THE UNIVERSE

SINCE MY BEAUTIFUL DAUGHTER Róisín was born, less than six months ago, I have found myself more in sympathy with the Labour Party. In the past, as you may recall, I have expressed scepticism when members of that party have tried to tell us that the relative they had just appointed to some public sinecure or other had got the job not on account of being related to a member of the Labour Party but because he or she was the "best person for the job". Until recently, such logic brought a thin smile to my lips, but now I understand not merely that it might be the truth but also the desperately frustrating difficulty in articulating it.

I have this problem telling people how beautiful my daughter is. I know that all babies are beautiful. And yes, I am aware that all parents believe their offspring to be the most beautiful children made by God, and that fathers are especially prone to being rendered hyperbolic by their daughters. But, you see, I have acknowledged all this and have already allowed for it. What I am saying is that, objectively speaking, Róisín Waters is the most beautiful baby there ever was. I have factored in the possible margin of error which statistical theory recommends in order to avoid running foul of probability aberrations. And at the other end of all this, I feel utterly confident in declaring that Róisín Waters is still, unquestionably, the most beautiful little girl the world has ever seen.

And still, some people refuse to believe it — that is, until they see her with their own eyes. Oh, they will nod and smile condescendingly when, in an attempt to prepare them, I say that of course Róisín is the most beautiful girl they will ever set eyes upon. I tell them that her mother and I spend most of our waking hours thinking about how ridiculously beautiful our daughter is. I say that, although I have already acknowledged how beautiful she is, it still takes me a few moments to recover every time I set eyes on her, so great is the difference between her beauty and the degree of beauty that the human mind is able to retain. I know they don't really believe me. They think I am simply saying what they would expect any father to say. But then when they meet her they just stare with their mouths open. "She is the most beautiful baby I've ever seen," they say. Even the ones who don't say it are thinking it but are too dumbstruck to speak. "What do you think I have been trying to tell you?", I say, with just the merest hint of exasperation. "Yes, but we thought you were only saying that because you are her father," they say. "I am a journalist," I reply. "I report the facts."

Of course, sometimes I detach myself from my objectivity and become simply a doting father. This state is nothing like I would have imagined, which is to say that is infinitely better than anything I have ever been told. For all of forty years I have laboured under the impression that babies are nothing but trouble. I had heard about the dirty nappies and the sleeplessness, but not about the magic of watching a human being unfold before your very eyes. I am willing to allow that, to an extent, this may have been because I was paying less than full attention. Perhaps, in the same way that I had shut myself off from the paeans of doting parents, I had let all information pertaining to the joys of parenting go in one ear and out the other. I do recall that from time to time it occurred to me to wonder why it was that people bothered to have babies at all, if it was such hard work. But now I believe the reason I have not been told how magical babies are is that this magic has been one of the great secrets of the human universe.

Men, for obvious reasons, have not known about it, and women, for even more obvious reasons, have wanted to keep it to themselves.

In truth the baby–parent relationship is almost ridiculously one-way. It is true that for those periods when Róisín is in my care, she is totally dependent on me for certain basic needs such as food and clean nappies. This is the version of the relationship we have been told about. What we have not been told is the extent to which the provision of these basic services is repaid in magic and joy. The things I bring to the relationship are as nothing compared to the things I get back. As yet, I do not even know what some of these elements are. All I know is that they are immense and that I am storing them away until I can better understand them.

Of the two of us, I am the more childish, the more troublesome, the more inadequate. I have read that certain forms of Eastern mysticism hold that babies come to Earth in a Godlike state and are only gradually infused with human shortcomings. I know now that this is true. From the moment Róisín was born, I have felt that she was already infinitely wise. She watches the world not with curiosity or wonder but with tolerance and amusement. I have never thought of her as a baby, in the sense of someone less knowing than myself. Although I know that I am expected to teach her things, in truth it is the other way around. Although I speak to her — mostly in my rudimentary Irish — I have found that silence is the best form of communication between us.

One of the things she is teaching me is how to live in the present moment. Because I have spent forty-one years living in what passes for civilisation, this trick has long escaped me. I can live in the past or in the future, often more than twenty or thirty years in either direction, but never in the now. This is the modern condition: the vacuous restlessness inculcated by advertising and market dynamics has opened a void within our souls which we try to fill with drugs of various kinds. When and where we are now is inadequate and ordinary — every other place or time or company is steeped in a seductive exoticism.

I don't believe it has been observed before that babies could be the most powerful antidote to modernity. Write it down — it's a good one. With babies, it appears, you have no choice but to be wherever you are. At the start of a day when Róisín and I are to be together, I am full of fear and apprehension on account of the responsibility involved. But once we are together, everything except the spark between us becomes dim and incidental. By the end of the day, though tired, I am totally there, and do not want it to end. Róisín is the only reality that is never disappointing.

There are two reasons why I wanted to write this. One is that it may alert other men to some things they have not been told about fatherhood. As evidenced by the amount of sneering propaganda targeted at men who would look after their children, the world is working very hard to keep us from knowing what we are missing.

Oh, and I wanted to thank God for sending us his angel.

(August 1996)

3

THE RUMMAGE FOR THE RIGHT COAT

DADDY ALWAYS SAYS GOODBYE. He stands at the gate, the door, the top of the stairs and smilingly waves day-day. He walks a little down the road, the path, the stairs, and turns to wave again. Daddy always leaves. Yes, he will return soon again, but his life is not of this place. He is of the other world outside. He is a part of your life but also apart from it. It has always been like this, but now it is more so.

I call it Raidió Róisín, the baby monitor that I place near my daughter's cot when she is asleep, to listen to in the living room. It reminds me of my own father, a traditional patriarch in a long black coat. It strikes me that it would have been an ideal way to check on him at night, on whether he was still breathing, rather than crouching at the bedroom door with my ear to the keyhole, listening for sounds that would reassure me he was still alive. He was always leaving too, which is perhaps why I worried so. He would go out in the early hours of the morning — to go, as I now understand, a-hunting. My fear was mixed with guilt on this account, for the dangers he faced were faced in part for me. Although as a child I feared for both parents, I feared mostly for him because he was not there. I listened to him leave in the morning and wondered if he would come back alive. When he said goodbye, he did so with a finger wetted with holy water from a bottle with green fungus on its neck. The echo of his sharpened nail throbbed in my forehead for as long as he was gone.

My father left our presence because he had to; the modern father leaves his child behind because he has no right not to. Today, when I say goodbye to Róisín, I do it with a wet kiss on her forehead. I do not leave in order to hunt. I simply leave. I hunt a little, yes, but from her viewpoint it is not essential. I come back empty-handed, more or less. My authority cannot derive from what I earn or what I give. As a father I have only one function: to love my daughter. Because all the existing models are now redundant, I need to learn this from the beginning.

Although conventional wisdom would have it that men have traditionally cared more for their work than for their children, the truth is that men have gone to work precisely in order to care for their children. Unfortunately, this imperative has inevitably drawn men away from direct involvement — as opposed to simple investment — in the lives of their children. Most men, according to what research exists on the subject, would much prefer to spend more time with their families, but that option has never been available. (According to US surveys, 80 per cent of working men would like to be able to take six months leave from work on the birth of a baby, to look after their children full-time.) In the past, the option was unavailable because there was hunting to be done; today it is unavailable because the culture that derived from the concept of man-as-hunter has, sincerely or otherwise, taken man's necessity for his free choice. In the old world, men had power over the external world, women over the internal world of the home. Men went out to work and women stayed home to mind the children. In the new world, women increasingly do both and the man increasingly makes his own arrangements. A woman can work in the modern workplace in the same way as any man, but a man can campaign until doomsday and never get to have a womb.

One difficulty is that, as increasing "equality" unveils the obsolescence of the traditional father, this is leading to the spurious belief that women going out to work is the reason for the crisis of fatherhood. In fact, the real problem has been that men have worked too much rather than that they now work less than they did.

Whether we like it or not, the issue focuses on different forms of power. In a world revolutionised by feminism, men find their economic power shrinking in inverse proportion to the increase in the economic power of women. But instead of the hoped-for holy grail of equality, what is emerging is an even more spectacular form of inequality. Since the domains of female power were never defined as such, but as evidence of women's enslavement, the transition from what we called patriarchy is depositing both external and domestic forms of power into the domain of the woman, and leaving a big question mark where the role of men used to be. Since it was never understood — even by men — that man's economic role was actually to do with his parenthood, this question hangs most ominously over the role of fatherhood. As the man's traditional bread-winning role is made obsolete by changing work patterns, the absence of any rules or understandings of what they did besides is leading to the effective marginalisation of fathers.

The nature of our answers is not hopeful. Men are buckling under the strain. Although I did not know it at the time, my fears for my father's welfare every time he left the house had a solid scientific basis. Although he lived to be nearly 84, he beat the bookies in doing so. Surveys in the United States have shown that, in the past 75 years or so, the gap between the life expectancies of men and women has widened remarkably. In 1920, women lived on average one year longer than men; today they live seven years longer.

Sexism against women is highly visible, but sexism against men is neither recognised nor acknowledged. Fathers, unlike mothers, have no antecedent rights by virtue of parenthood. If the reverse were true it would be a national scandal, but for the moment those who seek to redress it are swimming against the tide. Some men have recently started to organise themselves into groups, like Families Need Fathers in Britain and Parental Equality in Ireland. These groups exchange information and advice and are gradually brewing up a head of steam to bring the marginalisation of fatherhood to more widespread attention. They advise men on how to handle their defences in court, thus avoiding the bankruptcy that would make the entire exercise irrelevant. They set up day centres to which men can take their children during the hours of access, thus ensuring a safe, dry, warm and friendly environment for fathers and their children to mingle with others in the same situation. It is estimated that, every year, some 10,000 fathers find themselves facing effective banishment from the company of their children. Up to 20,000 children are added to the statistics every year. Because of the in camera rule, this remains an invisible epidemic.

An hour spent talking to a group of such men yields countless stories of discrimination and bias that would be federal issues if the victims were women. Separated men tell of being dragged through the courts by their former partners, firstly to be fleeced of any remaining economic resources and secondly to make it as difficult as possible for them to see their children. They tell, too, of a legal system that seems to see its role as the punishment of men and the veneration of women.

As with many problems, the legal difficulties facing the modern Irish father begin with the Constitution, which does not confer any specific rights on fathers vis-à-vis their children, nor indeed on children vis-à-vis their fathers. The constitutional provisions in respect of the family do give some protection to married fathers, but even these rights are in practice considered inferior to those of the mother. Moreover, the law effectively operates on a no-fault basis — which is to say that, even when the mother is to "blame" for the breakdown, she retains full rights and entitlements vis-à-vis the home and children. Almost invariably, she gets possession of the family home, which the father must continue to subsidise without retaining any right of access, even though it is the home of his children. The best a father can hope for is "reasonable" access, amounting to perhaps a few hours a week, usually taking the form of drives, walks or the fabled trip to McDonald's. A live-in boyfriend of the mother can quickly acquire de facto fatherhood of the children, with the natural father being gradually excluded.

Married fathers have limited rights, but unmarried fathers have even less. The judgement some years ago in the Keegan case, in which a young Irishman gained the right in the European Court for unmarried fathers to be consulted before their children were put up for adoption, has not yet been incorporated into Irish law. The position in our domestic law remains as stated in the case of *K v. W* (1990), which confirmed that Section 6A of the 1964 Guardianship of Infants Act does not confer on a natural father the automatic right to be guardian of his child. The Chief Justice said in that case that the extent and character of rights arising from the relationship of a father to his child in the event that he is not married should vary according to the circumstances in each individual case. "The range of variation," he said, "would, I am satisfied, extend from the situation of the father of a child conceived as the result of casual sexual intercourse, where the rights might well be so minimal as practically to be non-existent, to the situation of a child born as a result of a stable and established relationship and nurtured at the commencement of his life by his father and mother in a situation bearing nearly all the characteristics of a constitutionally protected family when the rights would be very extensive indeed."

The net result of this is that the mother has power to define the "situation" according to her own wishes, as to whether it was stable, established or otherwise. If she wishes to define the relationship as a short-term one, thereby excluding the father completely, she has the power to do this. If, on the other hand, she wishes to pursue the father for maintenance, she can do this also, while still seriously curtailing his rights of access to his children. There have been many cases of the mother having it both ways — excluding the father for a lengthy period and then seeking and obtaining retrospective maintenance for herself and the child. The mother can choose where the children will live, and she is free to move elsewhere, away from the father, with impunity.

If a father has not obtained guardianship of his children, he has no particular claim to his children in the event of the death of the mother and may have to fight the mother's family for custody. However, Section 6A of the 1964 Act does give fathers the right to apply to a court to be appointed as a guardian. The court has full discretion in this matter, and is theoretically supposed to regard the welfare of the child as the first and paramount consideration. In practice, however, the wishes and convenience of the mother get precedence. In breakdown situations, men are given custody in only the most extreme circumstances. The concept of joint custody, though gaining ground, has a long way to go before it is accepted as a plausible means of resolution in Ireland. Ninety per cent of cases result in the mother obtaining full custody, which in effect reduces the father to the status of a sort of visiting uncle. Since the mother is the one with whom the child resides, the court effectively confers on her the right to decide if and when contact will occur between the father and the child or children. This is true even in the context of the breakdown of what have been regarded as successful and happy marriages. Since most relationship breakdowns occur in acrimonious circumstances, a frequent outcome is that children are in effect held hostage by the mother in her dealings with the father. If she becomes unhappy with his performance or behaviour, irrespective of the basis of her unhappiness, she has the power to punish and banish. A court will make an order in respect of visitation rights, but a mother who seeks to frustrate the operation of this can do so with impunity. She can claim on any given day that the child is unwell, and turn the father away from her door. He is then faced with having to undertake further expensive and adversarial legal proceedings in order to restore what has been summarily taken away from him. This can go on forever.

The first thing lawyers say to fathers seeking help in gaining access to their children is, "You have no rights". A mother has the power to say to the father of her children, "I will decide whether you know your child or not", and he has no option but to accept this as an accurate summation of the legal situation. A father's best hope is to throw himself at the mercy of the mother and rely on her goodwill. If this is not forthcoming, he may as well walk away and wait until his children come to seek him out. A growing number of men are taking up this option, leading to further propaganda victories for those wishing to present men as feckless and unloving.

The overall problem is the result of an unhappy combination of bad law and a culture heavily biased in favour of mothers, with no comprehension at all of what the role of a father might be. The culture seems to presume that men are, by nature, delinquent and reluctant when it comes to direct responsibility for children. The rights of the mother are therefore considered to be synonymous with those of the child. Fathering is considered an "optional extra", a kind of service, which should ideally be provided for the child if the mother so decides, like piano lessons or judo.

But it would be wrong to see the situation as simply one of women keeping fathers away from their children. The society, through its culture, is what contrives to do so. Lazy thinking has led us to presume that female emancipation would result in equality, unity and universal harmony. Although for the moment women appear to win and men to lose, the truth is that both are equally victimised, though not as much as the children.

Men are silently attempting to redefine their roles. The problem is that they are unable to do so within the limits of a language constructed primarily to promote the idea that women are the only sex subject to discrimination. Anything a man might say to give voice to his frustration would come out in a politically incorrect form. So men keep silent, and are then accused of not expressing their feelings. When occasionally they do so, they are told that what they have said is not acceptable, and could they please try again? This article will be filed under that category, and it is likely that someone describing himself as a "new" man will be the first to make this point in public.

The New Man was a product of a search for new formulae within the existing language. Reacting against the failed patriarchal model, and finding himself with no answers to the endless stream of accusations, man beat his fallow breast and tried to fling out the chipped, enamel bath of traditional fatherhood, forgetting that it contained the baby. His baby. Because he was good, and determined to behave well, he witlessly helped create the context whereby his own children might never have access to his goodness. Confounded by the paradox of his position, he took the side of his own greatest disadvantage, wringing his hands in guilt and paying tribute to the courage and fortitude of womanhood, restating the wrongs of his fellow man until they had become as a forest of sin in which he himself, having forgotten how to hunt and climb and navigate the heights, was lost and helpless. He could not see that he himself had also been oppressed by the old world. Mea culpa, he sobbed, mea culpa, mea maxima culpa. Women had a vested interest in not begging to disagree.

Men became liabilities and all but superfluous. The man tried to make himself useful, offering to help with the nappies and other baby chores, but his presence was purely on sufferance by the women. More and more women, having obtained the requisite squirt of sperm, and the man's signature on the bank mandate, said "bye bye, sucker!"

New Man's failure to square the circle gave credence to those who said that the old ways were not just best but the sole options for existence. The pendulum would have to swing back. It was the way it was because there was no other way. The alternatives to orthodoxy were anarchy, disintegration and chaos. For quite a few men, the argument had about it a titter of plausibility, and some, rediscovering their Tarzan impulse, swung back to retrieve their long black coats.

Staring extinction in the face, Old Man and New Man accuse and harangue one another, each seeking to offload responsibility for their predicament. Old Man thinks his son lacks backbone and has failed to stand up for himself. New Man blames his father and the generations of males before him for having queered the pitch. Neither has the answer. Though they argue until Kingdom Come, Old Man and New Man could not agree. Old Man knows only one way to be Father. For him there is no discussion. The way to do it is the way it has always been done. New Man, however, offers not so much an alternative as a reaction. He knows how it should not be done. But all he offers by way of alternative is a fudge. And the long black coat hanging on the wardrobe both mocks and admonishes his woolliness. Outside the world is changing. New Man, having failed to advance a plausible fathering ethos of his own, may have no choice but to don his father's long black coat, though it is unlikely that he will concede that this means he has lost the argument.

Born into a time of maximised orthodoxy, men of my generation found themselves growing into a stratosphere of change. Pre-programmed with a sort of *Woman's Way* view of family life, in which mother stayed home and father worked all day and in the evening sat in his armchair smoking his pipe and reading a newspaper, all our efforts to realise it came to nothing. We were destined to be fathers in an era in which it was unclear what fathers actually did. In as far as we were prepared, it was with the ancient programme handed on to us by our own fathers, which we combined with a few woolly notions born of a deep hostility to that sensibility. We were determined to be different, but had no concrete ideas other than the ones we were bequeathed.

The admissible evidence against the orthodox nuclear family — child abuse, breakdown, addiction, violence of innumerable forms — was mounting and increasingly damning. The virus of violence, driven by the alleged patriarchal craving for control, which had been attacking the nuclear family from within, had burst the cork and escaped from the bottle, ricocheting through the generations in manifold forms.

The traditionalists declared that all this was the inevitable consequence of the amoral liberal society — the clamour for abortion, divorce, and other freedoms was destabilising the foundations of the nuclear family. This, too, had a ring of plausibility for, at face value at least, the evidence suggested a fairly widespread desire to throw hats, scarves and other forms of headgear at the nuclear family and seek the post-modern holy grail of limitless choice and minimal commitment.

There is another way of looking at what has been happening. To venture out at all into the acid rain of modernity, the human soul must clothe itself in garments appropriate to the blur. Perhaps rather than the fascination of the damned, what we call the postmodern condition is just a rummage for the right coat. Maybe our present confusion is an inchoate beginning to a new kind of response, which will yet mould the present chaos into new structures, at least as secure as the previous ones.

There may, in other words, exist the possibility that what we are undergoing is a positive disintegration, that, contrary to the apocalyptic prognostications of traditionalists, what we are experiencing is not the beginning of the end but the beginning of a whole new way of living, one not necessarily devoid of responsibility, though perhaps of the pseudo-responsibility which characterised the era of the long black coat. If men and women cannot live together, or at least not for the moment, and perhaps only ever again for some of the time, then we surely need to face these facts and try to deal with their consequences. Perhaps, then, we are in a period of purgation, flushing out the dirt and damage of the old and awaiting delivery of our brand new bathtub. Perhaps it is a little early for men to be getting too definitively steamed up about their banishment. But then again, perhaps the best way of abbreviating that period of banishment is to turn on the hot tap and allow the new era to blast itself into the world.

We need to begin a search for new visions, to redefine the social contract between men and women, beyond the shadow of victimology or control. But men do not know how to do this, and it is unlikely that they can do it without the help and sympathy of women. Unfortunately, the present culture tells women that, if they show weakness towards men, they will enable the rowing-back of the gains of feminism. This is why, increasingly, women are pursuing the winners-take-all options pressed on them by a sympathetic official culture and an adversarial legal system.

All men know is that they need to do something. What are fathers for? What do they do if not what their fathers did? How do they move? What do they wear?

There is no safe language available to men to express the nature of their longing to be with their children. Accused of being physically undemonstrative, they now must become less so for fear of inviting accusations of abuse. Increasingly in relationship breakdowns, it is the practice to suggest, either by accusation or innuendo, that the man cannot be trusted to be alone with his children.

A language to express a redefined notion of fatherhood can only evolve — it cannot be invented. One of the more modest objectives men need to aim for is the ability to carry out the everyday tasks of childrearing without exciting comment. There is little in the needs of a baby or child that a man cannot provide just as well as a woman, but the immense condescension of the culture continues to suggest that men are incapable, feckless, clumsy, undemonstrative and, really, not to be taken seriously when it comes to caring for children. In fact, in countries like Britain and the United States, the male is increasingly taking on the household responsibilities. Men are spending more time on housework and women less. Curiously, the extreme feminist propaganda campaign has managed to simultaneously complain about and patronise men, suggesting that they are unwilling to do the mundane work associated with child-rearing, and also that they are ill-equipped to do it. They are damned if they don't and laughed at if they do. What men are beginning to discover — too late, in some cases — is that looking after children, if you are able to dedicate yourself to it, is far more satisfying and fulfilling than almost any other form of work.

Things will change, because they have to. The rummage for the right coat will upend the smug wardrobes of orthodoxy in the culture and home, and the rigid production lines of the workplace. Both men and women have paid the price for the prevailing winds of nonsense. The search for new social forms, in which masculine and feminine sensibilities can find their most harmonic expression, must take us to hitherto unthought-of and even unthinkable places.

Because most of our present thinking, structures and ways of living developed out of the needs of the industrial society, it follows that if that form of society has reached its limits, it is time for a change of attitude. While the wrangle was proceeding between women and men, the world, left on automatic pilot, was going its own way, revolutionising the workplace and presenting mankind with a whole other set of ultimatums. Men, who for so long had the workplace virtually to themselves, were now finding themselves at home while their wives went out to work. It is estimated that, by the end of this decade, there will be more women than men working in the United States, with other western societies set to follow pretty smartly. It wasn't that men were left with nothing to do, more that the nature of economics had altered their value, changing the nature of work and the requirements of the workplace. So far, this process has revealed itself primarily in its disadvantages, but the advantages are now ripe for reaping.

Women, by virtue of their childbearing function, have a multiplicity of options — mothering, working, and various permutations of the two — while men have fewer and fewer. And because the workplace has been governed by the law of the jungle, few men have the luxury of experimenting. Those who try can risk running foul of hostile attitudes and bureaucratic structures which evolved to protect a corporate culture based on keeping men out of the house for as long as possible. We may be on the point of suddenly discovering the obvious — that men, and women, who have a happy home life make for the most effective corporate warriors.

Changes in societal attitudes and the culture of the workplace will be an essential part of any journey back to sanity. But legal changes are essential also. If we are to accept that we live in a divorce culture, should we not at least acknowledge the effects of this culture on children? This would seem to require some form of legislation that places the rights of the children to both their natural parents above the individual rights of either of the two parents to scrub the board and start again. At the moment, culture and law conspire to give the mother back as much of her freedom as possible, while utterly disregarding the rights of fathers and children. A constitutional amendment, if we could stand another such, might not be a bad place to start. Because the issue of fatherhood has primarily to do with the welfare of children, the emphasis of any such amendment should be on the right of the child to know his or her natural father, whether or not he is married to the mother. The debate would certainly help raise public awareness and provide the basis for future legislation. The introduction of the concept of joint custody for the generality of cases would restore fatherhood to its proper moral and social status.

We also need to look at the Family Courts, and in particular at their utterly unhelpful adversarial nature. A compulsory counselling system, with highly trained personnel given powers to enforce a set of guidelines designed to maximise the right of children to know both parents equally, would go a long way with those who campaign on these issues. But more than that, there is the need to educate public officialdom, from judges to social workers, in the importance of fatherhood. There would be no point in a form of compulsory counselling that would simply implement more efficiently the present skewed thinking.

It would be very stupid of the father of a beautiful little girl to paint women as the villains of the piece. It would be wrong to imply that women, still less feminists, are keeping fathers away from their children. The society, through its culture, is what contrives to do so. Woman and man are equal victims, though for the moment one appears to win and the other to lose.

We need to imagine new states of fatherhood, but have very little to go on. Do we become more like our mothers as we become less like our fathers? Is there a middle way? Is there any point in having two parents doing the same things in the same way? Will children react against a father who doesn't leave the cave to hunt for food?

Looking after babies is an immense responsibility. Men are conditioned to believe that it is beyond their capabilities. At the beginning I was fearful of the responsibility of caring for my daughter alone for even a few hours. I did not believe I could carry it off. Now I know I can. It is hard work, but there is no mystery about it. There is almost nothing my daughter needs now that I cannot give her. I can feed her, change her, bathe her, rock her to sleep, sing to her, play the melodeon while she sings or just sit and listen to her sing.

Talking to fathers who have survived the trauma of separation from and reconciliation with their children, the consensus is that the best relationship fathers have is with their adult daughters, when, having surrendered any notions of control or parental authority, they seek to know their children as people. But combining this ethos with the authority of parenthood during the formative years is something that has perhaps yet to be imagined, never mind achieved.

The modern father must be 101 per cent committed, 110 per cent available, and 200 per cent loving. In truth I have only the foggiest notion of how to be a father, and I know that probably a lot more than I imagine of what I will need to bring to it will still be stuff I picked up from my own father. It's not so much that there is only one way, but that the way it's been done up to now, however imperfect, must stand until either definitively disproved or improved upon. If in doubt, a long dark coat will still function until you have arrived at a fuller understanding of the need for a new identity. I bought one myself, just in case.

You can't go wrong with a long black coat.

(March 1997)

4

WHO NEEDS FATHERS?

TWO WEEKS AGO, *The Irish Times* carried, on its front page, the headline: "Who needs fathers when it comes to parenting?" As a father who tries to take his role seriously, the headline, and indeed the article it flagged, affronted me to my very soul. Both smacked of hate, of callousness, of irresponsibility, of indifference not merely to the feelings of half of mankind but to the consequences of present drifts for all human society. I was struck at once by my image of my daughter, who will be two in three weeks, being taken away from me, and of not a murmur of protest being raised to accompany my screams and hers.

Other fathers who are operating at the forgotten extremities of our liberal society took notice of the headline. These men, who for a cumulative aeon have been trying to love their children in the face of hostility and derision, were as horrified as I was. All I could say to those I spoke to was that I dissociated myself from the article. But as the silence reigned, as the headline settled down to find its place among the rest of the week's detritus, this response seemed increasingly inadequate.

In a healthy society, the headline would be met with the same horror as one asking, "Who needs Jews for civilisation?" or "Who needs blacks when it comes to human society?" Of course, it is unthinkable that such headlines would be published in *The Irish Times*, because Jewness and Blackness are on the list of conditions protected by our pseudo-liberal code. Fatherhood is not.

The article to which the headline referred purported to be about single motherhood. It was actually a diatribe against fathers and fatherhood, based on some new book, which I intend neither to mention nor discuss. The article was full — presumably because the book was — of the kind of half-baked statistics and pseudo-science which is invariably employed to disguise such man-hating. For those fortunate enough to have missed it, the assertion that "the average father could learn something from watching the monkeys in Dublin Zoo" was not untypical of the contents.

But I am interested in the background radiation. An individual or an institution found isolating a specific strain of humanity and subjecting it to hatred and contempt would quickly come under attack in the columns of this newspaper. A politician, for example, who attacked homosexuals or single mothers would be roundly condemned by our leader-writers and columnists.

It is at once a paradox and an inevitability that a newspaper that feels entitled to publish such hate-filled material against fathers is itself run almost exclusively by men. The Irish Times, numerically and culturally, is a male-dominated institution, albeit one intent upon self-preservation at a time when the pervasive ideas of the society — of which this newspaper is at the cutting edge — are in the opposite direction. Like many similar institutions at this modern moment, The Irish Times is deeply sensitive to its own contradictions. Although it is not intended as a criticism to observe that The Irish Times is a male-dominated institution, it will be interpreted as such by the men who run it. The fact that it is true is what will make them rush to deny it.

Of course, the fact that The Irish Times is male-dominated is inevitable, it being the product of a society that was similarly organised for many centuries, and with very good reasons. Culturally a product of British — rather than Irish — society, this newspaper reflects the general experience of the industrial world. Because industrial work was mainly of a heavy, manual nature, it was mainly done by men. Inevitably, the structures and hierarchy of society came to be what is now tendentiously termed "male-dominated".

But at this, the post-feminist moment, such institutions are beset by numerous contradictions and dilemmas. Although The Irish Times is assiduously attempting to advance as many females as it can find, the numbers do not yet add up to a gracing aspect. There is therefore a deep incongruency between the visible reality of the institution and its stated policies and outlook. Being poised at a moment of transition, it reflects the character of the old but espouses the ideals of the new. In many ways, this is indistinguishable from hypocrisy.

But an institution which cannot (yet) fully practise what it preaches can soft-focus its true nature by attacking more vulnerable elements of what is perceived as the old culture. We fathers are all of us individual human beings, relatively defenceless before God and our children. We make for easy targets to enable those seeking to cling to the old culture to show off their progressive credentials without personal cost.

The men who run *The Irish Times* know that the die is cast, that their positions are safe for only a little longer. The emerging culture of supposed equality and pluralism, which they have had such a central role in promoting, will eventually result in their own unseating. They are the last generation of men in power. Their ideology, their condition and their training tells them that this is a good thing, but their guts are filled with fear on account of their own vulnerability as human beings. Their ideal result, therefore, is the continued promulgation of their received ideologies, combined with the preservation of their positions. These objectives are ostensibly in conflict but are capable of temporary coexistence. Enabling attacks on the male sex is a way of buying time. Being poised on the precipice that marks the end of the old culture, they have a foot on the firm ground of the past, but also, through their willingness to insult other men, an insurance policy that will, they hope, protect them when the fall comes. They imagine that these years of appeasement will prompt the new regime to grant them leniency, for are they not, self-evidently, the "good men", the "nice men", the "progressive men"? I wish them well.

This explains also why the headline I mention provoked no public reaction among *Irish Times* readers. The culture and structure of *The Irish Times* reflects, generally speaking, that of the society inhabited by its readers: a society that says one thing and behaves in an altogether different fashion. The men and fathers who read this newspaper are also poised on the precipice, mostly attempting to extend the remit of the old culture for long enough to reach the sanctuary of their pensions. They live and breathe by the "culture of patriarchy" but think and speak as products of the feminist era. All day their heads are swimming with enlightened thoughts of the glass ceiling and the female eunuch, and at night they go home and have their dinners put in front of them. Although these men espouse what they consider "progressive" ideas, most of them are deeply threatened by men who talk sincerely about the process of fathering children in any more than a superficial manner. The post-industrial society has not yet come to knock on their doors.

Their pseudo-liberalism enables them also to exclude themselves from all discussion about the role or character of men. The idea that the world is full of unredeemable males, unworthy of compassion or respect, is something they feel free to support, because they are able to convince themselves that, being *Irish Times* readers who believe in progressive ideas, such criticisms could never be applied to themselves. Attacks on fathers read to them as attacks on other people.

The irony, of course, is that, although it is "other men" who are metaphysically affronted by such a headline, the ones who will suffer most are the very ones who see nothing wrong in leading attacks on their own sex. We, at least, are aware of what is happening to us, and when the hard rain comes, as it surely will, we at least will know why it is that we are expected to lie down and die.

(February 1998)

5

THE MAN WHO SAVED THE WORLD

THE WREATHED WHISPERS OF THE SISTERHOOD have issued forth for Bob Geldof since he assumed advocacy of the least PC human rights issue on Earth. I wondered if they would. He is, after all, the man who saved the world, put charisma into charity and gave rock 'n' roll back its conscience.

In an essay, "The Real Love that Dare Not Speak its Name", for a University of Cambridge Press book, *Children and Their Families: Contact, Rights and Welfare*, Geldof has attacked the bias in society's systems and culture which marginalises fathers and damages children. "The law," he wrote, "is creating vast wells of misery, massive discontent, an unstable society of feral children and feckless adolescents who have no understanding of authority, no knowledge of a man's love and how different but equal it is to a woman's."

The standard response to such interventions is to depict whoever has made them as hating woman and misusing children in the interests of power, ego and revenge. Geldof is already being targeted with both barrels.

This, he is told in the style of a nun discoursing on the Immaculate Conception, is not a male–female issue, and should not be turned into one. How an issue defined by the transfer of the natural rights of one person to the whim of another can be discussed without reference to the distinguishing characteristics of the respective parties is never explained. Similarly, a charge that men pursuing their right to parent is a misuse of children is levelled without any acknowledgment that the denial of fundamental human rights of both fathers and children is at least as damaging to children as fathers.

Inevitably, someone mentions Solomon. Geldof was the subject of one velvet-gloved assassination in a Sunday newspaper last week, when a female psychologist lectured him thus: "In the Old Testament tale about the judgement of King Solomon, two women claimed equal right to a baby. Solomon revealed the true parent when he called for his sword to cut the living child in two and give one half to one and half to the other — out of love for the child, the real mother relinquished her rights."

"Too many children," she concluded, "have already been sacrificed on the sword of inalienable 'rights'."

Two subtexts are detectable: (1) Mothers are "real" parents; fathers are not; (2) If fathers want to be seen as "real" parents, they should walk away from their children if that is what mothers decide.

Those who seek to deflect criticism of the moral corruption of family law are remarkably fond of this story, which in truth indicts precisely that which they defend. If mothers always behaved as implied, incidences of children being sacrificed on the sword of inalienable rights would be rare. It is women, overwhelmingly, who make applications to the family courts, for the simple and rational reason that family law is incentivised in their favour. Fathers respond, often because they have no choice; and usually they do so in pursuit of minimal concessions (not rights), which, even when extended by a court, are rarely enforced.

Within days of Geldof's recent appearance on *The Pat Kenny Show* to expand on his essay, the Irish government told the UN that it does not believe men should have the same rights as women in relation to guardianship, adoption, and custody of children. Fulfilling the objectives of UN conventions, it stated, "does not necessitate the extension to men of rights identical to those accorded by law to women".

If the government gave notice of its intention to discriminate against any other sub-group, uproar would ensue. The woman from the Irish Council for Civil Liberties would be on radio and TV from morning till night. An editorial in *The Irish Times* would thunder about, possibly, the wickedness of splitting the atom of justice. I do not note the absence of such responses in surprise, but simply observe that the hypocritical silence of Ireland's mouthpieces of liberal and moral indignation is the measure of what Geldof has taken on.

Thus far, one gathers he believes that the injustices he has noted are simply oversights. It appears not to occur to him that what he is describing is well known to those in power, and precisely as they intend. "Equality", he should be aware, comes in liberal society with the quotation marks attached, and removing these is more challenging than feeding the world. His decision to bring his considerable moral authority to this issue is already causing consternation in quarters which resist with extreme prejudice any challenge to their liberal gloss. If he persists, many who once spoke his name in awe will shake their heads and say what a pity it is that such a champion of the underdog has been embittered by personal experience.

(September 2003)

6

THE TRUTH BEHIND PESTER POWER

IF PROOF WERE NEEDED of how silly is the idea that attachment to certain life roles is "socially constructed", you only have to look at the characters and storylines appealing to young children. The latest craze is *Bob the Builder*, perhaps the most spectacular cartoon character success of recent times, now set to dwarf the *Tellytubbies*, *Rugrats* and maybe even *Barney and Friends*.

Bob the Builder, six months old, is already estimated to be worth £250 million. Sales of TV, video and merchandising rights have put HIT Entertainments among the most successful media companies in the UK. Bob's first single beat Westlife and Eminem to the coveted Christmas Number One spot, and the videos have also demolished all opposition. A recent article in *Investor Week* attributed Bob's success to "pester power", described as the exploitation of the increasing "purchasing power" exercised by young children.

As his name suggests, Bob is based on fairly unreconstructed notions of manhood: a wrench-wielding, hard-hatted archetype who, with friends Scoop, Muck, Lofty et al., clears up messes, gets a grip on sticky situations, saves the day and gets the job done. Meanwhile, Wendy runs the office and answers the phone. (Although, one day, when Bob has the flu and there's a major job to be done resurfacing the main road into the village, Wendy takes over and all goes smoothly until Dizzy gets stuck in some concrete.)

Children go mad for Bob in the same way as, in the past, they went mad for Postman Pat and Thomas the Tank Engine. These characters have in common their adherence to what might be termed the traditional male ethic of getting on with the job. Having worked for both CIÉ and An Post, what I observe, reading aloud the exploits of Thomas and Pat to my daughter, is how faithfully they record the spirit of the life of working men — their esteem for values like reliability, duty, co-operation, hard work and getting the job done because it is your job.

Bob, in his cunning, exploitative way, is a simple representation of what Camille Paglia has called "the sublime male poetry" of construction. Bob, to paraphrase the (sublime) Ms Paglia, ties us to Ancient Egypt, where monumental architecture was first imagined and achieved. He also brings to mind those beautiful words of Robert Bly, among the most moving ever written about loss: "Industrial circumstances took the father to a place where his sons and daughters could no longer watch him minute by minute, or hour by hour, as he fumbled incompetently with hoes, bolts, saws, shed doors, ploughs, wagons. His incompetence left holes or gaps where the sons and daughters could do better."

It is as though "pester power" is an expression of some deep hankering in the souls of our children, as though in these superficially superficial cartoon characters there is the recognition of some primal need of children, especially little boys, to encounter men who do and make things with their hands; who turn up on time — hail, rain or snow — and get the job finished; for whom the notion of service — to the public/customer/company — is a matter of pride and honour.

In his theory of language, the great American linguist and philosopher Noam Chomsky illustrated that linguistic capacity, for all the perceived difference between languages, is an innate, biological feature of the human mind. Observing that language structure follows the same deep-seated principles the world over, Chomsky demonstrated that the mind has a system of cognitive structures which develop in much the same way as the physical organs of the body. Noting many characteristics in language use and perception by children, where no relevant experience had occurred from which such knowledge could have been learned, he established that children acquire language in a manner suggesting that they are born with a large part of the linguistic apparatus already formed.

Attempts to adapt Chomsky's theories to music and other modes of expression have not moved far beyond the speculative, but his findings undoubtedly have profound implications for many aspects of human activity and expression. It is likely, as commonsense would have it anyway, that children are born with many innate and primal needs and characteristics — including what feminists call "gender-based" responses — and that these are reflected in the things they are attracted to. Such insights render nonsensical and dangerous the current emphasis on teaching which seems intent upon the deconstruction of certain unapproved elements of our culture — most notably masculinity — presumed to be "socially constructed".

Perhaps, though, we are better not drawing attention to such things, lest the feminists go after Bob. If this seems implausible, consider the case of Babar the Elephant, targeted by the custodians of political correctness in the US on account of the dangerous messages he is transmitting to the young. Babar, having lost his parents to a big game hunter, runs away from the jungle and ends up in the city, where he makes friends with a nice old lady, drives a car and wears a fetching green suit. Teachers in Massachusetts have been warned against using Babar, because he "extols the virtues of a European, middle-class lifestyle and disparages the animals and people who have remained in the jungle".

You think I'm making this up. Could I? Believe me, friends, this kind of thinking is coming soon to a kindergarten near you.

(February 2001)

7

THINKING DOUBLE

(A response to the judgement of Ms Justice Laffoy in respect of what she found was the unlawful adoption of a child by the proprietor of an adoption agency)

THE DEBATE OF THE PAST WEEK around the subject of adoption has once again touched on the doublethink of our society relating to children born out of wedlock. It demonstrates yet again how the assumptions about the relative rights of unmarried parents have been internalised to an extent that makes acceptable grotesque abuses of the human rights of fathers and children.

If I were to summarise the public perception of what is shocking about this matter, I would make a stab along the following lines: a young woman handed her child over to be adopted by the owner of a pregnancy counselling agency to which she had gone for advice, and the High Court found that the adoption was unlawful because the consent was neither informed or free and was therefore not a "real" consent.

This is fair enough in as far as it goes. The trouble is that is does not extend itself beyond the assumptions I mentioned before. To have it do so, a number of other questions would require to be asked. Foremost among these would be: Why it is that, even now that the detail of this case is public knowledge, nobody is asking why the father of Baby A was never asked if he wanted to take his child home?

Despite the moral outrage which has developed since the publication of Ms Justice Laffoy's judgement, while much attention has been focused on the alleged spiriting away of a child from its mother, little mention has been made of the fact that, morally speaking, the treatment of the child's father was far worse.

We know from Justice Laffoy's judgement that, shortly after the birth of Baby A, solicitors acting on behalf of the father wrote to the mother indicating that he wished to be made a joint guardian of his child. It seems that the mother disregarded this request, and indeed that nobody involved in the adoption transaction considered this request to have any bearing on what was being arranged.

The following sentence appears in the judgement of Ms Justice Laffoy: "The decision was made at a time when the mother had received no independent counselling or advice and, indeed, no proper advice at all in relation to the rights of Baby A, her own rights, the rights of the natural father, the law governing the care, welfare and custody and adoption of children and, most importantly, the restrictions imposed under the Act of 1998 in relation to private placements for adoption."

A cursory reading of this sentence might suggest that the issues I have raised above have been anticipated in our legal system and are being catered for now, albeit belatedly, in the legal proceedings arising out of the botched adoption attempt in the case of Baby A. It might also suggest that the Adoption Act 1998 is a remarkably enlightened piece of legislation, bestowing rights and entitlements equally on both natural parents. Such assumptions would be deeply erroneous.

The Adoption Act 1998 requires that steps be taken with a view to contacting the natural father before an adoption takes place. It does not demand that the father actually be consulted, but simply that the adoption agency "take such steps as are reasonably practicable" to consult him. If the mother withholds the father's name, it is possible for an adoption to proceed without any attempt being made to inform him. Even where contact is made with the father, the Act does not propose that he be consulted about whether or not he would be prepared to rear the child himself — only about whether he has any objections to the proposed adoption. There is no requirement in the 1998 Act to consider whether the "consent" of the father is "informed", "free" or "real".

The father, in effect, has the right to say yes to the adoption, or incur huge costs in an almost certainly doomed attempt to assert his own parenthood. In the event that he is actually consulted, and does not immediately indicate that he has no objection to the adoption, he will learn of his "potential rights" with regard to mounting a challenge to the adoption. Since a father has no automatic rights as a parent, merely the right to apply to a court for such rights, the only option open to a man in this situation is to immediately apply to the courts for joint-guardianship of his child. Without guardianship, he has no right to mount a legal challenge to the adoption. In the normal course of events, he requires the consent of the mother for an application for guardianship to be favourably considered, but it is open to him to try his luck with the court if this consent is not forthcoming. In practice, then, the only possibility of preventing an adoption of his own child resides in the likelihood that protracted court proceedings between the natural parents about guardianship and/or custody will almost certainly rule out the successful completion of an adoption. Nobody I have spoken to in this field can recall a single case in this country in which a father successfully prevented an adoption of his child and succeeded in obtaining custody for himself.

What this means, in substance and in effect, is that the mother has a virtually unchallengeable entitlement to dispose of "her" child in whatever way she pleases. She alone can decide that a child is to be banished not just from one side of his or her family, but from both. The father has no rights, other than a minor capacity to create a nuisance, which, in the Kafkaesque world of family law, would be seen as evidence that he was an unsuitable parent anyway. Thus, the clause in the 1998 Act referring to the father's right to be "consulted" is a fig leaf to conceal the State's refusal to treat all parents as equal human beings. Why is it shocking that a handful of mothers have been deprived of their children in dubious circumstances, and not at all shocking that many, many thousands of fathers have been treated far, far worse?

This element of the 1998 Act was cobbled together some four years after the State had been deeply embarrassed in the European Court, when a young Irishman, Joseph Keegan, took a case after his former girlfriend put their child up for adoption without his consent. He won the case, but did not get his child back, because the court found that in the six years it had taken to process the matter, the child had bonded with her adoptive parents and could be separated from them only at enormous emotional cost. Joseph Keegan had been willing to adopt (!) his own daughter. The mother and her family refused and the forces of the State were marshalled to deny Mr Keegan and his child their fundamental moral right to be together.

The adoption issue illustrates yet again the glaring double-standard which drives our cultural responses to unmarried parenthood in this society. Mothers are given virtually unrestricted rights over the future lives of children and simultaneously adjudged to be deserving of "compassion" and "support" no matter what they decide; fathers are either ignored and excluded or subjected to snide criticism and abuse because, usually, they will have behaved in precisely the manner the culture has dictated.

(September 1999)

8

THE SILENCE BROKEN

IN HIS COLUMN LAST TUESDAY, "Rise in family violence needs analysis", Fintan O'Toole used the previous weekend's tragedy, following which a man and his child were found stabbed to death, to condemn those who have highlighted the unjust treatment of fathers in the family law system. He listed a number of recent instances of children being, as he put it, "done to death", and concluded: "And although it is by no means an exclusively male phenomenon . . . it does seem that a majority of the perpetrators is male."

The word "seem" is interesting. In fact, most child-killings are perpetrated by mothers, who are rarely charged with this crime because there is an understanding that it is the act of a person of unsound mind. The media have entered into a similar undertaking not to report such killings by mothers as they would killings of other kinds. The silence makes possible Fintan's use of the word "seem". It would have been interesting to read his analysis of the assault resulting in a brain haemorrhage by a Limerick mother on her six-month-old son, reported in the same edition of *The Irish Times*. Judge Carroll Moran said the assaults were so abnormal that it was reasonable to think there were extraordinary factors behind the abuse and imposed a two-year suspended sentence.

Fintan, meanwhile, having constructed his straw man, went on: "The rising Men's Rights movement believes it has an explanation. It blames feminism, and in particular the operation of the family courts which it sees as a form of institutionalised discrimination against fathers." There followed a ritualistic nod towards the possibility that the alleged injustices might actually be taking place. Those who have, apparently, justified the killing of innocent children have "had an easy ride of late" because they have said things that needed saying. "They have drawn attention to the fact that men too can be victims of domestic violence, and that social attitudes can force them to suffer in silence. They have also made legitimate criticisms of the lack of transparency in the family court system. There is simply no objective information with which to test their allegations of bias against fathers in child custody cases because the secrecy of the courts does not allow for the scrutiny that every system needs. The service they have done in highlighting these two issues is considerable."

It is reassuring to know that, in the course of inciting other men to kill their children, I have been doing something useful, although I cannot recall the easy ride. I note in passing Fintan's belated acknowledgement of the truth. Regrettably, having previously criticised neither the social attitudes that force men to suffer in silence, nor the secrecy of the family courts system, his first intervention is to attack those who have spoken out.

The problem, he assures us, is not the arguments, it is "that these rational arguments often come wrapped in a hateful rhetoric that feeds the kind of paranoia, rage and infinite resentment that, in a deranged mind, can seem to justify horrific violence". There's that word "seem" again. It is clear that Fintan believes we must refrain from vehement denunciation of injustice on the off-chance that disturbed others might do something illegal.

Having conceded that he does not know the scale of injustice against fathers, Fintan goes on to allege that a "wildly exaggerated vision of a society ruled by mad feminists . . . in which men are emasculated and oppressed is being conjured up by the Men's Rights movement". He then attacks *Magill,* and an article in the November issue by Phil MacGiolla Bhain, about what Fintan calls "the appallingly high incidence of suicide among Irish men". Yes, it is appallingly high, but this is the first time Fintan has said so. "The subject," he says, "is an urgent one, and the predominance of male victims cries out for thoughtful analysis." I agree, but wonder, if he thinks it so urgent, why Fintan has remained silent about it for more than a decade. Where is his thoughtful analysis?

Fintan then rubbishes views expressed by Phil Mac Giolla Bhain, albeit having firstly attributed these to *Magill*, of which I am currently Consultant Editor. He disputes Phil's view that the elite running social policy in this State is governed by feminist ideas, quoting various statistics of female participation in senior positions. "If there is a man-hating elite, therefore, it is overwhelmingly male," Fintan argues. Well precisely — the social policy of this State is formulated and implemented largely by men who think like Fintan O'Toole.

Having suggested that those who protest about systematic denials of human rights have in doing so justified the killing of children, Fintan then claims not to have said this. "It would be absurd," he says, "to suggest that rhetorical distortions about the nature of Irish society cause anyone to kill children." Absurd is a good word, but scurrilous is better. Having made his allegation and withdrawn it, Fintan then repeats it. "What they [rhetorical distortions] do, however, is to feed into an already unstable mentality a picture of a world in which there is a vast conspiracy to deny men any kind of domestic justice. If you put wild resentment together with a paranoid sense of hopelessness, the result is bound to be explosive."

It is difficult to perceive the distinction between what Fintan is saying he is saying and what he is saying he is not saying. But is it at all possible that the resentment and sense of hopelessness he refers to are products of the injustices that Fintan, who has made a career out of denouncing injustice, refuses to condemn, as he has condemned those who have dared to expose them?

(November 2001)

9

A GUILT UNATTENUATED

U SUALLY, ONCE AN EMERGING PROBLEM is perceived, the tendency in seeking an answer is to focus on the particular factors that may point to a specific problem rather than looking at the more general picture. For example, if a particular type of aeroplane is involved in more than one crash over a short period of time, the response is to have all such aircraft pulled in and rigorously checked for faults specific to it. Never is there any suggestion that all aircraft should be grounded, or that the issue is the safety of air travel in general. This is obviously quite sensible.

And yet, when it comes to the subject of suicide, the glaring specifics are invariably overlooked, while all relevant bodies and institutions seek a generalised answer that might allow these specifics to be perhaps permanently ignored.

What is remarkable about the suicide figures that have emerged in recent years is the extent to which they indicate that the problem is primarily one concerning adult males. This, however, is one form of male domination that this society does not want to talk about.

Since 1990, there has been a fourfold increase in the number of deaths by suicide by men under the age of twenty-five. In some categories, male suicides outnumber female suicide by a factor of six or seven to one. Suicide now kills more young men, especially in the age-group between fifteen and twenty-nine, than accident or disease. For any parents of young sons, this should be a source of deep concern. And yet a society that would lay claim to compassionately responding to the requirements of its people — male and female, parents and children — wishes to brush this issue under the carpet.

These figures are even starker than they initially appear. Following steep rises through the 1970s and 1980s, the overall suicide rate has remained more or less constant since the start of the 1990s. Speaking at St Patrick's Hospital in Dublin in March 1990, the late Dr Michael J. Kelleher, a specialist in suicide issues, estimated the true rate of suicide to be "about 400 each year". In 1997, there were 433 suicide deaths. It is clear from the figures that, while other categories of people are less prone than previously to kill themselves, young men are much more liable to do so. Put another way, whereas living in our society has become more attractive to women and older men, it has become much less so for young adult males.

It should be obvious then that any discussion on this subject should be clearly focused on the fact that young men are killing themselves in ever greater numbers. This is what the problem is, and it is getting worse.

And yet, very rarely is the problem defined in these terms. Yes, there is discussion about suicide, and indeed a vague but growing sense that it is a greater problem than before. Except that it isn't, on the whole, a greater problem than before. And yes, it is now commonplace to hear the issue alluded to by politicians and commentators as one of the major issues of our time. Frequently it is couched in terms that imply that this issue is one that concerns primarily our "young people". But again, in point of fact, the major relevant issue of our time, about which we ought indeed to be concerned, is not suicide *per se*, or even suicide by "young people", but suicide by men, especially young men.

But when politicians, clerics, youth groups or even specialists in the subject come to pronounce in public on this issue, the elephant in the room — or the Jumbo falling from the sky — is almost invariably ignored. Yes, in the listing of relevant statistics, the fact that the suicide rate is now overwhelmingly male-dominated will be there for all to see. But then the discussion will go on as though this was a minor and somewhat irrelevant quirk of the statistics.

The reason for this is quite simple: it is ideologically inconvenient to a society that has just succeeded in convincing itself that only women suffer, to have to go back to basics in the manner which the suicide issue demands.

One of the most telling indicators is the fact that it has become standard to deal broadly with the subject in a way that treats as synonymous two issues generally regarded by specialists as separate and distinct. Suicide, as those who have to deal with it are fully aware, is an utterly different phenomenon from what is termed "parasuicide", or attempted suicide. However, if you deal with the issue by assuming that the two syndromes are connected, the problem suggests itself as being what is nowadays termed "gender-neutral". In general, "parasuicide" — i.e. the "unsuccessful" attempt to kill oneself — is a female phenomenon. This syndrome has a high survival rate, whereas when men "attempt" to kill themselves they rarely survive. Seen this way, it might be concluded that many more women than men actually attempt suicide, but more men "succeed". In general, it is women who threaten to kill themselves, and men who kill themselves. This idea is one the present ideology finds convenient. But if you perceive the two syndromes as two quite distinct phenomena — attempted suicide as a cry for help uttered in the hope or even certainty that help will be forthcoming, and suicide as an act of final and utter despair — then you are faced with the prospect of having to look sympathetically at men, and this is not something we are at all disposed to do.

As someone who has been writing about the maltreatment of men in this society for some time, this does not surprise me in the least. We have a society which, out of a distorted sense of what it calls "compassion", seeks always to placate and nurture what it perceives as "minorities". The problem is that, in each specific instance, these minorities are defined against a notional, unspecified majority, which is implicitly designated as being unworthy of compassion. And when you subtract the women, children, blind, infirm, insane and elderly (i.e. those minorities deserving of "compassion"), you are left with adult males, implicitly and explicitly defined as the "oppressive majority". Whereas our culture goes out of its way to tell young women on the verge of adulthood that they are, by nature, sensitive, caring, humane and compassionate, it tells its male young that they will grow up to be insensitive bastards, unworthy of sympathy or respect and possibly less than human. Young women are told that they have multiple lifestyle choices between career and motherhood, workplace and home. Young men are told that they must make way for their hitherto disadvantaged sisters and, by way of compensation for the sins of their grandfathers, forego the primal joy of fatherhood, if that is what their womenfolk decide. Young men are told that they must be strong unless where otherwise indicated; young women that the forces of the State and society will come to their rescue should anything go wrong.

Is it surprising that so many men, on the brink of the transition between childhood and adulthood, decide not to go on? As Schopenhauer put it: "It will generally be found that as soon as the terrors of life reach the point where they outweigh the terrors of death, a man will put an end to his life." Manhood is at risk of becoming a terminal illness, and the suicide statistics represent the cutting edge of this reality.

One of the traditional cop-outs about suicide has been that it is linked to mental illness. The purpose of emphasising this connection has been to spare the families of suicide victims, but also society at large, from the guilt arising from the accusation that suicide would otherwise represent. The idea that men are sicker than women would be grist to the mill of our present culture. But it is not true.

Of course, a proportion of suicide victims are people who have suffered from various mental disorders. But the vast majority have lived ostensibly normal lives, and indeed a common observation from family members of suicide victims is that they had no warning that anything was amiss. I have noticed of late an attempt to create a causal link between suicide and what is called "depression". Indeed, in an interview which formed part of a recent investigation of the suicide issue in the Catholic magazine *Reality*, Aware Chairman Dr Patrick McKeon reiterated the conventional official wisdom that the vast majority of suicide victims have been suffering from "some under-lying psychiatric problem, mainly depression or mood disorders". These remarks were widely reported, and, unfortunately, this is gen-erally as far as the headline writers seek to go. But later in the same interview, Dr McKeon spoke more specifically about the nature of what is called "depression". "Human beings, to live with themselves," he said, "actually have a natural infusion of positive perspectives on things, and that enables us to keep going in life. When that's taken away, that's actually called depression." And later in the interview: ". . . if anyone is really involved in life they are going to get de-pressed at some stage or other in their life. To anybody who says they don't get depressed . . . I say, are you really that switched off?"

This suggests that depression, in this sense, is not some clinical condition that descends on the individual as though a form of psycho-logical misfortune. It is inextricably related to the external conditions of that human being's life, and to his or her perception of these. To say that suicide victims are depressed tells us nothing. It is a tautol-ogy. Everyone gets depressed, but not everyone commits suicide. For a long time, it has been a central psychiatric belief that women have a greater tendency towards depression than men, and yet many fewer women end up killing themselves. This suggests that suicide has much less to do with depression *per se* than with the external, i.e. so-cietal, attitude to the depressed person. A depressed person who be-lieves that there is a listening ear out there is less likely to kill him- or herself than one who believes that there is not.

Close to the truth of this matter is the fact that women have an understanding with society that allows them to send warning signals, whereas men do not. Female depression and parasuicide exist in a public context of help and listening; male suicide in a public context of indifference and denial. The phenomenon of male suicide is pro-foundly linked to the paradoxical position of men in modern societies — to the fact that, while led to believe they are members of the domi-nant sex, many men, in their private experience, feel relatively power-less compared to women. Young men today live in a society that berates and denigrates their masculinity, and therefore the most fundamental element of their identities, at every twist and turn.

I am happy again to quote the late Dr Michael Kelleher, who in 1990 told the aforementioned gathering at St Patrick's Hospital in Dublin: "When an individual takes his own life it is not simply, as the Stoics thought, a personal statement; it is also a comment on the individual's social environment. With each death by suicide the question of responsibility should be considered. A society that can face questions such as: to what extent did the individual contribute to his own demise?; to what extent did his environment precipitate his death or fail to protect him from it?; to what extent was the treatment given to him inadequate for his needs?; and to what extent did society itself, including the formative forces of his youth, lead him to death by his own hand later?; is on the right pathway to better social and mental health."

Suicide, wrote Primo Levi, is born of a guilt that no punishment has attenuated. Guilt is born of shame, which in turn is born of denigration.

Manhood is now perhaps the most denigrated condition in our societies. Men, as a collective, are demonised and condemned, and nothing is said or done to reassure the innocent. Even the guilty can offload some of their individual guilt on their fellow males.

On the brink of manhood, a boy must understand that he has before him a lifetime of apologising for his existence, for his strength, for his intelligence, for his steadfastness, for his love of reason, for his lack of a womb. In the public discourse, in every conceivable way, men are shamed at every turn: in television dramas, sit-coms and adverts, in newspaper articles, in a political debate bending over backwards to appease an unappeasable feminist lobby. That these crimes against men are frequently committed by individuals themselves passing as men does little to mitigate their effects. Every holocaust has its collaborators.

(This essay is a amalgam of several pieces on male suicide published in The Irish Times *in 1998 and 1999.)*

10

THE CLAY CEILING

A RECENT *IRISH TIMES* REPORT of a conference on women's health, hosted in Dublin by the Irish College of General Practitioners and the Women's Health Council, cited a female English GP as stating that "more women than men die from diseases of the circulatory system". The clear inference arising from the need for a conference entitled "Women Taking Control of their Health" was that there exists some form of imbalance in health matters that adversely affects more women than men. Dr Ann McPherson's statement was factually true. But as an example of the distance that sometimes lies between fact and truth, it would be hard to beat.

Most years, more women than men do, in fact, die from diseases of the circulatory system. However, most of these deaths occur after the age of 75, when the average man has shoved up more daisies than he ever had hot dinners. In the long run, we'll all be dead of something or other. In an average year, roughly 35–40 per cent more women than men die from cerebrovascular disease and other diseases of the circulatory system, and about three-quarters of these female deaths occur past the age of 75. Only about 60 per cent of the men who succumb to these diseases survive past the age of 75. In every other age-group, significantly more men than women die from such forms of disease.

The pattern in relation to diseases of the circulatory system are significant only in that the male–female margins are less marked than is the case with other diseases. In other words, Dr Ann McPherson made mention of the condition that comes closest to implying that women's health is a more pressing, or a more ignored, issue than men's. In respect of all other significant conditions, the picture is much starker: men die younger and more frequently from almost anything you might think of.

It is difficult to imagine a disease that, though it could strike both sexes, tended to affect women significantly more than men, without this being alluded to at every possible opportunity. As a matter of fact, no such condition exists: all serious conditions that are capable of affecting both men and women tend to strike down men much earlier in life. We hear much about the "glass ceiling" affecting female opportunities in the workplace, and very little about the clay ceiling which awaits men long before their time.

There are some diseases — breast cancer, for instance — which affect women predominantly, and these are seldom off the news agenda. There are, by the same token, diseases — prostate cancer springs immediately to mind — which affect men exclusively, and these rarely rate a mention in public debate. Yet, prostate cancer affects men almost to the same extent as breast cancer affects women. Women are encouraged, through publicly funded advertising, to watch for early signs of breast cancer. Most victims of prostate cancer will never have heard of the disease until they have become seriously ill.

Heart disease provides the most striking example of the stark reality of this society's relative levels of concern about the health of males and females. If, without specialist knowledge, you were to get a question, in the course of, say, a game of Trivial Pursuit, about which of the sexes suffers most from heart disease, you might be forgiven for answering that both males and females were equally prone to the condition. After all, discussion of the disease in this society gives little indication that the situation is otherwise. Men and women get heart attacks, and sometimes die as a result. Indeed, in broad statistical terms, men and women are more or less equally prone to death from heart disease — except that, again, men tend to die in their youth and middle age, whereas women in general tend to die from heart failure in their seventies and beyond, by which time the average man has been dead for nearly a decade.

You would never have guessed this from the way heart disease is discussed in the media, or from special promotions by, for example, the Department of Health: invariably heart disease, like suicide, is discussed in sexually neutral terms, utterly denying the reality.

There is no Men's Health Council. Conferences about men's health are unheard of. In Ireland, as elsewhere in the western world, women's health is close to the top of the agenda for funding, research and public education; men's health is a non-issue.

There is something wrong here. After all, it is women, we are led to believe, who suffer disadvantage and discrimination in our society. It is men, we are told, who run our public institutions, including our media and our health services, allegedly for the benefit of themselves and other males. Why, then, are the dangers to men's health not highlighted in the same way as dangers to the health of women?

There is an extraordinary degree of evasion, both at official and public discourse levels, of the absolutely staggering statistical gap that exists between the physical well-being of men as compared to women. Two years ago, to mark the fiftieth anniversary of its existence, the Department of Health produced an impressive-looking book, *Reflections on Health*, containing a number of excellent essays about various aspects of health in Ireland. There were individual chapters on child welfare, health policy for women, services for the elderly, people with disabilities and the health service, and so forth. One group, however, was noticeably absent from the book, the one that, oddly enough, is most prone to premature death from all the main causes of death — men.

This was not an aberration. The approach of virtually all agencies charged with monitoring or protecting public health, throughout the western world, is to avoid mention of the startling differences between relative figures for males and females in respect of early death from major diseases. A typical quote is the following, from the World Health Organisation: "Irish men and women have the highest rate of death before the age of 65 from coronary heart disease (CHD) in the European Union — in 1993, 59 deaths per 100,000 population compared to the EU average of 32." This is true, in as far as it goes, but what it omits is that the overwhelming bulk of these fatalities are male. Women under the age of 65 die from heart disease at roughly a quarter the rate of men.

A recent survey by the British Office of Health Economics, using the same World Health Organisation figures for 1993, placed Ireland fourth in the world for premature death from coronary heart disease. In that year, Ireland had 310 deaths per 100,000 males between the ages of 45 and 64, and 82 deaths per 100,000 for females in the same age bracket. (These figures, because they relate to a smaller, maximum-risk age-segment, are obviously much higher than the overall figure for under-65s quoted above.)

To elicit this particular crumb of information from the media reports of the survey, however, you would have been better starting at the final paragraph and working back, since the main emphasis was again on the fact that Ireland now has the highest incidence of "premature death from heart disease in under-65-year-olds in the EU". The fact that the vast majority of these fatalities were males was a minor element of the story.

(October 1999)

11

A HEAVY HEART

IT IS REGARDED AS AN INDICATOR of the disadvantage of being female in Irish society until about seventy years ago that men tended to live longer than women. Since the 1930s, this pattern has undergone rapid reversal, to the extent that men now have a significantly lower life expectancy than women. Strangely, or perhaps not, this is not widely cited as evidence that men labour under a disadvantage in Irish society today. The standard analysis is that this pattern is attributable to men's inability to look after their health. Perhaps this is an instance of the feminisation of logic.

In virtually all spheres of human activity, low life expectancy is regarded as a classic indicator of underprivilege. The fact, for example, that black people have a low life expectancy compared to white people is regarded as a mark of the inequality that exists between races. The fact that Travellers have a significantly lower life expectancy than settled people is frequently cited as evidence of severe discrimination against Travellers in Irish society. Even between different classes of women, differing life expectancies and morbidity rates are seen as indicators of relative privilege or discrimination. But the same logic is never applied to men, who, despite being more likely than women to die young from each of the top fifteen causes of early death, are still regarded as privileged in every respect.

In western society, the average female now starts life with an expectation of living seven years longer than a man born in the same year. In pre-industrial society, men and women had about equal life-expectancies, but this changed with the onset of the twentieth century, when women began to live longer than men, the gap widening with every decade of the century.

In Ireland up to the 1930s, lower female life expectancy was partly accounted for by deaths during childbirth. In general, women who lived in rural areas had a higher susceptibility than men to diseases such as TB and pneumonia, but this marginal pattern was transposed in urban areas. By the early 1990s, however, the average Irish female could expect to live until she was seventy-eight, whereas the average Irish male would have been well advised to have his affairs in order by the time he reached his seventy-second birthday. Life expectancy patterns in Ireland are now almost in line with what we like to call "other developed societies". The fact that men die younger than women is now regarded by policy-makers, commentators and experts as a natural circumstance, something as inevitable as, say, the fact that ninety per cent of RUC members are Protestants. I would hazard that, if by some miracle we were to succeed in bringing the average Irish male's life expectancy into line with that of the average female, this would be denounced by feminists and their fellow travellers as an indicator of our oppression of women — compared, naturally, with "other developed countries".

Those with responsibility for public health in Ireland appear to imagine that there is nothing to be done about the fact that men are less healthy than women. The Irish Heart Foundation, for example, lists raised cholesterol, high blood pressure, smoking, lack of exercise and being overweight as risk-factors which "we can influence"; the risk factors which, apparently, we cannot counter are: family history of heart disease and our sex, age and race. This suggests that the so-called "gender" dimension of premature death is regarded as immutable and fixed.

The consensus among experts and responsible organisations is that the explanation for the disparity is that men do not take care of their health. A recent survey by the British Office of Health Economics, based on figures for 1993, placed Ireland fourth in the world for premature death from coronary heart disease, and quoted the main causes of heart disease as diet and lifestyle, in particular smoking and physical inactivity. But I don't think it would strike one as obvious that the diet and physical lifestyle of the average male is so significantly different from that of the average female as to result in four times as many men succumbing to premature coronary failure.

In 1992, the year before this survey was conducted, 29 per cent of Irish women were smokers, compared to 38 per cent of Irish men. This is a significant difference, certainly, but not nearly as significant as the disparity in fatalities from the supposedly directly related heart disease. In general, women were found to have a somewhat better diet, tending to eat more fruit and vegetables than men, and in general tended to be less overweight; but again it seems improbable that this, even in conjunction with the smoking factor, could amount to an explanation for the vast disparity in early fatalities.

And, whereas men come out relatively badly in the smoking and dietary categories, they do much better when it comes to physical exercise. According to 1994 figures compiled by the Irish Heart Foundation, one-third of women, as compared to a quarter of men, were likely to be sedentary during the working day, and similarly during leisure time. Tendency towards obesity — another major risk-indicator for heart disease — is about equal between the sexes, at about ten per cent. The evidence about diet and lifestyle, therefore, is neither conclusive nor convincing.

The things that kill men are not cigarettes, chips or settees, but duty, honour, risk, responsibility, drudgery, silent strength, loneliness, fear, dignity and ambition. All these translate into one quasi-medical word: stress — undoubtedly the most significantly common factor with heart failure and virtually every killer disease.

There are, of course, biological factors differentiating men and women in terms of susceptibility to disease, but the main difference has to do with the relative roles allotted the sexes by industrial society. The clay ceiling, affecting men, is as much a peculiarity of industrialisation as the glass ceiling affecting women is a feature of the post-industrial shakedown. And yet the one attracts negligible attention by comparison with the other.

Premature death in adult males is the consequence of the attempts of men and fathers to support their families in a merciless world. Men, who for a century or more have left the bosom of their families and walked through those factory gates in the rain, have paid the price in bearing — manfully — the physical expression of the mythical broken heart. The same technological revolution that liberated women enslaved men and banished them from the life-force that is the love of their mates and children.

But whereas the man walks slowly out his hall door and trudges through those gates, the ideology of the day presents him as skipping gaily down the path, leaving his wife washing his socks and his children crying at the windowpane.

In truth, he walks with a heavy heart, which drags him to an early grave.

(December 1999)

12

THE CORRECT ORDER OF HUMANITY

NOT LONG AGO, ONE COULD REGULARLY HEAR on national radio an advertising slogan, used to promote an organisation dedicated to helping female victims of domestic violence, which went: "Remember, it's a crime to beat a woman." From time to time, someone would ask naïve questions, like: "Does that mean it is not a crime to beat other kinds of people?" Following a minor public outcry (a *Liveline* discussion, to be precise), the slogan was tweaked a little to take it out of the realm of objective ludicrousness. A question now arises, however, as to whether or not this may not have been a mistake, since it appears that the official policy of the government could be reduced to something along the same lines.

Last week, the Minister for Justice, Mr John O'Donoghue, announced with a solemnity of which few are capable that he was extending the categories of offenders who shall not qualify for bail or temporary release from prison. At present, only armed robbers, drug importers and sex offenders are denied bail or temporary release. Henceforth, the minister announced, such benefits will be denied also to those convicted of: (1) violence against women; (2) violence against children; (3) attacks on the elderly and "other vulnerable members of the community"; (4) joyriding or persistent car-thieving.

If he was the type of person disposed to saving his wind, the Minister might just as easily have said that, henceforth, bail and temporary release will be extended only to persons convicted of violent offences against men between, say, the ages of 16 and 65. Unless I am missing something, this is the only category of person omitted from his list.

There is a message here for potential criminals: if you are going to beat someone up, make sure your victim is an adult male. If you take this elementary precaution, be assured that this State will look kindly on any requests for bail or temporary release, so that, presumably, you may be free to go back and finish off your man. Beware, however, that, having beaten your victim to a pulp, you do not afterwards make off in his motor vehicle, for then this State would have no option but to ensure that you face the full rigour of the law.

Let me put it another way: it is clear that the top four priorities of the Irish justice system are now, in descending order: women, children, the elderly and motor vehicles. I would say that after this come adult males under 65, except that there is no indication that the Minister for Justice has given any thought whatsoever to this category. Perhaps, if asked to extend the litany of his priorities, Mr O'Donoghue would go on to list racehorses, bicycles, ornamental shrubs, Charolais heifers without permanent teeth, golf balls, magpies and, then, at last, adult males; or perhaps he would not mention adult males until much further down, perhaps after hotel towels and company stationery. Since the Minister made no reference at all to how the system he presides over proposes to extend protection to this section of humanity, we just don't know.

I do not suggest that there is anything legally amiss with the Minister's logic; in fact, whereas Article 40.1 of the Irish Constitution asserts that "all citizens shall, as human persons, be held equal before the law", I have no doubt that Mr O'Donoghue's legal advice has laid emphasis on the qualifier which follows: "This shall not be held to mean that the State shall not in its enactments have due regard to differences of capacity, physical and moral, and of social function." And so, fellow adult males, be notified that it is the policy of this State that, if someone comes at you with a rampant chainsaw, the fact that you are theoretically bigger and stronger than certain others of the human species shall mean that you are expected to be a match for this attacker, and should not expect the justice system to waste its energies in vindicating your so-called rights. If your assailant is female, however, be warned to avoid doing her any undue violence in the course of this attempt to defend yourself, for this would result in the forfeiture of your rights to bail or early release.

Neither do I suggest that the Minister's statement lacks logic. In a society dominated by the strident demands of man-haters, it is extremely logical for politicians, male or female, to make statements like this and create policy in harmony with them.

What can be said, however, it that the logic of the Minister's position is contradicted by what we know of the facts. A man from Mars might conclude, listening to John O'Donoghue's statement, that most crimes of violence are committed against women, children and the elderly, and might accordingly compliment the Minister on the appropriateness of his response. The trouble is that most crimes of violence are committed against adult men. In every category of violent crime, with the exception of rape, the more violent the crime, the more likely the victim is to be male. It is true that the vast majority of inmates of our prison system are male, but mostly they are there for crimes against other men. Neither the Garda Síochána nor, oddly enough, Mr O'Donoghue's Department, is able to provide detailed breakdowns of the sex of either perpetrators or victims, but there are some telling indicators in the figures that are available. For example, in 1997, the latest year for which figures have been published to date, there were twice as many murders of males as of females, and four times as many manslaughters. In other words, seven out of every ten homicide victims are male. I should note that, of course, a significant minority of perpetrators of violent crimes do not end up in our prison system at all, because they are female. These, obviously, do not require to avail of bail or temporary release.

Why, when these facts are readily available to him, does an adult male Minister for Justice seek to imply that the situation is otherwise? The answer is that Mr O'Donoghue was doing no more than giving voice to the official policy of this State — that adult males do not deserve protection in the way other categories of human being do, and so had better be prepared to look out for themselves. If they can succeed in beating each other into oblivion, then so much, it seems, the better.

This form of public thought is the result of nearly thirty years of relentless campaigning by the misandrist forces that now dominate our public discourse, having created a multi-million-pound industry out of demonising men. It is an awesome achievement, for which those campaigners deserve full credit, and is all the more spectacular when one considers that this consciousness has been created to exist simultaneously with the widespread belief that men are the dominant sex.

The supreme irony is that if a female minister, known as a radical feminist, had made such a statement, it might well be met with public scepticism and even some anger. No greater tribute can be paid to the achievements of the ideologues of extreme feminism than that a man as unreconstructed as Mr John O'Donoghue is able to stand up in public, make such a statement and cause nobody to blink an eye.

(June 1999)

13

THE INDUSTRY OF UNTRUTH

SINCE THE PUBLICATION RECENTLY of the findings of a report commissioned by the Marriage and Relationship Counselling Services (MRCS) which again cast the gravest doubts on popular assumptions concerning domestic violence, the silence, both from official and political quarters and the normally vocal vested interests, has been deafening. The survey, conducted among 530 clients of MRCS, revealed that, of the troubled relationships in which they were called upon to assist, nearly fifty per cent involved domestic violence, and women were almost twice as likely to be the instigators of that violence. Broadly, the findings were that one in three of these relationships were subject to mutually inflicted violence, one in four demonstrated violence occasioned by the male, as against two in five in which the violence was initiated by the female partner.

A number of things need to be stated concerning these figures. Firstly, although this survey was not subject to the normal sampling requirements, its findings are remarkably in line with those of many international surveys, subject to the most rigorous standards in respect of quota-controls and so forth. Secondly, and most strikingly, the survey indicates that the level of female-instigated domestic violence may be higher here than elsewhere. Thirdly, these findings are utterly in conflict with the present official and cultural belief-system, which holds that in all but the most eccentric circumstances, violence between men and women is instigated by the male.

Belief in this "truth" is maintained in all the official institutions and agencies which become involved in tackling the difficulties experienced in relationships between men and women, including social services, the Garda Síochána, the medical profession, the legal profession and the judiciary. This belief is also held by the vast majority of politicians, who have responsibility for framing laws in this field.

This belief is utterly false. Its existence is the result not of the assimilation of the lived experience of human beings, but of the relentless propaganda of vested interests, primarily feminists and those involved in the highly lucrative violence-against-women industry.

This belief is not a harmless fallacy. Its consequences reach into the most intimate crevices of this society, affecting hugely the lives of men, women and children. Its corrosive effects act upon some of the most vital and sacred values of democratic society. The present belief-system casts a shadow over every set of proceedings affecting the lives of Irish families, because its assumptions impinge on the chances of every single adult male being perceived by the relevant authorities as a husband, father and human being. The belief that men are violent and women not means, in effect, that any man who shares a home with a woman is no more than an invited guest in that home for as long as that relationship endures in the eyes of the women, and that he can lose virtually all legal protection in that relationship at the whim of the woman. It means that married men continue to live in the homes they built or otherwise provided only for as long as their wives desire them to do so. It means that fathers can have satisfactory relationships with their children only for as long as their behaviour is congenial to the mother. It means that, year after year, more and more repressive legislation is being added to the statute books based on untruths and propaganda.

In an address to a family law conference earlier this year, a district justice, Judge Gerard Haughton, described the provisions for interim barring orders under Section 4 of the Domestic Violence Act 1996 as an infringement of the rights of men under the Constitution and the European Convention on Human Rights. In the Dublin

Metropolitan District, interim barring orders are handed out at the rate of about twelve a week. This means that, every week, twelve men have been forbidden, under pain of imprisonment, from entering their own homes, and this on the basis of *ex parte* orders issued on the un-corroborated word of women who have the most obvious vested interest in having them so restricted. Of ten orders extracted at random by Judge Haughton, the average duration of the order was more than six weeks, and one order was for four months. All were granted *ex parte*.

Judge Haughton commented: "There can be no argument with the proposition that to order an individual out of his family dwelling is almost as serious and far-reaching as taking children into care." He contrasted the provisions of the Child Care Act 1991, which stipulates that an emergency or interim care order in respect of a child can be granted for a maximum of eight days, with the provisions of the Domestic Violence Act 1996, which place no limit on the period for which an Interim Barring Order can be granted. Judge Haughton stated that he believed this raised questions as to the constitutionality of Section 4 of the Domestic Violence Act 1996. He said: "I am personally amazed that there has been neither challenge to the section nor any judicial review of the granting of Interim Barring Orders for such lengthy periods. . . . It seems to me that the granting of such orders on an *ex parte* basis for more than seven to fourteen days at the maximum is not defensible on constitutional grounds alone." Judge Haughton also stated his belief that this section is in breach of Article 16 of the European Convention on Human Rights which requires "a fair and public hearing within a reasonable time".

"How," asked Judge Haughton, "can a respondent who is the subject of such an order have either a fair trial or indeed fair procedures when he is not served with a copy of the information on foot of which the Interim Barring Order was granted, and indeed the District Court Rules do not provide for such a service?"

Judge Haughton's use of the word "he" was well advised. The Domestic Violence Act 1996 is virtually always used against men, which reflects its origins in the propagandistic clamouring of vested interests seeking to have all fault within male–female relationships deemed to be the fault of the men. That this piece of legislation ever got on to the statute books is both an extraordinary indictment of the quality of our concepts of justice and equality and an astonishing tribute to the propagandistic talents of Irish feminists.

Such injustices remain tolerable in a society with such a skewed notion of justice and compassion that it believes saints and sinners are identifiable on the basis of sex. At all costs, the logic of the truth must be evaded, lest it unseat the present paradigm.

Even in the MRCS report, there was contained the seed of the inevitable denial: "However, it needs to be emphasised that the outcomes of domestic violence in terms of physical and psychological injuries tend to be considerably more negative for female victims than for male." What possible basis could there be for such a statement? Are the consequences of being hit by a bus or a golf ball more "negative" for a woman than for a man, and does it matter if bus or ball was driven by a male or a female? In fact, all the evidence is that, because of the societal denial concerning the truth about domestic violence, the psychological effects on male victims of female violence may be much, much greater than those of a form of violence that is readily accepted at face value.

The notion that women suffer more as a result of domestic violence is itself part of the propaganda which in some respects is impervious to fact. What we have created is a system in which the facts matter less than the woman's perception of what has happened, or at least what she continues to maintain is her perception. If a woman feels she has been injured, then she has been, and the obvious solution is for the man to pack his bags. Imagine if such logic was applied to the criminal law, to the admission of asylum-seekers, or to the settlement of civil claims.

Last year, feminist groups like Women's Aid received about £10 million of taxpayers' money from the Department of Health and Children. That same Department also spent a more modest sum of £10,000 on a study of the factual position concerning domestic violence. This research revealed that the Department's policy of supporting only groups holding that men are the sole perpetrators of domestic violence is morally bankrupt. The Department responded by continuing that policy and burying its report.

The report I have in mind is entitled *Men and Domestic Violence: What Research Tells Us*. It was produced by Kieran McKeown and Philippa Kidd of Kieran McKeown Limited, Social and Economic Research Consultants. McKeown and Kidd studied research in the US, Britain, Canada and New Zealand, with particular reference to violence against men. Their report comprises 125 pages, but its central finding is: ". . . the results of representative studies are fairly consistent in showing that, in approximately half of all intimate relationships where domestic violence occurs, both partners use violent acts, with the remainder divided equally between male-only violence and female-only violence. As a result, the self-reported prevalence of domestic violence among men and women, both as victims and as perpetrators, is broadly similar for all types of violence, psychological and physical, minor and severe."

These facts, the report states, "can no longer be ignored", pointing as they do to "the need for a larger and more inclusive paradigm of domestic violence than is currently allowable within the existing consensus. By the same reasoning, these findings also make it extremely difficult to credibly sustain a perspective on domestic violence which assumes that, in the vast majority of cases, men are its only perpetrators and women its only victims."

For many years, feminist propagandists have maintained that all violence between men and women is the fault of men, and that all males are potential abusers of women. I have argued that the figures quoted are one-sided and misleading, and that a highly lucrative industry has, on the basis of untruths, been offering women the means of removing inconvenient men from their lives.

The report of Kieran McKeown and Philippa Kidd vindicates the position I have taken. I believe the Minister for Health, as an urgent matter of public interest, should order its immediate publication.

For many years, too, feminist propagandists have been seeking to stretch the definition of "abuse", which is a synonym for violence, to include virtually all behaviour, including silence and withdrawal, which adversely affects the female. Now that the truth has started to come out, feminists are seeking to narrow the ground between the goalposts to embrace only the physical effects of violence and the subjective responses of females. These factors, they believe, will continue to vindicate the present paradigm.

They are wrong. Just as investigation into the statistical nature of domestic violence has revealed the untruth about male monopoly of domestic abuse, so further research will reveal, as it has done elsewhere, that men suffer injuries just as serious as women as a consequence of domestic violence.

(This essay is an amalgam of two separate pieces on domestic violence, published in July and December 2001)

14

Bill Clinton's Predicament

(Thoughts on the Monica Lewinsky saga)

IT IS DIFFICULT TO IMAGINE A MORE comprehensive unveiling of the illusion of male dominance than the events concerning the Clinton Presidency of recent weeks. They bespoke a world changed utterly not merely from what it was but from what we still believe it to be — as evidenced by the global insistence on discussing the matter as though the old rules still obtained. This perspective focused most of the questions on the issue of why Hillary Clinton chose to "stand by her man". Ten seconds' consideration would have disposed of this question, even on its own slightly ludicrous terms. Long-suffering wives standing by wayward husbands is hardly a new phenomenon. Usually it occurs because such women know which side their bread is buttered on: a rational decision to hold on to what obtains rather than invite the less predictable.

And in this case we are talking about the woman who is married to supposedly the most powerful man in the world. What else would she be expected to do? Where do we think she might intend to go, or to achieve, in the coming three years, whereby she would be offered more opportunities for self-realisation than on the arm of the President of the US of A? Why do we waste time talking about such things?

Even in terms of old rules and perceptions, her actions make perfect sense. But we are not playing by the old rules. Was anybody listening, back in 1992, when Mrs Clinton told the world that she wasn't some little woman, "standing by her man like Tammy Wynette"? She meant that she had cut a deal. Her husband was a sad old sixties throwback who couldn't keep his dick in his trousers, but he stood a good chance of becoming the most powerful human being on the planet. She, although about fifty times smarter than he is, had zero chance of becoming President. They would go on. She would use the influence that his charisma delivered to make the presidency work for the things she believed in, and he would use what was left to get off with young ones. Hillary has an eye for the big picture and is not the type for turning.

One of the most striking things about the past week was the absence of even a hint of feminist criticism of Bill Clinton. On the face of it, this might appear strange, since the President stood accused of a string of crimes against women which, in almost any other conceivable instance, would have resulted in the roundest condemnation. We are talking about a society in which a woman is entitled, on waking up in bed beside a strange man after a night on the tiles, to immediately redefine the night's lovemaking as rape on the basis that it was the man's responsibility to know that she had had too much to drink; in such a culture, the allegations against Clinton amounted to a prima facie case of Misogyny One. And yet, there was not a dickybird out of the usual spokespersons for the sisterhood. Shere Hite, on Channel 4 News, put it all in perspective: President Clinton was a man who "supported rights for women". Asked to elaborate on this, she explained that he was a supporter of abortion. She seemed amused by Jon Snow's puzzlement about the relevance of this, and so she should be.

Apart from the television pictures of Clinton and his wife, the most intriguing images of recent weeks have been those of his accusers, who, by virtue of their accusations, have become figures of almost equal stature to the President himself. Each of them has spawned a multi-million dollar industry, on the scale of, say, a world-rating rock 'n' roll band. They are ferried around in limousines, accompanied by lawyers and other advisers. This is entirely appropriate, since they are the agents of a culture that delivers power to feminists without a quota in sight. Although feminists still play the numbers game, pointing out the distance still to be made up before full equality is delivered, the smarter ones know full well that their major objectives can be realised by more immediate methods. Hillary Clinton knows how far reality has moved on from those sixties' campus crusades, and is well versed in how the present period of transition allows feminists to maximise their strike capacity by employing tactics and weaponry from across the old and the new cultures. Women like this copped on long ago that it was possible to deliver their primary objectives without waiting for numerical equalisation — by using the oldest weapon in the history of man: the standing penis.

In truth, Bill Clinton, clearly the victim of a serious sexual addiction, is more to be pitied than laughed at. Without the support of his wife and other feminists, his trouser problem would render him unfit to govern. The old culture would have perceived his predicament with a mixture of amusement, disapproval and secret envy. What an ass, what a bastard, what a man! Woooggghhhh! And so forth. In the new, post-feminist culture, his previously celebrated macho sex-drive makes him a kitten in the hands of allegedly powerless women, and what would previously have been his macho/male-chauvinistic behaviour is seen as an opportunity to appropriate his power and make him pay for his weakness of character by doing what feminists ordain. It amounts to no more than the overt politicisation of the natural power of women over men.

The fact that the modern womaniser almost invariably tries to pass himself off as an ardent feminist has led to the myth that such men "just love women". Indeed, I heard more that one American feminist last week talking about what a "sensual" man Bill Clinton is. But the "feminism" of these men is a subterfuge to facilitate their addiction. Like all addicts, such men secretly despise that which enslaves them and, far from "loving" women, simply hide their contempt for what they are unable to resist behind uncritical acquiescence in the feminist perspective.

In the long run, all this will balance out, as the pretences drop away, one by one. In the meantime, the best ideal interim solution would be the creation of a mechanism by which political and other public figures who fall foul of feminist dogmas could be replaced by their wives. Under such a scheme, for example, Hillary Clinton would last week have become President of the United States, on the basis that her husband was too compromised to continue.

This would have three major advantages: one, the United States would have an infinitely more capable President; two, it would make open and visible what has happened anyway; and three, it would act as a salutary lesson to all those men who wish to retain what power they have: if they would do so, they must learn to keep John Thomas safely trousered.

(February 1998)

15

THE DIVINE RIGHT TO
PERFECT HAPPINESS

A FRIEND OF MINE RECENTLY MET UP with a noted French playwright who specialises in writing plays based on Greek mythology. In the course of their conversation, my friend asked him about the source of his fascination with this particular genre. He replied that what attracted him about myth was that it was actually pure truth. Everything else tells lies. History is misleading. Facts are fibs. Current affairs are two-faced. Everything we "know" from what we have garnered from such sources is wrong, because everything reaches us at the end of a process in which manipulation, distortion, salesmanship and vested interest have already had their evil way. But myth, because it has no purpose other than the revelation of its own story, is always truthful. The word "myth", therefore, has for him a meaning almost the opposite of its conventional one.

I have been thinking about this interesting perspective in relation to the celebration — I believe that is the right word — of the first anniversary of the death of the Princess of Wales. What is being remembered, we imagine, are the facts of Diana's life and personality. Indeed, the idea of Diana is often seen as what might colloquially be called a "myth", in the sense that her life and death have acquired the character of a Greek tragedy. But in the spirit of the French playwright's observations, I suggest that, considering the nature of the legend of Diana and the origins of so much of our knowledge of it, we should hesitate long before according this story the status of myth.

For this story is mainly lies. Indeed, it has been most interesting, observing the media coverage of these matters during the past week or so in London, how much attitudes towards Diana have changed in the twelve months since her death. Already there is a growing sense of public embarrassment at the indulgence and pretences that followed on our awakening to the news that the world's most famous woman had been killed in a car crash in Paris.

Within hours, a version of events was being created which seems, in retrospect, to have been fashioned out of the very character of Diana, to appease and gratify all those who had worshipped her most mindlessly when she was alive. The most disquieting aspect of this was not the attempted canonisation of Diana — an understandable response in the tragic circumstances of her death — but the search for a corresponding demon to act as counterpoint to her sainthood. Though no fan of the British royal family, I could still identify with the situation of her husband and mother-in-law, who were rapidly recruited as scapegoats in her downfall. A year down the road, the world is just beginning to see that Diana was the victim of nothing other that her own insatiable pursuit of gratification, which, by leading her into the proverbial bad company, made some kind of tragedy all but inevitable.

A colleague who has been engaged in some research here relating to the first anniversary of the death of the Princess of Wales has remarked upon an interesting division in attitudes on the subject between Irish women and Irish men. Women whom she interviewed, she told me, were almost invariably given to encomia of Diana. Men, although more reluctant to express clear-cut opinions, were much less prone to eulogy, and some appeared to harbour some profound anger on the subject. She didn't know why this was so, but I suggested that the reason men are angry with the cult of Diana is that they are tired of being held responsible for the unhappiness of women.

One of the few voices of sanity to cut through the nonsense of a year ago was that of Dr Oliver James, a British clinical psychologist who had only just delivered to his publishers a book which, without particularly setting out to do so, told the truth about the Princess of

Wales, or at least as much of it as any of us truly need to know. The book is *Britain on the Couch: Treating a Low Seratonin Society*, published by Century. James's thesis relates to the condition of what we call modern societies, and is utterly fascinating in the issues it raises. Briefly, what he suggests is that perhaps the principal difference between the 1990s and the 1950s is the fact that most or all of us now "know" far, far more people than would have been the case had we lived a generation ago. Whereas our grandparents "knew" just their immediate family, neighbours, a small circle of friends and acquaintances, most of us today, courtesy of the mass media society, have come to "know" hundreds, perhaps thousands, of people, from soap stars to royals. James argues, with great force and reason, that this has multiplied the effects of our natural tendency to compare ourselves with others. Being surrounded on a daily basis by the knowledge of our own relative lack of success in various endeavours, by virtue of the manifest "success" of the more famous, we are confronted at all times by the evidence of our own "failure". This constant, invariably negative comparison, James argues, creates chemical imbalances which attack our self-esteem, confidence and sense of self-possession, creating envy, depression and spiritual malfunction. It spawns drug addictions, eating disorders and insatiable appetites for newer and greater forms of gratification, which in turn destroy our capacity for healthy relationships with other people.

In this fine book, Dr James employed the otherwise unemployable female members of the British royal family to illustrate how this condition has swept through modern British society like a dose of salts. His thesis is founded on the notion that levels of the "happiness brain chemical" serotonin — on which human beings depend for their sense of well-being — are related to social status and the sense of self deriving from this. Negative social comparison, therefore, creates a spiral of diminishing self-esteem and depression, which in turn further deplete the serotonin levels. Dr James points to the remarkable irony that, although low levels of serotonin can result from the self-comparisons of the less privileged looking to the achievements of their betters, the condition actually increases in virulence as the social ladder is climbed. Those at the top are much more dissatisfied with their lot than those at the bottom. The winners in our societies feel more like losers than do the losers.

One of the most dangerous aspects of the creation of a myth of Diana is the promulgation of the notion that she was at one and the same time a heroine and a victim. In truth, she was neither. The pseudo-myth of Diana derived in part from her own very astute manipulation of the media, which created the raw material for the cult which has been promoted with even greater assiduity since her death. By this telling, she was the perfect mother, the selfless benefactor of the poor and underprivileged, the unhappy princess who was trapped in a bad marriage.

These ideas were very appealing to a particular element of popular sentiment among a certain class of British — and indeed Irish — women. But Princess Diana was not the perfect mother: she was a glamour-chasing, jet-setting, multi-millionairess, who spent most of her time in gyms, shops or lying on beaches. It rarely seems to occur to those who seek to present Diana as the ideal modern mother that, to remain in the public eye as much as she did, she must have been separated from her children for large chunks of the time.

Yes, she certainly was seen to help the "needy" and "voiceless", but that is because it was her chosen career, and "seen" is the operative word. She got back far more than she put in, not least the sense of moral satisfaction that comes from doing good deeds in public. It has not gone unremarked in the past week or so that Diana left not one penny of her considerable fortune to any of the charities which the rest of us are enjoined to support in her name.

As regards her alleged unhappiness: it never ceases to amaze me that grown-up people can seriously put forward the notion that this hugely privileged woman would make it into a list of the top billion unhappy people on earth. She was one of the richest women in the world and certainly the best-known. She had everything she ever wanted, or at least everything desired by the vast majority of those who fawned over her — ah, yes, except a good marriage. Why this should single her out for special sympathy in a world in which this is rapidly becoming the norm, is unclear. Was her husband happy, and does this matter? Presumably, he too was the victim of a bad marriage. Why has the world no sympathy to offer him? Was he responsible for his wife's alleged unhappiness? If so, why was she in turn not judged to be responsible for his? Indeed, was Princess Diana responsible for anything at all that happened to her? Was there one bad thing that occurred in her life that was not the fault of her father, her husband or some other man?

The Princess of Wales was an icon to female irresponsibility. She was the personification of the idea that women have a divine right to perfect happiness, which popular culture aimed at women has reduced to the aspiration to hourglass figures, multiple orgasms and platinum credit cards. What the cult of Lady Di says to us is that women, by virtue of being women, are automatically entitled to be happy. If they are not, it is the fault of somebody else, almost certainly some adult male. If a woman is as allegedly beautiful as Diana and is still unhappy, it proves the case beyond doubt: who but an outright bastard could reject such a paragon of beauty and virtue? The subtext of the exaltation of Diana, therefore, is the accusation that men have failed women. This is modern society's most notorious crime.

Diana's life and the treatment of her death present a case study in the incapacity of elements of what we term modern society to accept the ineluctable realities of human existence — that life is a bitch and then you die. It is something of a generalisation to say that this is primarily a female condition, but not much. The vast bulk of female popular culture is now directed at the modern woman's growing sense of victimhood and disgruntlement — from the plethora of increasingly ludicrous women's magazines inciting narcissism and self-absorption, to the growing popularity of man-hating television shows like *Ally McBeal*, to the rash of misandrist TV adverts for everything from car insurance to sausages. As the demands created by this culture become more and more insatiable, so does the anger at the consequent lack of fulfilment. At the cutting edge of this phenomenon are the cults of a handful of female celebrities, of whom Diana was the most prominent. With the collaboration of the popular media, these women present themselves as — simultaneously — victims, saints, "strong women" and selfless carers for their children. In the vast majority of cases, the truth is the opposite of everything the cult suggests: in truth, such women are extremely selfish, manipulative and abusive. The problem is that, increasingly, these cults are used as ideological battering rams to promote within our societies ideas that serve nothing except hedonism and spite, and ultimately risk making all of us more unhappy than we already are.

(September 1998)

16

THE FEEBLE CONCEIT OF
MRS MARY ROBINSON

IT IS NOT EASY, WHEN YOU HAVE BEEN WRONG, to come out and admit the error. But that is what I must do this morning.

Ten years ago, I devoted a section of my first book, *Jiving at the Crossroads*, to welcoming the election as President of Mrs Mary Robinson just a few months before. While disapproving of the treatment of her chief opponent, the late Brian Lenihan, I had approved strongly of Mrs Robinson and had given her my number one vote. During the campaign, I had written a number of articles extolling her merits and indicating an enthusiastic welcome for the development her election would herald for this society. This extract from my book gives a sense of why I did so:

> [S]he was saying that there did not have to be winners or losers, there did not have to be sides. By fighting against the perceived conservative forces in Irish society, she had come to appreciate the nature of those forces: that they were not merely the preserve of a diehard minority, but an essential part of the equilibrium of the society. Conversely, the liberal forces to which Dublin 4 had claimed ownership did not belong to them alone. Conservatism and liberalism were not exterior forces, but intrinsic parts of herself, of her own experience and outlook; just as they were parts of me, of all of us.

At the time, I believed this to be true, but now I know it is gibberish. I believe this because of comments by Mrs Robinson, now the United Nations Commissioner for Human Rights, to mark International

91

Women's Day. That day, 8 March, Mrs Robinson was reported in the "breaking news" section of the *Irish Times* website as stating: "Apparently there are small boys in Ireland who are complaining to their mothers, 'Why can't I grow up to be President?' That seems to me to be an excellent experience for small boys in Ireland."

Consider the implications of the fact that a public servant, charged with overseeing the universal extension of human rights, gloats in public that a sub-group is suffering from a new potential discrimination. This is far from the picture I painted of a woman so committed to human progress that she was prepared to embrace erstwhile political opponents and accommodate views with which she disagreed.

Consider that when Mrs Robinson was elected President of this Republic she undertook to become guardian of the Irish Constitution, in which the following two passages appear: (1) Article 4:1: "Every citizen who has reached his thirty-fifth year of age is eligible for election to the office of President"; and (2) Article 40:1: "All citizens shall, as human persons, be held equal before the law".

It is clear from her own words that Mrs Robinson does not subscribe to these guarantees, that she is a female chauvinist of the most extreme kind, who desires not equality but feminist supremacy. In the ten years since she became President, the suicide figures for young men have multiplied fourfold, a factor which, among others, indicates that young males are possibly the most vulnerable group in this society. Anyone who can pick out any category of human being, still less a group as guiltless and exposed as little boys, and crow about their future disenfranchisement is not a fit person to hold any kind of public office, still less those to which Mrs Robinson has had the privilege of being appointed. That a public figure of Mrs Robinson's seniority regards the possibility of further discrimination against boys as a source of satisfaction is beyond belief. That it should go unnoticed is a separate and equally grievous outrage.

If she had said this eleven years ago, how many of us would have voted for her? How many men? How many women with "small" sons and nephews? I have no doubt that, had she displayed this female chauvinism in the campaign of 1990, she would have come in at the bottom of the field. She therefore obtained the office of President, with help from gullible people like me, by misleading the electorate as to her true outlook.

Inevitably, someone will pop up to accuse me of lacking a sense of humour. Mrs Robinson was joking, of course.

Of course. But imagine, if you will, if a leading public figure, a man, were to declare how pleased he was that little girls could look forward to being excluded from some significant public office or other. I cannot imagine a man saying such a thing, but if he did, could he hope to rely upon the good humour of the public? I don't doubt that before he had closed his mouth, the feminist ayatollahs would have taken to the airwaves in their droves, condemning his remarks, demanding his resignation or dismissal, and calling for all male public figures to undergo "gender sensitivity retraining".

Of course, it goes without saying that Mrs Robinson's comments are without any basis, that they are no more than a feeble conceit, a self-aggrandising effort to enhance retrospectively the significance of the events of 1990 and her own role in these. In truth, small boys are much too busy fishing and playing football to worry about being President.

But underlying her words is a deeply disquieting hostility — surpassing the everyday feminist rancour towards males, and, by virtue of being specifically directed at young boys, acquiring a quite dangerous and unwomanly disposition. This moment of chilling pseudo-humour was also one of unguarded truth, allowing a brief flash of the inhospitable fangs behind the fixed smile of modern feminism.

(March 2001)

17

THE POLITICS OF HANDCUFFS

A MINOR SKIRMISH OCCURRED in Seanad Éireann last week about the inconsistent use of handcuffs when prisoners are being taken from court. The discussion was provoked by the fact that the former Christian brother, Maurice Tobin, convicted of the sexual abuse of twenty-five boys in Letterfrack, was not handcuffed when led from court in Galway, whereas George Redmond, convicted the previous week on charges of corruption, had been handcuffed to a prison officer when he was led away to prison.

I have a more arresting comparison. On the same day as Mr Redmond was taken from the Circuit Criminal Court, a twenty-five-year-old Welshwoman, Christina Williams, was escorted from the Central Criminal Court to begin a life sentence for the murder of Andrew Foley on 7 May 2002. She was accompanied by a single female prison warder, and walked with her arms dangling by her sides.

Mr Redmond's misdeeds are perhaps more notorious than those of Ms Williams. He had been found guilty of corruption relating to matters which first came to public attention in the hearings of the Flood Tribunal. Specifically, he was convicted of accepting a bribe of £10,000 in return for facilitating the purchase from the local authority of a right-of-way to link a filling station with the Lucan bypass.

Ms Williams had been convicted of murder. The details of the last minutes of Andrew Foley have been published in most of the newspapers, though rather less graphically in some than in others. In case you missed it: Ms Williams, apparently offended because Mr Foley asked her for sex, stabbed her victim in the eye, arms, shoulders, chest and genitals. As he lay bleeding to death on the sofa in his own flat, she filled his electric kettle, waited for it to boil, and poured the boiling water over him. Asked why she did this, Ms Williams explained that Mr Foley had shouted at her, pushed her and told her to leave his flat. "I just got carried away," she said.

Although I had, to be honest, a reasonable suspicion about why Ms Williams was not handcuffed, I couldn't completely shake off a worry that the handcuffing of Mr Redmond might have been the result of an order from on high that he be paraded in a state of maximised humiliation for the delectation of the indignant classes.

Mr Redmond, whatever you may think of him, is nearly eighty years of age and had been convicted in relation to the acceptance of a brown envelope, whereas Ms Williams had committed one of the most barbaric murders in the history of the State. Happily, a few hours spent foraging in the labyrinth that is the Department of Justice was sufficient to restore my prejudices to their proper order. A spokeswoman for the Department of Justice informed me that the decision about whether or not to handcuff a prisoner is "an operational matter for prison officers on a particular day". A spokesman for the Irish Prison Service was more precise: although he is unaware of any legislative or regulatory basis for this, the policy is that male prisoners are handcuffed "almost always", and female prisoners "almost never". And no, he emphasised, there is no question that handcuffs are part of the punishment of a prisoner, in the sense of adding to the indignity of his being led away. It is purely a matter of security — that of prisoners and prisoner officers, as well as an added precaution to prevent drugs being passed to prisoners as they are being led from court.

But, I countered, as far as Mr Redmond and Ms Williams were concerned, there could be no question as to which of the two posed the greater threat: Mr Redmond is an elderly man, incapable of boxing his way out of a brown paper bag, and Ms Williams, in addition to the brutal murder of Mr Foley, had previous convictions in her native country of assault on a landlady, a taxi driver and, oh yes, a

police officer. Sorry — did I not mention her conviction for assault-
ing a police officer? At this point, the spokesman for the Irish Prison
Service had the good grace to laugh. In fact, we both had a good old
bellylaugh for a minute or so.

So, I summarised, getting my breath back, we can safely ignore
the notion that the issuing of handcuffs to male prisoners has to do
with either objective considerations of security or, er, drugs, and decide that it is purely a matter of old-fashioned sexism? In as far as it is
possible for a spokesman for the Irish Prison Service to agree with
such a contention, I got the distinct impression that he did so.

You can't imagine how relieved I was to clear that up.

(November 2003)

18

SWIVEL-HEADS TO YOU TOO

IT'S REASONABLE, I THINK, TO SUGGEST that the world is in something of a sorry state when it is not possible to flog a few teabags
without insulting half the human race. I refer to the television advert
for Lyons "pyramid" teabags, the one with the man twittering on
about "hydrodynamics" and the secret of the pyramid shape residing
in the "geometric effect", while his female partner makes the tea and
very sensibly points out that it's just that "more space gives it more
flavour". In the end the man comes round to her way of thinking:
more space gives the tea more flavour, he declares. "You're a gen-
ius," she says. Cue laughter and applause.

I assume the "point" of this "joke" is something like this: the man,
incapable of boiling a kettle, is as ridiculous as he is incapable, while
the woman, solid and sensible, makes the tea and gets to the heart of
the matter. The trouble is that it was mostly men who, for what it is
worth, developed the tetrahedral teabag. (If you think this a minor
achievement, let me tell you that Lyons's bumf informs us that "the
3D shape of the pyramid means that the tea within the bag has up to
fifty per cent more room to move, more closely mirroring the brewing
action of loose leaf tea in a teapot. Additionally, the bag floats just
below the surface of the water rather than on the top, this speeds up
the brewing process as the liquid can circulate inside the bag much
faster. An independent view was obtained from the Imperial College
in London, whose thermo-fluid section carried out tests on the new
shape alongside flat, square and round bags. Their tests confirmed

that the brewing action which takes place inside the tetrahedral bag is much closer to that of loose leaf in a teapot.")

The "hook" used in this advert is a standard technique in about thirty to forty per cent of television advertising at the present moment: take a middle-aged, straight, white male, put him with a woman, any woman, and make him look stupid/ignorant/incompetent. If you can dress him in a ridiculous apron, so much the better. Obviously, given that it is a technique used repeatedly by advertisers to sell everything from sausages to cars, it must have been found to work. This being the case, it tells us a lot about the advertisers, the "creative" minds behind the adverts and the people they seek to sell their products to. In short, it tells us a great deal about the kind of culture we now inhabit. (A friend close to the industry, incidentally, points out that the vast majority of marketing managers in industry are now women in their thirties, which he believes accounts for the tone and content of much advertising on radio and television.)

People I have spoken to within the industry, when they admit to having noticed the phenomenon in question at all, invariably seek to argue that it is happening by way of counterbalancing an earlier trend of advertising which was offensive to women. But when challenged to name a television advert which insulted females as much as, say, the current ad for the SuperValu chain of supermarkets insults adult white males, they have no answer.

If you know the advert, forgive the blow-by-blow summary. Two women are sitting in the café of a SuperValu outlet, drinking coffee and eating cake. One of them is speaking on her mobile telephone to a man who is clearly her husband/partner, and the father of her children. "It's not exactly a piece of cake here either", she smirks, as she shovels, yes, cake into her mouth. Cut to adult straight white male in the midst of utter bedlam at home, surrounded by bawling children, and clearly unable to cope. He says something into the telephone which we are unable to hear. "I have my hands full here too, you know," replies the woman, grinning at her companion, who giggles uncontrollably. The adult straight white male asks the woman to bring him home a packet of razor blades — and she rings off. "Swivel-heads to you too," she says to her companion, and the two collapse in paroxysms of mirth.

Imagine the ad with the sexual roles reversed and, instead of "swivel-heads", insert some personal item related to female hygiene. Not nice? No, I didn't think you'd like it much, any more than you might like the corollary of the current advert for Renault cars, featuring the charming lady with the steel tape measure and the slogan "Size Matters".

There is, as you may know, a mechanism whereby complaints about advertising can be adjudicated. It might well be worth submitting a few complaints were it not for the fact that the relevant body, the Advertising Standards Authority for Ireland, appears to have an inbuilt blindspot with regard to sexism against males. The Authority's rules about standards in advertising are very specific with regard to what is termed "sexism and stereotyping", but it does not appear to have occurred to anyone that these phenomena can work both ways. The relevant section starts off promisingly enough: "Advertising should respect the principle of the equality of men and women and the dignity of all persons." It would be hard to argue with that. But then it goes on: "Advertisements should recognise and reflect women's role in society and should avoid stereotyping." It is clear that "equality" in this context means "equality for women", with the virtual certainty that "stereotyping" would be evaluated from the same perspective. There is a veneer of neutrality in the emphasis on "the dignity of all persons" and in the assertion that "Men and women perform and share household management and domestic tasks", but these aspirations quite clearly have no practical effect.

When pinned down on the subject, advertising people offer two arguments by way of defence: one, that most of the "creative" people in advertising are men, to which the obvious answer is that quislings are not a new phenomenon, and two, that such portrayals of men have no effect. But if this is the case, why do people bother to advertise at all? Advertising is about contagion, about spreading ideas among the maximum numbers of potential customers. Why should it be any less effective in disseminating stereotypes than in promoting commercial messages?

Standards in advertising, like standards in anything else are, it is to be presumed, formulated for very good reasons. For example, when the Code of the Advertising Standards Authority sets forth that advertising should respect the dignity of persons "who are vulnerable by reason of age or other condition or circumstance", it can be presumed that there are dangers attached to such standards not being enforced. Clearly, the authority takes the view that advertising is capable of doing serious damage to vulnerable people, unless high standards are upheld. Similarly when it says that advertising should not undermine the confidence of vulnerable persons, or that advertising should "avoid stereotyping or other insensitive approaches which could promote negative images or prove hurtful or distressing to such person or their families", or that advertising should not subject such persons to "ridicule or offensive humour", it is reasonable to assume that if such things are not avoided, the consequences are likely to be inimical to human dignity or well-being.

We could all perhaps have a laugh at incompetent/ridiculous males were it not for the fact that we have a family law system in place which, on a daily basis, deprives children of the care and protection of their fathers as the result of precisely the kind of stereotyping favoured by advertising agencies and their clients. We could all have a giggle at the adult straight white male were it not for the fact that young men on the verge of this condition are opting in ever increasing numbers not to go on, a circumstance which almost certainly has more than a little to do with the culture of denigration surrounding straight white adult manhood.

(September 1999)

19

SPOKESPERSONS FOR THE MARKET

TALKING TO AN ACQUAINTANCE down the West recently, we got to discussing the beauty and refinement of late-twentieth-century advanced capitalism. For sheer order and consistency, for the manner in which it adapts to protect itself against every new twitch in the jungle around it, there are few things in nature to equal it.

The wealth-generating system which governs our societies is now, and has been for a long time, the self-declared most important aspect of human existence, and everything that threatens to reduce either its capacity or influence is treated as hostile. But what is even more fascinating is the manner in which the system is able to recruit to its defence even those elements that have previously shown a tendency to threaten it. In many cases, these become the system's most able protectors.

Take feminism. Once upon a time, feminism threatened to redefine the nature of human desire. In seeking to equalise opportunity for women and men, it was setting out, we fondly imagined, to break down the barriers which confined the sexes to preordained roles. As well as seeking to liberate women into the world of fulfilling paid employment, it demanded that we unblock also the channel in the opposite direction, which separated men from the intimate elements of raising their children. What feminism seemed to hold out was a world utterly transformed in its priorities: men and women would share equally the burdens and joys of family life, and stand shoulder to shoulder in the workplace. The result would be previously undreamt of harmony and balance, not just as a consequence of the immediate readjustments between the sexes, but also of the deep, long-term benefits to be accrued to future generations by virtue of the new enlightenment about the raising of children.

Now, we find that feminists are arguing not for changes that would improve the lot of women, men or children, but for changes that would maximise the efficiency of the market. In the continuing debate about child-minding, for example, what is being called for by leading feminist voices is the immediate creation of conditions in which not only will each family make available to the market the maximum number of operatives, but the maximum further economic activity will be generated in looking after children. Previously, families tended to send forth one operative into the economy, generally the father. Now the market is demanding not only that the mother, too, be liberated to put nuts on Volvos, but that her place in the raising of her children be taken by an outsider, who will also be part of the economy. What the alleged spokespersons on behalf of women are demanding, therefore, is precisely what the market would ask for if it could speak.

The extraordinary thing is that, in doing so, feminists have been seeking to suggest that they speak not merely on behalf of women but also of children. This is an awesome and pernicious arrogance. If women's groups, in seeking to liberate women into paid employment were simultaneously seeking to ensure that fathers were given the opportunity to take over those aspects of the parenting function rendered vacant by the absence of mothers, then there could be no quarrel. But the same interests who seek an equal place for women in the public sphere are also, strangely — or perhaps not — the same ones who seek to deny fathers the society of their own children.

What has happened is that, having achieved some headway with one strand of its agenda, feminism has opted to settle for temporary power-sharing, with a view to eventual supremacy. Having made significant inroads in improving the position of women in the workplace, feminists have changed tack. It is now clear that creating a world in which men and women can achieve more fulfilled lives is no longer the agenda. Feminists have no ambitions for the lives of men, other than that they be ground into the dust of history.

I have seen this at first hand in recent times as I attempted to draw public attention to the situation of men who have been banished from the society of their children. In the beginning, I rather naïvely thought that this issue would bring feminists to my aid. After all, what I was asking was that this somewhat overlooked dimension of their revolution be attended to. But what I found was that, far from getting support from feminists, the only significant resistance was coming from feminists and the political leaders who live in fear of them.

Talking to men of my generation in recent times I have made some rather startling discoveries about the commonality of our experience. We were the first generation of men that not only did not resist the emancipation of women but actively supported it. We took feminism at face value, imagining that it would liberate us also from some of the responsibility of providing and enable us to live more fulfilled lives in harmony with women and children. But now we find that, all the time, we have been sawing off the branch on which we were sitting, while our cheerleading sisters urged us onwards to greater efforts. We find that there is not, after all, any intention of implementing the second part of the feminist agenda.

I was at first quite taken aback when, in highlighting the fatherhood issue, I was accused of attacking feminists. I was genuinely nonplussed that anyone could think that this is what I was doing. I was also, I quickly noticed, anxious to rebut the allegation, as it seemed to me that attacking feminism might be seen as a reactionary activity. Now, I realise that, since actually existing feminism is perhaps the most reactionary force in our society, the only proper course for anyone seeking to promote truly progressive ideas is to attack it without qualification.

The virus that once threatened to destroy the system has now merged with it and is strengthening its resistance to attack. What the system desires above all is that its interests, rather than the interests of human beings, continue to be the priority of human civilisation. And because any move by men to find a place outside the system would still be deeply threatening to its interests, it is necessary for all those with the system's interests at heart to ensure that men do not find it easy to retreat to the bosom of their families. This is why feminism is not interested in helping men to be better fathers and why it is now fundamentally a philosophy about the demonisation of men, creating inter-sexual rancour, and appropriating everyday social issues — like child abuse, domestic violence and even poverty — as primarily issues affecting only women. It is also why leading women's groups are to the fore in demanding repressive state action — always against men.

Yet again, we see the almost perfect nature of George Orwell's fable, *Animal Farm*. The leading feminists of our age, while imagining that they are continuing to promote a radical and progressive agenda, are now the Squealers and the Napoleons of our society.

(May 1999)

20

THE NOOKIE PRINCIPLE

I FIND IT ENDLESSLY FASCINATING THAT, whenever I attempt to make an argument about something unorthodox or new, I find myself confronted by a phalanx of respondents whose tactic is to represent me as the opposite of themselves. Invariably, they are self-styled liberals, pluralists, feminists and so forth, and I, by definition, am the antithesis. Because they are so convinced of their own rightness about everything, anything that challenges their views can only be reactionary and wrong.

The most recent occasion of this experience has been my attempt to put forward some tentative perspectives on the changing relationships between the sexes. Although I have explored many aspects, general and specific, of the changing balance of power between men and women, I have yet to encounter a single voice of opposition prepared to engage with what I have actually written or said.

For several years now, I have been writing about the frightening increase in male suicides, the discrimination against fathers in the family courts, the depiction of adult straight white males in media advertising and the neglect of men's health. Not once in that time has anyone responded with a coherent rebuttal of the facts I have outlined. Invariably, the responses to my articles have been personalised attacks on my character or motivations. Often, critics have sought to engage with me on the basis of positions that I had not advanced at all, but which, clearly, they would like me to have adopted, so as to make my arguments easier to knock down. A frequent tactic is to represent what I have written about fatherhood and men as an attack on women, which is a bit like saying that it is an attack on Galway to suggest that Roscommon needs better roads.

In response to one article I wrote about men and suicide, a male writer of a letter to the editor wrote that I was ignoring the damaging effect of male suicides on female survivors, and therefore I was being irresponsible. It did not seem to occur to him that, in his utter indifference to the plight of the boys and men who had actually died, he was making my point far more graphically than I was. Another man wrote that "we don't need people who tell us to defend our outdated and indefensible privileges".

I have never suggested that men should move to defend their privileges. In my view, the privileges of men, where they have existed at all, have been poisoned chalices. The "dominance" of the male in politics, economics and work has come with a heavy price tag. Not only has it alienated men from the core meaning of their existence, which resides in the role of fatherhood, but it has set them up as the scapegoats of a deeply spiteful backlash which refuses to acknowledge that such "dominance" occurred out of the prevailing circumstances in a world where the nature of work suggested that men were, all other things being equal, the more appropriate breadwinners.

In large part, of course, the refusal to engage with the substance of my arguments arises because the points I have made have been incontrovertible, the mere articulation of the everyday experience of people in the real world. My only attack has been on society and its dangerously skewed thinking. Attempts to smear me as a "misogynist" are typical of this thinking. (Isn't it remarkable that such accusations now issue forth, without irony, from the adherents of an ideology that for thirty years has been creating inter-sexual rancour by demonising men?)

I find it interesting, too, that the most vociferous voices against me in this argument are male. Most intelligent women, even some convinced feminists, know in their hearts that what I say is true. My late *Irish Times* colleague, Mary Cummins, for example, one of those who spearheaded women's struggle for equality in Ireland since the 1960s, told me several times that what I was saying about the treatment of men in society was so obvious that she could not see how anyone found it objectionable.

I would imagine that most sensible women find the present culture of the sanctified female and the demonised male offensive — not because it oppresses them but because it patronises them mercilessly and denies their truth as much as it denies that of their men. It is also forgotten by those who elect to speak on behalf of womankind that most women have fathers, brothers, husbands, sons and nephews, in whose happiness they have a vested interest.

Most men, too, know in their hearts that our sex faces serious problems that are not being acknowledged. Some who live with these realities on a daily basis shrug and say, "What's new?" But others, precisely because they recognise in what I say the substance of a fear that has long been within themselves, must shout me down in order to suppress that voice inside. Because the culture tells them so, they believe that their own redemption resides in further self-flagellation. Most of these men are well-educated, genuinely privileged people. For them, in their individual lives, survival for the moment resides in repeating the lie, in pretending that everything is as the culture describes it. Why rock the boat when it's much easier to say what they think women want to hear? People who insist on describing reality as it is represent a serious threat to their sexual, political, emotional and economic security.

In the field of personal relationships, this syndrome is known as "the nookie principle", a self-explanatory concept. But it also has a political expression. Usually, the men who push themselves to the fore in attacking those who seek more balance in inter-sexual matters are academic hacks whose careers have flourished because of a strict adherence to feminist orthodoxy. (I also, incidentally, find it bizarre that people who seek to lecture me about my alleged "privileges" almost invariably do so from behind university degrees and addresses, the irony arising from the fact that, my alleged manly dominance notwithstanding, a university education is a privilege of which I have never had the privilege. But then again, perhaps this just goes to explain my lack of enlightenment.)

Just as their personal lives are dominated by the belief that women must be flattered and uncritically appeased, experience tells these honorary Sisters that they will not fail to prosper professionally if they continue to say the right things. These men are not stupid. They see, as I do, the writing on the wall, but believe that the system that has favoured them thus far can bury the truth for another few years — long enough for them to negotiate the greasy pole. Their present objective is to create a bogus, castrated "men's movement" which would have men crawling around on their hands and knees, apologising for their existence. This would result in the frustration of any real engagement with these issues for another generation.

I hope it keeps fine for them. I hope, sincerely, that they never have to cut one of their sons down from the rafters of an outhouse or scrape a loved brother's brains from a bathroom wall.

(December 1999)

II

Millennial Revisions:
Changes and Contradictions

I

NEUTRALITY AS MORAL INDEPENDENCE

IT WILL PERHAPS COME AS SOMETHING of a shock to John Bruton to be told that he has in recent times become one of the most eloquent exponents of Irish neutrality. The element of surprise might arise from the fact that Mr Bruton and his party, Fine Gael, have for a long time been to the fore in pushing or dragging Ireland into various forms of alliance with the military power blocs, all the time seeking to undermine the credibility of Irish neutrality so as to soften us up for such mergers. For several years now, leading members of Fine Gael have been chipping away at the concept of Irish neutrality in terms suggesting that it is no more than a sentimental hankering after a less knowing past. But last week, Mr Bruton did Ireland and its tradition of military neutrality a great service by his criticisms of the NATO bombing of Yugoslavia and his calls for a humane response to the refugee crisis. Mr Bruton's remarks about the predictability of the vast exodus from Kosovo and his attack on the British Foreign Secretary, Robin Cook, for saying that the refugee crisis could not have been foreseen, were courageous and well observed. His call for a cessation of the bombing over the Orthodox Easter period, to allow for a negotiated settlement, was sensible and decent. This was a long way from the conventional image of Irish neutrality — as portrayed by its opponents — of the slinking, mealy-mouthed fence-sitter, dispensing blessings in scrupulously equal measure on both sides of a conflict, regardless of considerations of relative strength or objective morality.

Mr Bruton's remarks were fully in the spirit of Article 29.1 of the Irish Constitution, which states that "Ireland affirms its devotion to the ideal of peace and friendly co-operation amongst nations founded on international justice and morality".

The irony is that, if his party had already won the argument about Irish neutrality, Mr Bruton would be less free to make such statements. His subsequent assertion — that if Ireland had not been "sitting on the sidelines" when the decisions about military action in Yugoslavia were being made, it would have had a greater opportunity to counter the "simplistic view" which led to the NATO decision to intervene — seems naïve. If Mr Bruton were Taoiseach of a Republic of Ireland with full membership of NATO (not an entirely improbable scenario, the way things are going), he would have had no choice but to bite his tongue and acquiesce in the dropping of hell from the heavens over Yugoslavia. He would not have been in any position to criticise our military partners, still less accuse them of telling untruths.

This highlights something that for a long time should have been obvious, but which the disingenuousness of many of those seeking to sell out on Irish neutrality has served to conceal: being neutral does not mean standing idly by. There is, therefore, undoubtedly an urgent need to re-examine the fundamentals of our neutral stance, but without assuming in advance that the outcome of such discussions will be stronger links with military alliances, as opposed to clarification of the principles of Irish neutrality with a view to enhancing our independence.

To the credit of Fine Gael and its recent leaders, let it be noted that they have been consistent on this issue for a long time, maintaining that Ireland had a moral duty to participate in the military life of its allies in Europe and beyond. For all that one might disagree, this is a straightforward and essentially proper position, which cannot be faulted on the basis that it is dishonest or cynical. Where I would find fault with this stance is on the basis that it is mistaken, that it is a knee-jerk response to the guilt engendered by dishonest and misplaced criticism, and that it is an unnecessary selling-out of an important freedom to interests over which we would afterwards have less rather than more influence than at present.

It is true that Irish neutrality has become the source of much cant and hypocrisy in the distant and recent past, but that does not mean it does not contain something valuable and worthy of retention. It is true, for example, that both Fianna Fáil and the Labour Party have for years treated Irish neutrality as something to be, in opposition, paraded as a virtue and, in government, offered for sale. The present government's efforts to present as a moral issue its proposal to enlist Ireland in the NATO-sponsored Partnership For Peace, for example, are threadbare and bankrupt. There can be no morality in seeking to barter off what is left of Ireland's decency and independence, and this lack of morality is nowhere as visible as in the lack of integrity of those politicians who have suddenly been "persuaded" that the changing nature of international affairs now calls on them to renege on every principle they previously pronounced upon in this connection. Three years ago, speaking as Leader of the Opposition in a Dáil debate on the Partnership For Peace, Bertie Ahern said that any attempt to join without a referendum would be "a serious breach of faith and fundamentally undemocratic". More recently, in his capacity as Taoiseach, Mr Ahern announced his intention to resile from this and other previous commitments, including a 1997 Fianna Fáil election manifesto promise, in respect of Ireland's relationship with the PFP. "I would envisage, all going well," he told the Dáil earlier this year, "that Ireland will join the Partnership For Peace on a mutually agreed basis in the second half of this year."

As usual, what debate there has been has followed the line of maximum cynicism. I noticed a letter on the Letters to the Editor page last week from a prospective Labour Party local representative, berating Fianna Fáil for its lack of principle. But Labour Party activists would do well to keep their guns in their holsters when it comes to pointing up U-turns on this issue. For Mr Ahern is not the first to play the game of advocating neutrality in opposition and attacking it in government: the former Labour Party leader, Dick Spring, has won in perpetuity the T-shirt for this form of two-timing. Once among the most passionate upholders of Irish neutrality, as exemplified by its proposal to amend the Maastricht Treaty to oppose "any involvement by Ireland in military structures derived from NATO or the Western European Union", the Labour Party has little to be smug about in this regard. The party's Constitution states: "The Labour Party's commitment to peace means that we will seek to solve disputes through peaceful means, turn our backs on the barbarism of war, and strengthen our position as a militarily neutral nation outside all military alliances." In its manifesto for the 1992 election, the Labour Party pledged to take "all steps necessary", including seeking a constitutional affirmation, to defend Irish neutrality, claiming that it was obvious that "other Irish political parties are prepared to make very major concessions on the status of our neutrality in response to the views of other political forces within the NATO/WEU ambit". In government between 1993 and 1997, Mr Spring was the most active ever advocate of Ireland's membership of the PFP, leaving Mr Ahern's government with a difficult act to follow in the matter of crawling before the world's military superpowers.

It is obvious that the only purpose of the PFP is to be an antechamber of NATO. It was established five years ago by NATO as part of a conscious strategy of enlargement, to facilitate military co-operation between existing NATO countries, those currently adopting neutral stances, and the emerging democracies of eastern Europe. The only purpose of Ireland's joining the PFP would be to provide a *fait accompli* to later be presented to the Irish electorate as evidence that we had already technically lost our virginity and should now go all the way. As in other matters relating to European integration, the Irish electorate is being forced to yield another slice of salami under the pretence that it represents a minor and rather harmless development of the existing position. The next slice will be fatal to Irish neutrality, but it will be levied in the same way and by the same logic. This is not a debate, but a process with one end only: outright acquiescence in the wishes of the warmongers. The "options" are carefully crafted so as to exclude any redefinition of the position in a way that might enhance rather than dilute Irish neutrality.

There is undoubtedly an urgent need to renew and update the concept of Irish neutrality in the post-Cold War world. But this does not necessarily imply, as those who oppose neutrality relentlessly suggest, that neutrality is now outmoded and should be surrendered. Perhaps a more accurate description of Ireland's position would be a word like "uncommitted", conveying a sense that, while we are prepared to participate on the side of good against evil, we are not about to sign up uncritically to one side regardless of future circumstances. Such a word could without difficulty have been applied to last week's courageous and timely remarks by John Bruton, which maintained a balance between standing up to Milosevic and criticising his enemies. Just because we do not want to sell our souls does not mean we should not point out the difference between right and wrong.

(April 1999)

2

TERROR, TERROR IS THIS DAY

(Thoughts in the frozen moments after 9/11)

MY FATHER WAS BURIED ON the same day as the Ayatollah Khomeini, who died the day after him. Cut off from the news media, I knew nothing of this until I caught sight of a television in a pub after we had returned from the graveyard.

Some years later, reading Don DeLillo's novel *Mao II*, I came upon the following description of that June day in 1989, from the viewpoint of a character called Karen: "The living forced their way into the burial site, bloodying their hands and tearing at their hair, choking in the thick dust, and the body of Khomeini rested in a flimsy box, a kind of litter with low sides, and Karen found she could go into the slums of south Teheran, backwards into people's lives, and hear them saying, We have lost our father. All the dispossessed waking to the morning call. Sorrow, sorrow is this day."

Terror, terror is this day. I could see in the faces of those hundreds of thousands of people who sought that day to prevent the body of their father going into the ground that what consumed them was not sorrow but fear. They did not want, any more than I did, their father to leave them, for how could they face the terrors of the world without him? DeLillo wrote: "The living touched the body, they pressed the imam's flesh to keep him warm."

I remember as a teenager that a great-aunt who lived on Long Island, NYC, took for a while to sending us postcards of the newly constructed World Trade Centre. We had not been to New York, but those postcards told us our aunt was more proud that she lived within sight of those towers than of anything else. "Look," she said, "I am at the heart of the world, our world, your world."

Fear begets fear. Vertigo, the fear of heights, might now be redefined as a fear of getting above oneself. Until last week, I had imagined that my fear of heights was irrational to the point of superstition. The trepidation I felt on the upper storeys of tall buildings was a measure of a fear, I was persuaded, that defied logic. Now I know all it defied was experience, a different thing. We have been shown that our deepest fears have a sound basis in reality.

Looking at my great-aunt's postcards, I used to puzzle: why, if this was the centre of our world, was it necessary to build these towers up into the sky, when the whole of Connacht was crying out for people? Why, if this was the same world as ours, was my great-aunt living thousands of miles away from where she longed to be? The magnetism of capital had sucked her in to live beside this human geyser, shooting its human contents up into the clouds. We imagined we had mastered the earth, but in truth we had ourselves been mastered.

The battle between Islam and the West is the world's last battle between tradition and modernity. Faith, devotion and authority of the old kind confront science, reason and materialism and the most violent must bear everything away. Last Tuesday was a meeting of the unstoppable force and the immoveable object. Strangely, the inertia of tradition was represented by a moving aeroplane, while the driving whirlwind of progress was depicted in the seemingly indestructible twin towers of the World Trade Centre. We saw what happened. We are left with our fears.

For several decades now, Islam has been under bombardment from the western media, from Hollywood, CNN, and the liberal voices of postmodern cynicism. Besieged by values which not merely seek to contradict its faith and unsettle its austerity, but to undermine the very essence of its devotion and mysticism, Islam has retreated into a cocoon of paranoia, yes, but also self-sufficiency. Other traditions have crumbled, but Islam has not. It has been observed that the West does not have an answer to suicide bombers, to the characteristic of indifference to personal welfare upon which its enemy is able to call. It has not been widely observed that those who destroyed the World Trade Centre were also using as a weapon the very instrument of media power that had been used for so long against them. Without television, this act would have been meaningless, and therefore unthinkable. Its awesome evil resided not simply in the ingeniousness of its turning of the crudest of technologies against the heart of modernity, but in its calculated strike against the western imagination, using the very instruments which had seemed to make the West omnipotent.

There are only two known antidotes to fear: action and prayer. Each on its own is useless. In its hour of grief, America fell back upon values that the logic of consumerism has done so much to erode: faith in God and belief in authority of the old kind. The most impressive people of the past week have been George W. Bush and Billy Graham. Just as its enemy, driven by fears of engulfment, surrendered a little to the anti-values that threatened it, so the West, in its terror, rushed backwards to embrace the values it had all but abandoned. Western liberalism lies buried in the rubble of the World Trade Centre, and at the pulpit are the figures of men who walk in the old way, uttering words of war in the pauses between prayers. Our fathers are risen and walk among us.

(September 2001)

3

FALLING IN LOVE

I THOUGHT I HAD COMPREHENDED the awfulness of what happened in Manhattan until someone drew my attention to a photograph in one of the American news weeklies. It showed people jumping from one of the towers before it collapsed. Of the figures of several men and women plummeting to their deaths, two, a man and a woman, appeared to be holding hands.

It is cliché to say that the calamity of the World Trade Centre resembled the most unbelievable horror sci-fi movie. I watched from within minutes of the first plane hitting the first tower. There was something unreal, unreachable, about it. The thought crossed my mind that we have evolved forms of technology to watch such calamities but no means of intervening in them.

When the towers began to fall, there was a, yes, spectacularity about it, and one had to deliberately remind oneself that there were still possibly thousands of people inside. So many times we had seen comparable sights created by special effects, acquiring the ability to be shocked without feeling anything real. That dual emotional response did not disperse in me until I forced myself to look at that photograph.

And I had to force myself. This image was beyond words, belief or comprehension, and yet somehow made possible the beginnings of comprehension. Its horror, it began to dawn on me, resided in the story that might lie behind it.

Who were they, this man and this woman? What did they mean to one another? Were they lovers or good friends? What had been their thoughts, that morning, brushing their teeth? Had they arrived at the World Trade Centre a short time before, hand in hand? Did they ascend in the lift together? Were they alone and, if so, did they smooch on the way up? Did they linger a moment in a corridor before going to their separate desks, planning to meet for lunch? Did one of them ring the other just after they parted? And in the fateful moments after the plane hit their tower did they seek one another out, understanding immediately that this was the end? What did they say to begin to comprehend what had happened to their beautiful lives, to their hopes and dreams, to their plans of being together? What words did they use, this man and this woman, to set in train the beginning of the end of their lives? Which of them made the first move, beginning the short process of setting out the awful logic of their situation? Did the man say to the woman, or the woman to the man, "We are going to die"? How did this notion begin to root itself between them? Did their lives flash before them, both at the same time? Did they have time to look into the awful chasm now opening up between what they had imagined their lives might be like and what their remaining minutes or hours were likely to be like unless they took their lives into their own hands? How did they come to terms with that enormity in the little time they had to make up their minds? Or were they just too terrified for words? Was the situation and its awful solution so obvious that no words were necessary or even possible? Were tears their only exchange? Did the man lead the woman, or the woman lead the man, in silence towards the window and to their mutual doom? What was it like, in those stricken rooms in those fatally wounded towers in those final minutes as the world looked on, unable to do anything, unable even to register the emotional difference between this and a Spiderman movie? Was there a logic to that final act? Was it based on the ineluctable knowledge of the reality which we now know only too well? Did they know for sure the tower would fall? Was there nothing of hope? Did they make a conscious choice that falling to their deaths

was better than being roasted alive? Did they pray for a miracle, perhaps being blown onto a ledge below the fire beneath them. Did God
come into it? Did they decide to depart this world hand-in-hand, so as
to enter the next in the same way? Did they jump at the same instant
or had one of them to pull the other after him or her? Did they utter
final words of love? Were there other people queuing up for the ledge
and did they have to jump hurriedly without saying goodbye, or safe
home or see you on the other side? Did they speak on the way down?
How long did it take before they hit the ground — how long, I mean,
in real time — the length of time it takes to — what? — turn the page
of a newspaper or change the channel on a TV set? Did they have
time to look around, one last time, at the world they had so suddenly
to depart? Did one of them perhaps catch a glimpse of what might
have been, in the distance, a camera flash, before that first blaze of
heaven exploded in their brains?

I hope and pray they are together now, that man and woman we
saw falling in togetherness, and that they can remember their dreams
of love on Earth and laugh at how little they had been prepared to settle for. May they rest in peace and love.

(September 2001)

4

CHANGED UTTERLY

SEPTEMBER 11 IN MANHATTAN rendered Irish neutrality finally redundant, at least for this long-time defender of that policy. Loy-
alty and duty require from us that we now support the United States. I
believe there are several reasons why the present situation is, in political and military terms, utterly different from anything in the past.
But the primary reason we should support the Americans is that not to
do so would be wrong.

Irish neutrality was never intended to be an opting out of moral
responsibility. It was, rather, a somewhat vague but nevertheless sincere effort to retain our independence, the better to avoid involvement
in conflicts into which we had no input and over which we had no
control. It was the practical articulation of Article 29.1 of the Irish
Constitution, which states: "Ireland affirms its devotion to the ideal of
peace and friendly co-operation amongst nations founded on international justice and morality."

Although beset by many contradictions, Irish neutrality was never
a matter of pragmatism, cowardice or hypocrisy. The origins of the
policy were undoubtedly pragmatic, but it endured during times when
the restraining voice of Ireland was an important one against nuclear
proliferation and increasing militarisation in the world. It represented,
quite simply, a reservation of the Irish position pending the emergence of clarity about each or any situation. In impeding conscription
to organisations such as NATO and Partnership For Peace, neutrality
stood for the very simple principle of not desiring to be committed in

advance. It had to do with raising a voice of conscience, restraint or refusal, as opposed to meek acquiescence in whatever our more powerful allies decided. As such, I believe it was an admirable and clearsighted philosophy. Those who have defended it I would count as among the most idealistic people in the land.

But the world after September 11 is utterly changed. The ferocity, cunning, callousness and inhumanity of that act surpassed anything we have seen. Certainly, there are arguments to be had about American foreign policy, about the bombing of Iraq, about the effect of trade sanctions on innocent people. But while these debates are continuing, there can be no doubt about our duty: we must be on the side of those who were so grievously assaulted in New York on September 11. There can be no moral trade-off on the basis of the relative inhumanity of atrocities. We cannot claim to be sincere in our professed concern for Iraqi children if we can conceive of the utter barbarity of what occurred in New York and see that it cannot go unanswered. The United States is morally entitled to respond to these attacks, in whatever way its leaders, having taken due counsel and after appropriate reflection, decide.

It is clear also, of course, that our interests, including our economic interests, reside in supporting the United States. We are part of the western world, and therefore part of what has been attacked. Our neutrality would mean nothing to those who carried out this outrage. They would destroy us without compunction. Unless we support the United States against this barbarism, we are not entitled to the protection we will surely need if these agents of evil are not dealt with for good. We should, of course, argue for compliance with the established rules of military conflict, but no more than that.

Fundamentally, our foreign policy has always been pragmatic. It was based, sensibly, as much on self-interest as on principled objection to gratuitous militarism. What was sometimes disquieting was the extent to which Irish politicians were prepared to pay lip-service to neutrality while in opposition, and in office sell it down the river. Even more worrying was that the sell-outs were invariably made not in the face of some pressing moral imperative but in the sole interests of nurturing economic and political bonds with other western nations. Over the years, we have continued to elect political leaders who had either no understanding of Irish neutrality or no genuine commitment to it. As a result, we have entered into tacit understandings with the United States, Britain and other European nations which it would be wrong to renege on now. Since we failed to call a halt to the sell-out, it is now, as well as being an inappropriate time to plead Irish neutrality, far too late for this to have any credibility.

There is no loss of face here for those who have defended our neutral stance. In fact, the present situation raises, in this context, an opportunity for a truly moral and pragmatic arrangement between hawks and doves: the prospect of the closure of Sellafield on the grounds that it represents the most likely target for terrorists intent upon wreaking in these islands the kind of havoc they created in New York.

Irish neutrality is not the only thing beset by contradictions: western military alliances have long laboured under the contradiction that, while ostensibly seeking to limit nuclear proliferation, they were also enabling the spread of nuclear technology for civil purposes. Those who opposed nuclear technology have pointed out many times that the availability of plutonium at plants like Sellafield seriously increases the risk of nuclear terrorism in the world. In New York on September 11 we witnessed the handiwork of terrorists who have mastered the judo-fighter's trick of using his opponent's strengths against him. It does not take much to imagine what might happen if such logic were to be directed at Sellafield, the closure and dismantling of which is therefore now an urgent military imperative.

(October 2001)

5

LETTING GO OF THE DREAM

SEPTEMBER 11. I DOUBT IF THERE WILL come a time when we will need to reinstate the year, for only a greater hurt could dilute the power of that date, and such a thing is unimaginable. I nearly wrote "almost unimaginable" but shy away from tempting evil.

These autumn days used to be associated with the return to school, a sufficiency of horror of itself for those who had not yet lost their innocence. But no more. These days of low clouds, stolen sunshine and blackberry jam — previously coloured by what has now resumed the status of mere childish horror — will, for those whose lives were transfixed by the unspeakable calamity of a year ago, forever carry this new moroseness as its dominant shade. And in that number is included, surely, anyone with a human heart.

The moment has not yet passed. Maybe on Thursday morning it can begin to. Today it remains a dull ache in the gut, even for those who watched from afar and, having watched, could still hold their loved ones to them. Such days had been identified, promised, dreaded in the past, but this was surely one we feared beyond imagining.

The era since the 1960s could be characterised as the age of peace, love and understanding. For all the conflict and bloodshed of those years, there had been, underlying it all, an undercurrent of hope, a belief that reason and positivity might help to usher in a new dispensation. This optimism emerged from the pop revolution of the sixties, the All-You-Need-Is-Love revolution, which at the time seemed like an unexceptionable and rather nice idea. This youth-driven utopianism grew and was nurtured and grew still more in the art schools and campuses of London, Paris, California and New York, and was carried on the airwaves to the furthermost recesses of the western world. It was also, strangely and paradoxically, a rather aggressive idea, a renunciation, a repudiation, a refusal. It rejected the authority of the past, of the Father, of the Leader, of the imperfectly human, and suggested in its place the authority of fellow feeling, of belief in the essential goodness of all humanity.

The problem was that it rarely engaged with its quarry other than in an abstract way. It was detached, luxuriously so. It rested blithely on the soft upholstery of western civilisation, the entity it attacked with such scorn and sanctity, assuming peace and safety to be natural states of affairs. And strangely, too, it took on almost the precise colours and contours of the paternalism exhibited by the discredited and fallen elders it condemned. Thus, the moral dilemmas of the world, not to mention their consequences, were all happening somewhere else, in places where, as what analysis there was would have it, the flow of peace, love and understanding had been curtailed by the venality and vested interests of the failed elders. The passion of this new politics was born of, above all, distance from the war zone and was emblemised by a strident refusal to perceive imperialism other than that which began at home. In this new politics, too, there was a redefinition of heroism, in the valorisation of draft-dodging and the sexualisation of refusal: the girls who said Yes to the guys who said No.

Virtually all our present-day western political cultures are products of the fusion of this sixties' utopianism with the hard-headedness of established power. In recent times, every country in the western hemisphere has aspired to being run by a coalition between student politics and the permanent government. These arrangements are propelled by a woolly positivism based on the belief that human beings really are basically good if unprovoked, a fallacy sustained by the absence of real danger. And although representing an undoubtedly sincere pursuit of idealism, the nature of the coalitions enables reactionism to be held in reserve.

It has been both startling and strangely reassuring to observe the recent subsuming of popular utopianism by the natural bellicosity of power, but also intriguing to observe that this has met with almost total public approval. It was noticeable how, in the immediate wake of September 11, the initial sense of absolute horror seemed to buckle slightly in the public arena, mainly as a result of the what-aboutery of America's enemies. But, other than in the hearts of the professional oppositionists, this attempt to accommodate to the new frontier of outrage failed to gain a foothold in the beating hearts of real people.

Among the many deaths of September 11, then, was the death of sixties' utopianism. Even casual encounters now between the erstwhile adherents of this pseudo-radicalism are visited by an uncertainty that rarely troubled them in the past. There is such a significant possibility that one or other party will have been transformed by the events of a year ago that it is unsafe to make assumptions about anything. There remains the shadow of the old iconoclasm, but it usually lacks either conviction or sincerity, and what occurs is a variation on the standard dance between two people unsure of each other's intentions until one of them comes clean and enables a new commonality to reveal itself. I have such encounters all the time now, characterised above all by the realisation that the dream is indeed over, that those of us who nourished ourselves on the luxurious radicalism of the remote are finally obliged to grow up. Once you have watched the beginning of the end of the world with someone you love, it is impossible to return to humbug.

(September 2002)

6

THE REDUNDANCY OF PACIFISM

THE TENOR OF THE CONDEMNATION BY alleged advocates of peace of the leaders of the US/UK alliance has been too personalised, too intense, too rude and too, yes, violent, to be accepted as genuine pacifism. It is an odd brand of pacifism that majors in daubing things with red paint. The attempt at symbolism is crude and hackneyed, but the unintended semiotics are inescapable also. Although there is a degree of side-stepping with regard to Mr Blair, it is clear that most of those who oppose the war seem to have much stronger feelings against the US President, George Bush, than against the tyrant Saddam. People walk up and expect me to agree with them when they fulminate about Mr Bush's "madness", "stupidity" or bad English. When I shake my head, they begin to shake all over.

There is, then, behind the rhetoric of concern for Iraqi children, some more profound feelings: rage and fear. The fear I wrote about some weeks back — a sublimated knowingness that we in the West are dealing with perhaps the greatest threat we have ever faced. There is a sense of a syndrome that often accompanies attempts to deal with bullies: when the brave stand up and say "Enough!", less valiant souls shrink back and plead: "Go easy!"

The rage aspect is even more interesting. There are, clearly, elements within the anti-war movement intent upon exploiting the situation to create political disruption. There is also a huge amount of genuine sentiment, much of it emanating from the young, or at least reflecting a youthful viewpoint based on idealism and hope. But mixed in with this idealism is a more malignant strain — an almost hysterical opposition to the clarity of an authority which would set limits on the freedoms western culture has promised all its subjects. This manifests itself in the expression of arguably coherent political viewpoints, but is in reality a repudiation of rule by principle rather than populism. In our media-saturated age, we are moving towards government by phone-in talk-show, and anyone who would draw a line in the land is to be condemned as a dictator. Even the presence in the equation of a real dictator does not quell those who spit venom towards the voices of reason and reality.

The most persuasive argument — not merely as to why this war is both necessary and moral but why also those protesting against it are out of touch with the present — was articulated by Mr Blair in his televised address on the night after the first wave of bombing. "The threat to Britain today is not that of my father's generation," he said. Instantly, we must know what he meant.

All of us who grew up in the shadow of the Cold War had a sense of the clear moral dimensions of global conflict. Nuclear weapons were to be used only as a response to their use; first use was illegal and was understood, more or less on both sides, to be morally wrong. Moreover, the concept of mutual deterrence provided a reasonable degree of security in the West based on the idea that fear of retaliation in kind would prevent our enemies from using the technology they were known to possess. This support-arch of mutual fear enabled the world to avoid an apocalypse.

These conditions do not exist in the new global hostilities. Mr Blair spelt out, broadly, the altered conditions in which we now live, pitted against a culture, or at least a significant part of one, which does not share our values or perceptions. Whether that Muslim world is justified in its repudiation of the — in its eyes — morally degenerate West is an interesting philosophical question, but the answer, whatever it is, will not save us or our children from the almost certain consequences of this antagonism. Moreover, within that world there exists a cultural and religious perception with regard to the very meaning of life, which destroys any hope of a coexistence based on mutual deterrence. The reality suggested by suicide bombers prepared to destroy themselves as well as the perceived enemies of Islam renders impossible a Cold War-style stand-off. September 11 left the matter beyond any doubt: if the West did not eliminate its enemies, its enemies would eliminate it. It is not nice that this is the case. It would be better if the world could live in harmony. That it cannot is sad. But this is where we find ourselves.

The new realities are stark, and Mr Blair sketched them out coherently while seeking to avoid inviting the inevitable backlash a more explicit diagram would have attracted. The combination of suicide-bombers, profound hatred and actual weaponry of mass destruction amounts no longer to a political problem: it threatens the end of the world. The idea, therefore, implicit in both the anti-war rhetoric and United Nations procrastination, that the West must wait to be sure of its facts, is like advocating a check for live wires using a moistened finger.

There is a sense, then, that the anti-war movement exists in a time-warp, that its heart is living in the sixties still. It is, in a way, encouraging that people still care enough about their world to go out and protest. But the protestors are naïve, and Mr Blair and Mr Bush are right to ignore them. For the first time in a generation, the West has as its leaders men who are prepared to do what they know to be right even at the expense of their personal or political popularity. They, not the protestors, have responsibility for protecting America and Europe from the attentions of its sworn enemies, and they alone would be blamed if they failed to act in time.

(*March 2003*)

7

MELODRAMOCRACY

(On the Inquiry into the death of the British scientist, Dr David Kelly)

O N HIS WAY IN TO TESTIFY at the Hutton Inquiry last week, Tony Blair turned to look towards the media cameras vulturing from a distance. The image of the British Prime Minister's face, carried throughout the world, was a picture of the unhealth of western democracy at perhaps its most critical moment for fifty years. That fleeting glance betrayed an emotion somewhere between defiance and pleading, an expression of beleaguered incomprehension, which, for all that it was personal, was also profoundly political, the look of a leader caught up in a madness he does not rightly understand.

Mr Blair was attending to give evidence at an inquiry he had himself established to investigate the circumstances of the apparent suicide of a government official. He had, in other words, appeared to invoke and co-operate with one of the checks retained by British democracy for its protection. Yet, the mood was suggestive of a hanging party — a mob of placard-waving malcontents, a pressgang dripping with cynicism, and a general sense that he was fighting for his political life.

The idea that someone in authority must be "to blame" for something as incomprehensible as a lone suicide belongs in one of the dottier plots in *Coronation Street*. It is the product of a tabloidised society, in which collective thought reaches critical mass at the level of cheap melodrama and saloon bar spite. By the logic of the Hutton Inquiry, no scrutiny will in future be possible of the behaviour of any individual, lest that individual go on to self-destruct. This promises, to begin with, the end of jurisprudence and workplace discipline.

The presence in the equation of a Law Lord does nothing to diminish the silliness of it all. It is silly that public controversy over a decision to take a nation to war has telescoped down into scrutiny of the private pain of one individual. It is even sillier that people see this as democracy in action. The Hutton Inquiry circus makes sense to political opportunists, conspiracy theorists, existential anoraks and the terminally disgruntled. To sensible people it makes no sense. Once, a British PM would have dealt with such an event in a terse statement to the House of Commons, leaving the rest to the coroner. But politics has been replaced by something called "the optics", a miasma of distortion created by the fog of public ennui hitting the cold pane of media cynicism. Hence, Hutton, all that fallout, and the potentially lethal consequences for the capacity of leadership to make important decisions in the public interest.

Perhaps dictionaries of political phenomena will in time identify the 1990s as the era when something to be named, perhaps, "hyperdemocracy" or "melodramocracy" surfaced in advanced western societies. For now, we perceive things fuzzily, vaguely, paradoxically. In the mix, certainly, is creeping tabloidisation, with its debasement of public thought. Today's public demands, through its duly elected media, that its "leaders" answer to the most simple-minded logic while evincing the lower forms of emotional response. The result is government by taxi-driver, characterised by piety, sincerity and populism, rather than intelligence, responsibility, and resolve.

Several years ago, mistaking some conspicuous trees for the wood, I warned that Blair's attempts to ingratiate himself with the Murdoch press would be his undoing. Today, Murdoch remains embedded with the Blair government, but the infection he unleashed into the British body politic has seeped upwards to contaminate even the "quality" press and the national broadcaster.

Even the talents of the brilliant Alastair Campbell have proved insufficient to protect Tony Blair from the intrusion of the new hyperdemocracy, in which government derives from the cynical exploitation by a voracious media of the sub-intelligent whims of an idle, bored and insatiable public. Campbell's job was to anticipate the doltishness of the public mood and pander to it before it could be exploited by media scrambling for material and mischief. In New Labour's first term he delivered with aplomb. But, inevitably, his undisguised contempt for media hypocrisy caused the tamed animals to turn on the ringmaster, with the results we now observe.

It all warns that, in the future, we may retain a form of democracy, but not the representation by intelligent people of the will of the people. Instead, we will have the hyperventilating response of a beleaguered political establishment to a public clamour for this, that, the other and the opposite, all at the same time, a process governed by rage, fear, piety, stupidity and sentimentality. In these conditions, the steady knit-one-purl-one of responsible government will unravel in a succession of dropped stitches, as the leaders of democracy dance to the loudest, most witless voices in the land.

(September 2003)

8

FEAR OF PASSION

A FEW YEARS AGO, WHEN A PLAY of mine was staged in Kilkenny, we had a problem about costumes. The play was set vaguely around 2020, and we were searching for a useful putative concept of the appropriate dress sense. It was important that the clothes not attract attention for the wrong reasons, but also that they carry a sense of a future a little like the present, while allowing for speculative possibilities about how present-day notions of linear "progress" might become unseated. We didn't resolve the issue, largely because of a sense that fashion never follows predictable lines; hence any attempt at anticipating a specific future would entrap the play in whatever is the antithesis of nostalgia — a bit like those essays we wrote in school about "Life in 2000 AD".

I had, I imagined, one good idea. I thought it would be fun to dress one of the characters, a man born perhaps in the 1990s, in a white T-shirt, emblazoned with the head of Padraic Pearse, and the legend "1916–2016". The idea was to communicate a sense of a future normality in which a young man might, casually and without any manifest motivation, wear an emblem that was not condemnatory of the Irish revolution. My plan was for the T-shirt to provide a deliberately puzzling counterpoint to a play with no overt references to such issues. Some critics drew all sorts of inferences about the "message". Others decided that the T-shirt was a device to signal that the play was set in 2016, whereas I thought everyone knew commemorative T-shirts are never worn, other than by zealots and nerds, until years after the events they proclaim. I wanted to convey a sense of a young man for whom the notion of 1916 was not contaminated, or was at least protected by a certain ironic ambiguity, signifying the possibility of a change in public thought between the present and the period of the play. The shirt was anticipating a possible course of history in which the damage of the past thirty years had been undone, perhaps by the passage of two decades of peace, followed by the genuine maturity of an understanding that the past was not the enemy after all. The critics' obsession with literal fact, however, meant that I lost the argument, and the character wore a woolly jumper for the second performance.

Today, Easter Monday, falls on the same date as in 1916. This should mean something, but we don't talk much about all that nowadays, so the celebrations are likely to be muted. With sixteen Easters to go, the T-shirt seems as elusive as ever. We, the citizens of a Republic built upon the bones of 1916, who next month will feel a warm glow of pride in our tolerance and pluralism as we watch Orangemen march down Dawson Street, Dublin, no longer feel entitled to celebrate our own historical moments of valour and glory.

It is as though fear of the power of our own history and mythology is so great it must be subdued, lest it drive us into renewed bursts of passion and violence. Those who seek to suppress all nationalist sentiment say precisely that: the Easter Rising remains the most potent argument for the legitimacy of political violence, and its power must be obliterated before civilisation can descend. This warning is invariably delivered as a preamble to deconstructions of the history on which the claims of modern Irish republicanism are based. Calumnies about the pernicious legacy of Pearse and the other leaders are followed by assertions that the revolution was an armed coup, undertaken in the face of opposition from the majority of Irish people; that only following the execution of the leaders did public sympathy shift towards the revolutionaries; and that the Rising was given bogus retrospective sanction by the attainment of Irish independence.

It all depends on which history book you're reading. But my interest is in why, if the significance of 1916 is so easily disposed of, we are so terrified of its mythology.

I believe repugnance of violence is but a superficial reason. More critical is that we do not trust the passions in ourselves that once burst forth in the knowledge of certain truths, so these must be suppressed in the interests of modernity. But that means that, deep down, we believe them to be valid. This is perhaps the greatest tribute we can be pay the 1916 leaders today: that the truth they represent is still so potent, it must be twisted and denied.

Those who would have us ignore what Thomas Davis called "the passion and deeds of the past", and live influenced only "by wind and sun and tree", have unsurprisingly put things back-to-front: it is not that this dark, heroic past is a dangerous incitement in the present, but that present exigencies dictate the colour and meaning we ascribe to history. Just as a myth of 1916 was employed in the green-tinted post-independence reconstruction, a caricatured notion of the 1966 commemorations was similarly utilised, from the early 1970s, to deconstruct the nationalist version so as to rationalise our abandonment of Northern nationalists. Thus, we are at the mercy of a kind of propagandist ricochet, which hits off the surfaces of particular moments according to the angle of prevailing desires and beliefs.

More worrying than the threat of political violence, for those who would discredit 1916, is the notion, central to the philosophy of the 1916 leadership, that the battle they fought was for the Irish national ideal, what Pearse called "the national soul". This, we have allowed ourselves to be convinced, was narrow, insular, even racist, and therefore to be left behind on the scrapheap of history. Ironically, recent violence has played into the hands of those peddling this neo-unionist agenda, by giving them a fig leaf of morality in their repudiation not just of gunmen past and present, but of the entire baggage of ideas and beliefs which motivated the long fight for Irish freedom.

But what mostly exercises such people is not so much the immorality of violence, as the likelihood that, in the absence of violence, the mythology of the past will rise again and they will have no easy answers with which to repudiate it. Just as they have it back-to-front when they warn of the insidious influence of republican commemoration, they have it likewise with regard to the likely course of events in the event of a settlement of the Northern conflict. This, when it comes, will not bring the "maturity" of Sticky wet dreams, but the opportunity to again celebrate the Irish nation without prejudice or embarrassment. In certain quarters, this prospect is much worse than bullets and bombs.

(April 2000)

9

A Rebel Song

ONE OF THE STICKS MOST FREQUENTLY used to beat the memory of Padraic Pearse is the misinterpretation of his poetry. Pearse's essays are extraordinarily clear and specific. They outline in detail the specifications of true freedom, and the process by which it is to be attained. They leave very little room for ambiguity about what the author saw as being necessary. They are shocking and subversive, by virtue of the ultimate banality of their truths. This is why they have been allowed go out of print. Enabling them to be read would open to question some of the necessary falsehoods about the Irish revolution and its present-day aftermath, which are essential to the preservation of the delusions and short-term interest of the ruling elite. But the poems are allowed to survive, because they can be twisted and appropriated in order to prove what we are required to believe.

The abusive misinterpretation of one poem in particular, "The Rebel", is probably the main plank of the discrediting not merely of Pearse but of the 1916 Rising itself. Those who set themselves up to judge and condemn the men and women who made them free citizens of an independent republic feel free to lavish their pronouncements without undue onus of proof. But when pushed to provide evidence of Padraic Pearse's alleged racist tendencies, the most literate among them will advance this poem in support of their charge.

These are the lines cited in support of this contention:

> I say to my people that they are holy, that they are august, despite
> their chains.

> That they are greater than those that hold them, and stronger and
> purer, . . .

In these lines, undoubtedly, Padraic Pearse addresses the Irish people and tells them they are better than their English oppressors. In a certain pedantic sense this corresponds to what we now define as racism. But to describe it as such, in the true context in which this poem was written, amounts either to dishonesty or stupidity.

It goes almost without saying that "The Rebel" is primarily addressed not to people but to what Pearse himself described as "Things". Pearse speaks to his fellow slaves, who "have no treasure but hope", and urges them to throw off their manacles. He speaks as one of "the blood of serfs", who nonetheless has "a soul greater than the souls of my people's masters", and gives notice both to oppressed and oppressor of the retribution that approaches. When speaking to slaves, is it not necessary to take into account the possibility that, by virtue of their enslavement, their self-esteem may not be all it might? And what, by way of encouragement, is the leader of slaves to say in order to jolly them along? Is he, in the interests of absolute political correctness, to confine himself to the assertion that they may very well be the "equal" of those enlightened chappies with their boots at their throats? Moreover, to contend that the slave is "greater" than his master is, in this context, no more than a simple observation of truth. The slave is indeed better — morally, at least — if only because he is not, at that precise moment, attempting to subjugate someone else.

But there is a deeper context to this poem which, in fairness to those who misappropriate it, is not immediately visible without a particular kind of viewfinder. I have in mind the kind of viewfinder that is available through the understanding of the true nature of colonialism. Pearse was examining the same condition identified and diagnosed some forty years later by the Caribbean-born psychiatrist Frantz Fanon. Fanon identified the cornerstone of slavery as the inculcation of the belief in the colonised native that civilisation is only possible through imitation and emulation of his oppressor. Thus, in a certain sense, to

suggest that liberation resides in parity between the slave and his oppressor is to argue for the completion of the colonial project. What then
is the would-be liberator to suggest? The acceptance of a degree of inferiority by the native in order to preserve his distinctive identity?
Clearly, the only option, within the limits that language allows, is to
advise the slave that he is capable of being better than his master. Only
in this way can the manifold complexes associated with the process of
perverted identification of slave with master be dispersed.

The "Troubles" foreclosed all such discussions. One of the great
tragedies for Pearse, the memory of the Easter Rising, and this society's well-being, lies in the fact that Fanon's ideas, which began to be
published in the 1960s, did not achieve general currency until the present outbreak of conflict in the North had begun. Otherwise, we might
have seen the extraordinary symmetry between the two men.

The natural tendency of peoples whose culture has been denied by
colonisation is to assert the value of that buried culture until the hills
roar with its worth and wonder. But this, as Fanon never tired of
pointing out, is always the wrong approach. "It would be easy to
prove, or to win the admission, that the black is the equal of the
white," he elaborated in a remarkable echo of "The Rebel". But, he
continued, "my purpose is quite different: What I want to do is help
the black man to free himself of the arsenal of complexes that has
been developed by the colonial environment." Fanon was urging a
process of what he called "tearing away" from the influence of the
coloniser: by negating the sense of inferiority which the native felt
about himself and his own culture, he could recreate himself and so
be enabled to embrace his erstwhile master as a full human being.

This, too, was Pearse's objective. The "tearing away" that was required was not from England or the English, but from the process of
identification and imitation, and from the slavishness which imprisoned
the Irishman in the abusive relationship with his perceived betters.

In his essay "The Murder Machine", about the effects of the
English education system in Ireland, written nearly fifty years before
Fanon's groundbreaking analyses of the effects of colonialism in

Africa, Pearse outlined the psychological effects of the same process in Ireland. This "Murder Machine" had, in effect, created in Ireland the conditions of slavery. "Certain of the slaves among us are appointed jailors over the common herd of slaves. And they are trained from their youth for this degrading office. The ordinary slaves are trained for their lowly tasks in dingy places called schools; the buildings in which the higher trained slaves are trained are called colleges and universities." The Murder Machine "aimed at the substitution for men and women of mere Things. It has not been an entire success. There are still a great many thousand men and women in Ireland. But a great many thousand of what, by way of courtesy, we call men and women, are simply Things. Men and women, however depraved, have kindly human allegiances. But these Things have no allegiance. Like other Things, they are for sale."

And yet, this same murderous system conditioned us to defend it as the very essence of civilisation. "To invent such a system of teaching and to persuade us that it is an education system, an *Irish* education system to be defended by Irishmen against attack, is the most wonderful thing the English have accomplished in Ireland," he wrote, "and the most wicked." The English, he wrote, "are too wise a people to attempt to educate the Irish in any worthy sense". Instead, they had "planned and established an education system which more wickedly does violence to the elementary human rights of Irish children than would an edict for the general castration of Irish males".

This is the kind of stuff that, in the disingenuousness of Modern Ireland, will always be interpreted as the irredentist myopia of a simple-minded nationalist. But Pearse was not a simple-minded man, and in truth he was not talking about nationalism in any sense related to our present-day concept of it. He was talking about the future capacity of Irish people not simply to be Irish but to be human. To be.

(April 1999)

10

THE MURDER MACHINE

(The Bombing of Omagh)

G LOBAL, COLLECTIVE OR POLITICAL CONCEPTS survive only with great difficulty in the domain of personal pain. If an event such as Omagh had harmed as much as a hair on my child's head, I doubt if I could ever again acquire the will to care about the configuration of Ireland's political options or solutions. If anything of the horror of last Saturday week were to be visited on those whom I hold dearest, I do not believe that I would care a jot if lumps of Ireland started to fall away into the sea.

But I might, however, be grateful if someone else could summon up the energy to go back to thinking about those matters which still stand between us and a final resolution. It would be a great mistake if, in our desire to dissociate ourselves from the bombers at Omagh, we responded in ways which will, in the long term, serve to ensure that such atrocities will happen again. It would be a mistake, too, to again seek to jettison those values that, in uncontaminated form, are crucial to our capacity to recover from these obscenities. I mean, in particular, the willingness to entertain freedom of democratic debate, and the desire to foster a true spirit of patriotism.

This is a difficult time to talk about patriotism. In the wake of atrocities like Omagh, the word acquires for a time a deep texture of malign and mocking irony. It becomes an unspeakable thing. And in those moments, the inevitable voices emerge to tell us that it is something we are better off without. But sooner or later, it must be rescued again, and cleansed in the truth of our necessity for some form of idealism to hold us together.

It is understandable, at times like this, that people will decide that the process is not worth the candle. It is understandable, too, that people will issue demands for simplistic solutions. It is understandable that people will be ashamed enough of the deeds of some of their fellow human beings to want to surrender anything of their own beliefs that implies even the slightest degree of affinity between themselves and the perpetrators of such barbarism. Last week, in this column, I asked the question myself: is it possible to share any of the beliefs of the people who planted the bomb in Omagh and remain part of the human family?

The answer is: it has to be. For the day we allow the bombers to shame us into repudiating our beliefs for fear of sharing them with such monsters is the day we give power to the terrorist to recreate our hearts and our minds.

I heard people on the radio during the week demanding that those voters in the Republic who had voted against the Belfast Agreement show themselves and explain their actions now, in the shadow of Omagh. Such thinking, however understandable in the grief of the moment, is deeply dangerous to democracy. For surely nothing in a democratic society is as far from the mark of a pencil on a ballot paper as a car-bomb in a crowded street. To suggest that the act of the first suggests a complicity in the second is to say that, far from being an antidote to terrorism, democracy is merely its synonym. This is dangerous nonsense. To give an example removed from the emotion of the Northern issue: the fact that a crazed zealot may shoot dead a doctor who has carried out abortions does not retrospectively mean that it was wrong for an Irish voter to support the 1983 amendment to the Constitution extending rights to the unborn. If there is to be any hope of solving the underlying issues that led to the Omagh bombing, it will surely be through the expression of political difference by means other than violence.

Once again, we can see, in the wake of Omagh, the deep reservoirs of national shame as they swirl and toss under the assault of a degradation that no thoughts or words can dissipate. The idea that there is a concept of nationhood, of sovereignty, of patriotism, that is sole and indivisible, and that this should now be jettisoned for good because it has shown itself capable of such barbarism, is one that is difficult to argue with right now. But argue with it we must. For patriotism is not some optional extra to the smooth running of an already functioning society. It is the very blood that runs through the veins of our collective humanity. Patriotism, far from being the cause of such outrages as Omagh, is the quality that stands to protect us from such things. Patriotism is the love of our country and our countrymen. At its best it unites us in fellow-feeling with other peoples. True patriotism has no place for hatred.

Quite soon, as part of the continuing peace efforts, we will need to begin a process of enquiry into the reasons why the concepts of Irish nationhood and patriotism have become so contaminated by barbarism. This should not take the form of the standard comparisons between the deeds of the present and the deeds of the past, but be an honest examination of why it is that the arena of patriotism has fallen into the hands of thugs, blackguards and pitiable wretches. Those among the leadership of the republican movement who have lately walked away from violence have a responsibility to help us explore these questions with truth and courage.

I have seen it alleged that the planters of the Omagh bomb could not be called cowardly because they risked capture or self-destruction in planting their bomb. To this I respond that there is some factor to be accounted for in explanation of why such alleged patriots, who might once have been expected to be found engaged in mortal combat with the might of the British army, are now mainly associated with the killing and maiming of passing children, women and men. I fail to see how this can be distinguished from cowardice.

It often seems that the greatest damage inflicted on the Irish nation has not been at the hands of the occupying forces of the British crown, but by some of the self-appointed would-be liberators of the Irish people from such occupation. This has certainly been true of the most recent phase of this unfortunate historical circumstance. But that does not mean that the occupation of Irish lands and hearts and minds was virtuous and proper. It does not mean that the Irish people should have stood idly by and allowed themselves to be walked into the ground. It does not mean that all those who, at various times in our history, stood and fought invasion and interference and the criminality of the invader were villains or fools, or that their resistance was immoral or wrong.

The message of Omagh is not that we should abandon our sense of nationhood, or the cause of our collective realisation, or our patriotism or our national pride. The message of Omagh is surely that we must pray all the harder that no one who claims to serve such causes will ever again dishonour them by cowardice, inhumanity or rapine.

(August 1998)

11

POINTING FINGERS AT OURSELVES

THERE WAS A STRANGE OMISSION from the lists of the indicted in media treatments of last week's report of the Comptroller and Auditor General in relation to the national epidemic of bogus non-resident accounts. It was noticeable that the finger of blame was consistently pointed at the banks and other financial institutions, at the Revenue Commissioners, at the Central Bank, at the proverbial "successive governments", at political and State institutions, but that there was little mention of the people who held the bogus accounts and presumably profited more than any of the aforementioned. The closest we got to an indictment of the account-holders was when the editorial writer in Wednesday's *Irish Independent* briefly acknowledged that "ordinary citizens who held these accounts behaved disgracefully", before moving on to the less "ordinary" culprits.

There is a good reason why newspapers or radio and television programmes might wish to gloss over this aspect of the matter: a fair percentage of their readers/listeners/viewers are likely to be among the guilty parties. In all, we appear to be talking about a minimum of a quarter of a million bogus accounts, which, assuming they were mostly held by different individuals, amounts to a significant proportion of the adult population. The "ordinary citizens" who "behaved disgracefully", therefore, were as likely as not to be readers of the *Irish Independent*. Indeed, considering the likely socio-economic profile of account-holders, it is probable that an even higher proportion may be among the readers of *The Irish Times* — perhaps one in four

146

of you, at a conservative estimate. In fact, it is theoretically possible that a bogus account was held by at least one member of every second family in the State. This scandal, therefore, is quite different to the others we have been contemplating of late. This one involves pointing the finger inwards towards ourselves rather than outwards towards others.

But something else it may do is draw attention to the futility of finger-pointing in the first place. In her book *Economic Philosophy*, Joan Robinson explores the basis of what we regard as socio-economic morality, arguing that the rules of the economy are not absolute moral values, but mechanisms of cohesion that make social life possible.

The point about dishonesty, she says, is not that it is morally repugnant, but that it is a "nuisance": it makes social life difficult. Teaching honesty is therefore a technical rather than a moral requirement. By this logic, compliance with tax law is a social contract rather than a moral obligation: only if it can be shown that evasion of taxes causes pain or loss to others, and that this was a foreseeable consequence of the evasion, does it become a moral question.

The reason we have saturated this territory with concepts of morality is that socio-economic cohesion is not of itself a sufficient incentive to prevent individuals from opting out of the collective contract. Without the pseudo-moral dimension, it might be persuasive for the individual to decide that social cohesion could function fine and dandy if everyone else observed the necessary requirements of correct social behaviour, leaving the individual the opportunity of opting out of the social contract while availing fully of its benefits. The ideal situation for the individual in relation to matters fiscal is if everyone else observes the social obligation to pay tax, leaving him free to avoid it without significant damage to the social fabric. But, clearly, if everyone took this view, social life would disintegrate. There is therefore a conflict between collective and individual interest, which is why we have introduced concepts of morality to what are essentially technical issues.

If anyone doubts the logic of this, consider the fact that the reason advanced by financial institutions and State agencies for the failure to put a stop to bogus non-resident accounts was that to do so would have undermined the economy: any attempt to deal with the issue might have resulted in a flight of capital. The wholesale evasion of Deposit Interest Retention Tax (DIRT), therefore, was regarded as the lesser of evils: the "moral" dimension was placed second to the need for economic cohesion. This should not surprise us, since economic cohesion is the point of taxation in the first place.

There is something of a mystery, then, as to precisely what codes we now imagine have been breached by the DIRT scandal. Most of us cannot truly feel offended by people dodging DIRT, especially when these "offenders" might be our brothers, sisters, friends or readers. I believe we also have a strong collective sense that DIRT is perhaps the most repugnant tax ever devised by the Irish exchequer, drawing as it does on the measly returns on funds on which income tax has already — theoretically at least — been levied.

You have to delve deep into the undergrowth before you can get your arms around any of the primary moral principles purportedly at stake here. Like virtually all aspects of our economic life, taxation of non-resident accounts is a matter of rules and regulations rather than absolute moral principles. Maybe the only moral issue here is why accounts held by non-residents were deemed to be free from DIRT in the first place. And maybe the reason we become outraged on hearing that someone has evaded tax is not because of some offence to our moral sensibility, but because this person has broken the rule which we have felt constrained to observe.

Who, then, takes issue with what has occurred? Who is offended by it, and why? The authorities, clearly, do not feel aggrieved, or at least did not do so until the scam was exposed. The banks have been quite happy to facilitate their customers, thereby allegedly preventing the collapse of the Irish economy. The customers, those in the know at least, can have few complaints, especially since it is the banks that must now pay the back tax. Certainly, there is much pious talk about "compliant taxpayers", but these, in the main, seem to be people like myself who did not know about the benefits of having a bogus non-resident account. And nobody, I notice, is proposing to compensate us in the only manner in which the "moral" equilibrium of this situation might conceivably be restored: the refunding of all taxation levied under the DIRT scheme.

Mostly what is offended by all this, then, is the bogus morality our societies have created around the issue of rendering unto Caesar. The reason we seek to make much of this issue, and in particular why we seek to fix the blame on the various institutions and authorities involved, is that we wish to exercise our collective grievance at having to pay tax at all. This scandal, we reasonably believe, shows the duplicity and hypocrisy of the authorities, and the bogus nature of the supposed moral imperative to pay tax. Thus, the point of public outrage is not to create conditions wherein there will be less tax evasion, but to create a rationalisation for still more: for if the authorities have sanctioned this behaviour in the past, how can they seriously adopt a righteous approach to evasion in the future?

(July 1999)

12

THE FISCAL CLERGY

TAX IS THE NEW SEX. Once, pinch-faced men with fiercely cropped grey heads policed the prescribed moralism of the day by beating fornicating couples out of hedges with hawthorn sticks; nowadays, individuals of indeterminate sexuality but disquietingly familiar fanaticism pore over reports of tribunals and High Court inspectors in pursuit of transgressors of the new Sixth Commandment: Thou shalt not evade thy taxes without risk of hanging thy Armani jacket on the back of a cell door in Mountjoy.

They are a fearsome lot, this new clergy, brooking neither dissent nor moral equivocation. The rules, they say, are simple and absolute: everyone has a moral duty to pay tax; personal conscience or circumstances are irrelevant.

Underlying the Ansbacher circus is an unspoken set of rules, without which the discussion would, lacking a moral engine, become stalled by a constellation of caveats and qualifiers. Any attempt to question these rules is repudiated as "amoral", so it is clear that these rules are not merely technocratic regulations to be contested on the basis of logic or subjective reason. They are moral rules.

So, let us have a stab at naming them. The first rule, obviously, is that the payment of taxes is a moral obligation, deriving from one's membership of society, and having to do with the responsibility to contribute to society on the basis of relative wealth. The scale of this responsibility is to be determined by the State, which, by virtue of having a democratically elected government, has an absolute right to levy and demand payment of taxes and punish those who refuse to pay. There shall be no capacity in this arrangement for opting out on the basis of subjective assessments of either personal or public interest. Any such refusal shall be regarded as fraud.

Very well. It can be taken from this admittedly crude summary that the issues arising from Ansbacher are not merely ones of fairness, equality or, less still, personal pique. The anger being directed at tax defaulters is not simply the righteous anger of those who have paid till they bled, but a moral anger, arising from a constant and immutable principle, transcending all other considerations, including, presumably, national boundaries. We do not condemn tax evasion merely because the Irish State may have been defrauded — any evasion of tax deemed by the relevant authorities to be due to any state with a democratically elected government is morally wrong.

Very well, then, a simple question: when is the government going to appoint a High Court inspector to investigate the activities of transnational corporations (TNCs) operating in Ireland?

I am not suggesting that such corporations are engaged in defrauding the Irish State. I have no doubt that all of them pay their fair share of taxes to the Irish exchequer. Indeed there is ample evidence that many of them pay more than their fair share of taxes in this country. That's all right then, is it not?; they have fulfilled their moral obligation.

In his fine book, *Inside the Celtic Tiger*, Denis O'Hearn drew attention to the phenomena of profit-shifting and transfer-pricing as practised by TNCs operating in this jurisdiction. Because Ireland has one of the lowest rates of profit taxation in the world, many such companies come here to avail of these benefits and in return provide employment in the Irish economy. Nothing wrong so far, since our tax rates are legitimate and approved, albeit reluctantly, by our international partners.

However, studies of the sector have uncovered a tendency on the part of mainly US companies to employ creative accounting practices to shift their profits from high- to low-taxation economies, and there is considerable evidence that some utilise the low Irish tax rates to avoid taxation in their home territories. The device employed is a paper transaction by which components are sold to subsidiaries in low-tax economies at artificially low prices, while prices of finished products are artificially inflated to ensure that a disproportionate element of overall profits qualifies for the lowest rates of tax. These practices are surreptitious, and many TNCs are said to have two sets of books, one for the tax authorities, another to keep track of the viability of their activities. Profit levels for US TNCs in Ireland have been running at three times the level of other TNCs operating here, up to five times the level achieved by the same companies in other economies, and some ten times the level of our indigenous firms. There is, then, considerable evidence that Irish taxation conditions are being improperly used by US-owned firms to evade taxation in the United States. Wouldn't it be hilarious if, in the future, a US court report were to find that Ireland during the 1990s became the industrial equivalent of the Cayman Islands?

A number of academic commentators have for more that a decade been drawing attention to these disquieting practices, but to no avail. This is perplexing, given the appetite for fiscal probity we have shown in recent times. Surely it is not possible that our desire to expose tax evasion wherever we may find it is in the least compromised by the possibility that US TNCs might simply withdraw from the Irish economy if we started to apply our clearly established moral principles to their activities? That we are among the net beneficiaries and that the consequences of these evasions are visited not on this society but on the citizens of the United States can surely have no bearing on the application of what are, after all, clear moral principles. Boom, boom!

(July 2002)

13

THE COVERT REVOLUTION

M R JUSTICE SMITH WARNS THAT evidence given in the various tribunals is damaging Ireland's reputation abroad, and endangering its status as a location for business. He points out that Ireland has entered the world Corruption Perception Index at number 23 with a bullet, and that last year's report of the Joseph Rowntree Trust lists Ireland as among the most corrupt states in Europe. Questioning these perceptions, he urges a more balanced perspective.

I believe he misses the point. The destruction of Ireland's international reputation is among the objectives of those driving the tribunal bandwagon — mainly left-wing journalists and politicians harbouring resentments about the nature of Irish society who have been denied other means of gaining power.

Tribunals are the cutting-edge of a recent covert revolution in Irish life, a consolation prize to left-wing sentiment disappointed at the failure to create a left–right divide. Tribunals emerged in the early 1990s as a collateral aspect of Fianna Fáil-led coalitions, intended to police FF's value system but also providing FF with a convenient earthing device to disable the negative energies which threatened the stability of government. FF had electoral power, but its opponents had an arguably more potent weapon: the ability to manipulate both public discourse and the minority factions upon which FF depended to remain in power.

Mr Justice Smith is right when he suggests that, compared with other societies, Ireland is not unduly affected by corruption. The comparison being made, however, is not with other societies, but between real life and a standard unique to Irish society.

This story, like many others, began in the reconstruction that followed the Great Famine of the 1840s, when the Catholic Church took on full stewardship of the material and moral life of the nation. Among the ingenious devices of that reconstruction was the creation of a new currency of social status, demoting materialist comparison as an indicator of human dignity. The core of this reconstructed culture formed, until recently, part of the core ideology of the State, asserting that the dignity of an individual was not to be judged from what he had, but from what he was. The prescribed virtues were: industry, chastity, frugality, passivity and inoffensiveness. It wasn't that money didn't matter — it did, but in the sense that wealth endangered the moral standing of an individual unless accompanied by a sufficiency of the prescribed virtues.

Having arrived at 2003, and having passed through two periods of relative national prosperity on the way, one might cynically observe that the Irish eschewal of wealth was a sour-grapes frugality predicated on the absence of money. But there is a real cultural problem with regard to acclimatising ourselves to prosperity in a society that culturally disparages the pursuit or attainment of material acquisition.

Nobody or nothing since Independence has straightforwardly squared this circle. Among the many achievements of FF in riding Irish reality was the accommodation of frugality and materialism within the same belief-system. Conscious that we needed to get real to get rich, but mindful of the impediment of cultural frugality, the party forged a middle way, pursuing a broadly materialist agenda while paying lip-service to the old pieties for fear of frightening the cultural horses. Thus, the creation of wealth came to involve various sleights-of-hand. For example, wealth was OK if the wealth-creating initiative was external, thus avoiding upset to the local balance. Among natives, underhandedness became something admirable, thus lessening envy and resentment. A local could have and flaunt wealth by remaining culturally connected with the community in a manner exaggerated in proportion to his wad. Hence the cute-hoor syndrome, which drew the community into a conspiracy of celebration at the shady enrichment of one of its own. Fianna Fáil's support for this mutant value system has provided the focus for its opponents for the past several decades.

The revolution represented by the tribunals is the cutting edge of a dialectic that seeks to reconcile piety and prosperity in a new way. It has failed — mainly because of the dishonesty of its stated intentions and because the virus of the national materialist doublethink has infected the tribunal process itself, with lawyers getting rich from investigating the phenomenon of covert enrichment.

Having emerged somewhat by accident, the tribunals persist in their revolution at the insistence of a relatively small group of ideologically motivated zealots who carry deep resentments about a culture which allowed those who refused to take it literally to become wealthy, while they, the virtuously frugal, remained poor. Part of their agenda is indeed the shaming of Ireland in the eyes of the world. And, yes, this revolution now threatens to strangle any hope of sustaining Irish prosperity, because it attacks the only way we know of getting rich.

(April 2003)

14

TRIBUNALS: THE BASTARD
CHILD OF COALITION

A CYNIC, OBSERVING THE TREND OF media commentary, might predict that one or other of the tribunals will shortly deliver some unanticipated sensation. I say this not from inside knowledge of these mysterious bodies but observation of what happens when criticism of tribunal culture reaches a certain level. At such moments, we can expect a new star to parade before cameras on the way to sing like Gigli.

Since the start of the year, the muttering about the cost, wisdom, usefulness and dangers of tribunals has again been rising, crescendo-like. Some commentators — not all tribunal sceptics — have been advancing cogent arguments as to why it may be time for a rethink. If I had a vested interest in the longevity of the tribunal instrument, and an inside track on the timing of strategic revelation (if such a cynical concept might be imagined to exist), I'd be thinking it was time to play an ace or two.

The tribunal is indeed one of the most mysterious elements to emerge in recent Irish public life. An outsider, cursorily observing the daily tribunal fest, might understandably conclude that Ireland had recently undergone some kind of cultural revolution, that a new broom has set about cleaning up the moral life of the nation, that this society is hell-bent on getting to the truth. However, not only is the moral life of the nation no better — in truth, the evolution of tribunal culture had little to do with morality in the first place.

The tribunal is the illegitimate offspring of coalition governments involving Fianna Fáil. Because of the chronic instability of these arrangements, a necessity arose for a device to deal with problematic issues that might, if left to unravel in an uncontrolled fashion, threaten relations between the partners. The tribunal enabled such issues to be rendered unthreatening.

Arguably, though, the greatest benefits of tribunals have accrued to the media, for whom tribunal-revelations have been a cheap, ready-made product. And it is not a coincidence that the most fervent champions of tribunalism have been journalists with a broadly left-wing perspective, for whom the tribunals have provided both a means of flailing their ideological enemies — while themselves earning reputations as the guardians of public integrity — and also a way of deflecting scrutiny of flaws in their own ideological prescriptions. It should be obvious why such individuals would depict Irish society as corrupt in certain respects, while ignoring less convenient forms of dishonesty. For example, it is arguable that the welfare state enables a far more widespread and damaging dishonesty than anything involving brown envelopes, but this cannot be confronted while Flood and Moriarty continue to sit. In this respect, the tribunals have actively suppressed a rounded debate about corruption in Irish life.

A society intent upon the truth would not be easy with this, any more than it would tolerate lawyers becoming fabulously wealthy by investigating minor backhanders several decades in the past. A healthy society might ask why its police force is considered unfit to investigate such matters, or why, in the event that a previously undreamt-of wrongdoing has come to light of recent times, some new kind of policing could not be developed to meet this need.

The inherent inconsistency of tribunal culture, too, has damaged the public perception of the legal system. There is an incoherence in the way, for example, one tribunal will rigorously target an individual, whereas another will confine itself to generalities, refusing to point fingers; and it is disturbing that rigour appears to exist in inverse proportion to the gravity of the matter at hand.

There is also the matter of the disjunction between the moralistic language providing the background radiation to the tribunal-fest and the consequences that arise — or do not arise — as a result of tribunal proceedings. Some citizens have been disgruntled by the failure of particular tribunals to deliver them justice, while others are named and shamed in a manner devoid of the normal judicial sanction. Very often it seems the tribunals operate as an arm of the media, providing a quasi-legal procedure on which journalists deliver the ultimate verdict and dole out the punishment in public excoriation of institutions or individuals. This results in, yes, a corruption of the public perception of what wrongdoing signifies.

I met recently an individual who, having regaled me with the tricks he had employed to outfox the taxman, asked me if I was following the tribunals. I muttered about not being a great fan and he immediately upbraided me for my lack of public-spiritedness. "We'd never have known about all this corruption if it hadn't been for them tribunals!" he declared.

For some citizens, then, the tribunal represents less a way of purging dishonesty from Irish life, as of providing a fund of justification for the moral economies of the smaller operator. So long as Flood and Moriarty are doing their stuff for the *Nine O'Clock News*, the common or garden tax-dodger or social welfare fraudster can feel secure in the knowledge that he is only trotting after the big fry.

(February 2003)

15

THE SENSITIVITIES OF THE TRANSMISSION SYSTEM

ONCE IN A WHILE A VOICE IS RAISED to restore faith in the capacity of public servants to be more than job-minding automatons, mouthing spin-doctored bureauspeak and inane platitudes. Such an occasion was the recent remarks by the Taxing Master of the High Court, James Flynn, in describing tribunals as "Frankenstein monsters" and "Star Chambers". The immediate response was: "What? Did he say that?" Here, clearly, was someone with a mind of his own, saying things the dogs in the street know to be true. It was obvious Master Flynn was alive, and human. If only, one thought forlornly, we could have more of this in public life, things — even mad, mistaken or wrong things — might get said, and society grow a little as a result. This, after all, is the theory of democracy and free speech.

But it was inevitable, given the set-up he was describing, that Master Flynn would be made to eat crow. If his remarks were allowed stand, other public servants might take to speaking their minds. The true nature of Irish public life, and the mechanisms which propel it in particular directions, would inch further into view. And the many who regard tribunals as expensive, time-wasting charades would begin to understand that they are not alone.

The mechanism whereby the retraction was extracted was instructive. Key players with vested interests immediately began orchestrating pressure for sanctions. Politicians who gained power by accusing others made solemn statements of their "concern". Attacks were launched by journalists whom tribunals have made into stars. The odd thing was the slow-burning nature of the official response. There was a slight hiatus between the initial splurge of articles and statements, and a second onslaught a few days later, as though the first response was mere irritation, coupled with a wearied sense that this was part of the cut-and-thrust of political life; whereas the second resulted from the realisation that, if these comments were let stand, the whole edifice might fall.

One can observe in the response of the Tánaiste, Mary Harney, the contrived nature of the pressure for sanctions. Ms Harney described Master Flynn's comments as "clearly offensive" to the Oireachtas and judges presiding over tribunals. But the Houses of the Oireachtas are not some thin-skinned entity, which takes to its bed at the slightest hint of criticism: it is the national parliament, where trenchant debate takes place from dawn till dusk. If members of the Oireachtas are so easily offended, those who elected them are entitled to ask whether they shouldn't be in some other line of work. Moreover, some members of the Oireachtas agree with Master Flynn.

I don't doubt certain judges were offended. But I thought we were coming around to the view that judges are over-privileged deities who have been beyond criticism for too long. The notion that men, or indeed women, who send people off to jail in chains the way the rest of us put sugar on our cornflakes have a right to be "offended" by statements devoid of malice or personal reference is not merely silly, it is retrograde and dangerous.

The public should scrutinise this episode for its important lessons about the public life of this State. This case exposed the transmission system operated by the engineers of our society: the media are the engine; the Progressive Democrats — a party founded on the principle of appealing to public perception — function as the clutch; and the government — ostensibly elected by the people and dominated by Fianna Fáil, but in reality run by the transmission system — is engaged to do the will of the true rulers of society. The wheels move. Once we heard that the (PD) Attorney General had conveyed the government's "deep concern" to the President of the High Court, Master Flynn's climbdown or removal was a matter of time.

The objection to public servants speaking their minds relates not to their breaching codes of silence, but to the content of their views. Only when certain interests are in disagreement with their opinions do problems arise. We saw this during Mary Robinson's presidency when, despite some of her statements breaking the spirit and letter of the Constitution, no move was made to sanction her. Invariably, she expressed views congenial to the transmission system.

Two months ago, another public servant, Peter Finlay SC, resigned from the position of refugee appeals adjudicator, shortly after making a ferocious attack on the asylum process. He said that he could not serve in a system he did not believe in, since to do so would be inconsistent with the views he expressed. But there was no suggestion of government pressure on Mr Finlay to retract, because there was no media pressure, because the views he expressed found favour with the media: both statement and principled resignation were widely praised.

The classic instance of this syndrome is the case of the now retired High Court Judge, Rory O'Hanlon, sacked as President of the Law Reform Commission for making comments about abortion and the Maastricht Treaty. Some years later, the State paid Mr O'Hanlon a significant six-figure sum following the settlement of an action in which he claimed his dismissal was unconstitutional. When he made his remarks, Mr O'Hanlon came under splenetic attack from politicians and journalists, who accused him of "scaremongering", of "undermining democracy" and of "insulting the intelligence of the Irish people".

Mr O'Hanlon is opposed to abortion. His dismissal followed his rejection of a government "request" to "stay out of controversy". That selfsame government (also a FF/PD coalition) remained inert when another judge, Ms Justice Mella Carroll, went public on precisely the same issue by signing a statement issued by the Commission on the Status of Women which made recommendations on abortion in the wake of the Supreme Court ruling in the X Case. The difference was that the transmission system agreed with Miss Justice Carroll.

Had Master Flynn not apologised, he too might have been dismissed, and in a few years a couple of column inches in the newspapers would inform us that this episode, too, had cost the Irish taxpayer perhaps a million pounds in damages and costs.

What this teaches us is that, for all our cant about free speech, we have little space for anyone with genuinely independent views. I do not doubt that, as the Moriarty and Flood tribunals meander on, the public mind will more and more come around to the views expressed by Master Flynn.

(April 2000)

16

THE PORNOGRAPHY OF PROBITY

*(Written in 1999, during a brief period when I had all but decamped
to London to be closer to my daughter)*

I HAD IMAGINED THAT MY ATTITUDE to events in Ireland would be
unaffected by being in London, so long as I listened to the radio and
bought *The Irish Times* every day. But it isn't the case. As it happens,
my house in London came with a satellite dish, a thing I would not
normally be interested in possessing. To my surprise, I find I am able
to receive RTÉ Radio One on my television set, as clear as a bell.
Again, I at first thought this would mean I hadn't really left Ireland at
all. I could get up in the morning, switch on *Morning Ireland*, and
continue to believe that I was still at home. But it doesn't work. Perspective, I'm finding, has nothing to do with the quality of reception.

At no time during the past week, listening to David Hanly and
Richard Crowley talking to Michael Noonan, Mary Harney or Bertie
Ahern, did I have any sense that the ongoing tribunal circus, on which
the quality of Irish public life is alleged to depend, was anything other
than a high farce in a somewhat distant State. Would the PDs pull out
of government? Would the State be "plunged" into a general election?
I didn't care.

At first I thought the change was simply to do with myself. Perhaps I felt less engaged? Perhaps my not caring whether or not the
government would fall was to do with my personal boredom thresh-
old after many years listening to the same old nonsense? Perhaps,

since I am much more likely to have a vote in the next British general election than the next Irish general election, I had the beginning of a sense that my stake had been surrendered?

Yes and no. Such elements were present but they were not dominant. My overwhelming sense was of what an enormous scam it all was.

The tribunal culture is a business based on the creation, promotion and sale of gossip. It may or may not bring down governments, but either way it will make no difference. It is the music in the game of musical chairs. That is all.

From a distance, it is possible to sense the truth. If you go right in, to the tribunal chamber, to Leinster House, to the political meeting, you come away thinking about what those participating in the game would like you to be thinking about. If you stand back and listen, you hear the things they avoid saying.

The leader of the Party of Principle, Mary Harney, for example, has been telling us why she will not bring down the government of which she is deputy leader. "As of now, we have no reason not to believe the Taoiseach," she said. In other words, they are waiting for conclusive proof before pulling the plug. But those of us with the irritating capacity to retain longish memories can recall several occasions in the past when the Party of Principle did not wait to acquire proof of wrongdoing before pulling the plug. On those occasions, the Party of Principle laid much store on the necessity of "restoring public confidence in the integrity of the political system".

The explanations for things being different now are twofold. Firstly, on those previous occasions, the Party of Principle was motivated by deep personal and political malice towards particular individuals, and this element is not present on this occasion. Secondly, the Party of Principle stands to be wiped out in the next election.

But even more pertinent is the fact that the next election, when it is fought, will be fought by all parties using funds which have been acquired in a same manner resembling those transactions which the Moriarty tribunal is now seeking to "investigate". All parties depend on donations from "admirers". All parties indulge those who support them. All parties are beholden to the sector of Irish society with the deepest pockets. To pretend otherwise is ludicrous. Moreover, the newspapers and broadcasting organisations which report on these proceedings are just as much at the whim of corporate favour, albeit mostly in the form of advertising revenue, as are the politicians. That is why they must pretend there is a line somewhere which has been breached on this occasion.

Such distinctions, however retroactive, are necessary in the interests of preserving the integrity of the product which is now on sale to the Irish people. What is on sale is the illusion that Irish society is run, or was at some time intended to be run, according to elevated principles. Everybody knows that such principles are believed in only by children and simpletons. Everybody knows that money makes the world go round. The purpose of pretending that it doesn't, oddly enough, is to make more money.

After a decade of tribunal culture, nothing has changed in Irish society or politics as a result of these protracted investigations. After each election, the same politicians change places with one another. Those who have been under a cloud spend a short term in the political sin-bin before re-entering the playing pitch of government. Only two politicians implicated in these events have left office: one of them was to retire anyway; the other resigned in a fit of pique. Thus, it is not possible to trace one single beneficial development to any of the four massively expensive tribunals that have dominated Irish political life in this decade. It is probable that we will discover things from the Moriarty and Flood tribunals that we do not already know. It is even possible that we will discover things that will shock us, or annoy us, or confirm our worst suspicions. But it is unlikely that, no matter what happens at these tribunals, we shall discover anything that will change anything about the way this State functions.

If those who run our public affairs wanted to bring about change, they have every opportunity to do so. If politicians, for example, wished to reform the planning system, they could do so with the minimum of delay. In the past decade, every one of the five main parties in the State has been in government for at least one extended period. To the extent that these parties express dissatisfaction with the way things are done in this State, each of them has had ample opportunity to bring about changes in accordance with their analysis.

Tribunal culture is essential to the survival of politics, not because of the requirement to restore truth and principle to public life, but because there is now nothing else for politics to be concerned about. Globalisation, European unity and the death of left–right ideology have ensured that politicians have virtually no differences about any of the issues that politics is supposed to be about. They therefore need material to present themselves before the public, just as a singer needs songs or a juggler needs skittles. Similarly with the media. Newspapers, for example, having rowed in with virtually every consensus on the important questions of life, must find something to entice people to hand hard currency across the newsagent's counter.

That is why I use the word "gossip". Scrutiny of "matters of public interest", such as those before the various tribunals, may have a much more elevated-sounding sense of importance than trivia about the lives of soap stars — but it has the same purpose.

In any society or community, gossip fulfils a very useful function. When we gossip, as the German psychoanalyst and writer Alexander Mitscherlich has observed, we are concerned "not so much with the facts as with the effects that they arouse in us; we are concerned with the gaining, not of knowledge, but of pleasure". It is, he added, a hook on which to hang all our "unpleasure" and a way of temporarily forgetting our own miseries.

Thus, when Padraig Flynn goes on the *Late Late Show* to boast about his three houses, we imagine we are outraged by his brass neck, while in fact we are titillated by our envy and sense of outrage against someone who is a source of annoyance to us. He allows us to feel superior, even if only in our relative deprivation. "Gossiping", Mitscherlich concludes, is a way of "gaining enjoyment for one's pride for which there are no opportunities in actuality".

Tribunals, therefore, are a kind of political pornography, which allow us to work off all our pent-up feelings of outrage, curiosity, envy and spite, without having to engage in any meaningful way with what is happening around us. That is why tribunals never have any effect: voters rarely if ever take them into account when placing marks on ballot papers. An additional reason for the growth of tribunal culture in Ireland is the escalating urbanisation of our society. In previous eras, the appetite for gossip was satisfied at the parish pump; today, in our increasingly atomised society, there are less opportunities for gossip because there is no longer the intimacy at local level to provide the kind of common knowledge off which gossip feeds. Thus, we depend on the media for a constant fund of prurience and surprise, and politicians, celebrities and other public figures have become as ciphers in the dramas which allow us to live by proxy.

So, enjoy the tribunals — but don't fool yourself that they matter one whit.

(February 1999)

17

THE NATIONAL RATCATCHERS

I SEE MY COLLEAGUE EMILY O'REILLY, the political editor of the *Sunday Business Post*, has been going out on a limb to call for sympathy and mercy for the former Taoiseach, Charles Haughey. This, as I have discovered from time to time myself, is a rather sticky wicket. It is not easy to call for restraint when the blood of vengefulness is up.

The tribunal of inquiry has been Irish society's greatest discovery of the 1990s. It was a perfect device for media and the new breed of politician to carry on the various kinds of pretence which they so earnestly desired to maintain. It allowed us to dig up the past in a selective way, so as to dramatise our imagined progression without admitting what was really at the root of our collective ill-health.

All the issues which tribunals have been instituted to investigate have been the inevitable consequence of a history that many of the advocates of the inquiry have simultaneously been intent upon denying. All the inquiries have centred on aspects of Irish life that might be called the direct consequence of colonialism, interference and slavery, but the purpose of investigating such phenomena in this way is to conceal rather than expose their true nature.

When a country suffers eight hundred years of slavery, it is prudent to expect certain things and not to be too surprised by certain others. There is a pattern to all such experience, which will perhaps one day be recognised as scientific reality. A country recently freed from slavery will begin to behave in an inevitable and predictable fashion. Firstly it will spawn an elite of its own, to replace that which has been driven back to the mother country. This elite will inevitably be marked by certain characteristics: arrogance coupled with incompetence, greed combined with an inability to produce anything worthwhile or marketable, and a craven desire to ingratiate itself to outsiders which is matched only by its contempt for the native people. With such a band at the controls, the new society lurches forward along predestined lines. In the first surges of patriotism, a crude and primitive indigenous economy is subjected to the life support of protectionism in the hope that some spontaneous convalescence will occur. When this fails, as it always does, the elite turns outwards to the wider world and begins to investigate ways of supporting itself without having to undergo the discomfort of a full cultural realisation from within. An economy is constructed which is, in effect, a cuckoo economy. More and more, the affairs of the nation are arranged so as to accommodate the wishes of external interests. The education system, being part of the colonial heritage, perpetuates the process of imitation, ingratiation and subservience. Even the culture of the nation is designed for tourists and foreign academics. The absence of a civic culture will result in the emergence of family fiefdoms and dynasties, characterised by grandiosity and pretension. The political movements that led the people to their nominal independence will descend into cynicism, petty corruption and private advantage, combining autocracy with a shallow populism based on sentiment and greed.

But because of the nature of the underlying condition, many of these disintegrations will present themselves as positive changes. The breaking away of the political system from the wishes of the people, for example, will be presented as the expression of a modern impulse to generate conditions of legality and egalitarianism in place of clientelism and patronage. Meanwhile, these same political parties remain in the grip of a patronage all the more sinister because it is legal.

Of course, aspects of the life of the nation will be characterised by genuine attempts to realise some autonomous life, but these will seem to be deeply flawed by comparison with the imported models. They will therefore be subject to the suspicion and contempt of the ruling elite.

Everything we now seek to investigate has its roots in this condition: planning abuses, tax evasion, the petty corruption of the beef industry, Charles Haughey's subsidised lifestyle. The function of the public inquiries, however, is to bury this truth rather than to uncover it once and for all. What we are saying with these tribunals, to ourselves and, even more importantly, to the wider world, is that we are shocked to find such evidence of primitive abuses in a modern society. We wish to articulate this sense of shock to the whole world, so that everyone will know how civilised and modern we are. Imitating the legalistic approaches of our European neighbours, we affect to be surprised and indignant to uncover such scandal in our midst.

In truth, we should be investigating not why the beef industry is subject to corruption, but how on earth we managed to have an Irish beef industry at all. We should be congratulating ourselves that this, at least, remains in native hands, and seeking to find ways in which we could replicate this success in other areas. Similarly, the story of Charles Haughey might more usefully be studied for its lessons in what occurs to societies which have no experience of democracy other than through imitation of external models, for its blurring of the lines between what is regal and what is legal, and for its less than flattering reflection of our own craven desires for the comforting signs of opulence in our leaders. It is not an accident that the three Taoisigh before the present incumbent were all millionaires.

Public life in this country is characterised by one impulse above all others: the desire to pretend that the centuries of our slavery did not occur. The main function of politics, apart from organising our affairs, is to teach us about ourselves. But this is the last thing we want of it. All the time, we attempt to extract from political affairs the kind of lesson that will make us feel better about how we are now. What we seek is vindication rather than intelligence.

And this is profoundly related to our difficulty with self-description. There has been a strong tendency in the age of self-awareness which dawned with the 1960s to present the trajectory of our political affairs as emerging from the darkness of sub-modernity and moving towards the light of the final European home. This sub-modernity, however, was rarely if ever given its true context, in the historical experience of occupation, interference and abuse, but was credited, as its architects had ordained, to the intrinsic backwardness of the native people.

Irish politics is always slightly revolting, precisely because, as a people, we are revolting against all existing images of ourselves. Likewise, all attempts at political analysis seek either to revolt or re-form — never simply to understand. All the time, we imagine our-selves temporarily on the outside looking in, suggesting alterations and amendments to bring us in line with our ideal image of ourselves, oblivious that these ideal images derive from our enslavers.

Thus, we believe, Goodman, Haughey, Lowry and the others rep-resent just imperfections in an otherwise constantly improving situa-tion. If we can simply expunge the wrongdoer, we can be as pure as the blueprint has promised. It is as though we are waiting for the rat-catcher to make the house safe to return to, and are shouting advice through the letterbox. In truth, of course, we are both rat and rat-catcher, and with the same set of interdependencies.

The post-tribal society is the most tribal of all. The new tribe sets about defeating the old, but in a manner as to suggest that it is en-gaged in something entirely new and utterly virtuous. In its attempt to rewrite reality in accordance with its own interests, it rides roughshod over language and truth. To the objective observer, what is going on appears to have all the hallmarks of the skulduggery of old, but be-cause it is encased in the sanctimonious language of modernity, it cannot be questioned other than by those willing to risk the damna-tion of public disapprobation.

(January 1998)

18

THE BANEFUL CONSEQUENCES
OF THE QUARK

THE PERCEPTION PERSISTS THAT THE current epidemic of scandals is symptomatic of the allegedly sub-modern ethos of parish-pump politics, so denigrated by those who also are to the fore in unmasking the unethical and corrupt. In fact, the corruption is a consequence of the modernisation of Irish politics over the past three decades.

The worldwide infestation of modern politics by corruption is chiefly a function of what political scientists call "the quark". It is appropriate, perhaps, since the word has its origins in the work of an Irish writer, that Irish politics is now dominated by this phenomenon also. The word comes from the phrase "Three quarks for Muster Mark", in *Finnegans Wake*. The concept was adapted to the study of physics to designate a subatomic particle believed to be one of the essential building blocks of matter. Although the concept has apparently proved very useful in the understanding of elementary particles, nobody has ever succeeded in finding a distinct, self-standing quark.

The political quark relates to the unit of public opinion on a given subject at a frozen moment, the holy grail to which modern politics is addicted. The obsession with focus groups, opinion polls, advertising, consultants and spin-doctors is all about chasing the quark. In a typical general election campaign, the main political parties might between them spend in the region of £1 million on opinion polling alone, in ascertaining its momentary state. On factoring in the cost of advertising designed to influence, appease, massage and reassure the quark, it becomes clear that the main distortion in political life arises not from the inherent venality of politicians or public officials but from a culture of politics which favours following rather than leading.

The scandals under investigation at present relate to the 1970s, 1980s and 1990s. It is not a coincidence that the first public poll conducted of Irish political opinion was in 1969. The emergence of the quark was the reason political parties began to require more and more funding, and is therefore the context in which most of our political corruption must be seen. The reason political parties need to put the hammer on business for money is to compete with other parties to discover and tap into the quark. Even those instances of money being accepted by individual politicians for their own enrichment owes its enabling ambiguity to the necessity of funding the pursuit of the quark. This is what allows businessmen and politicians to talk about "supporting the democratic process", when really they mean greasing the wheels of opportunity for themselves.

What is the quark an alternative to? Leadership, perhaps; but, more pertinently, that which distinguishes the leadership model of politics from an obsession with the public mood: connection with real people, what we disparagingly refer to as "the politics of the parish-pump". This is what sets the Lemass, Cosgrave and de Valera eras apart from those of Haughey, FitzGerald, Bruton and Ahern.

It is a cliché that modern politics lacks leadership, but the alternative notion that politics today is led by the public view is rather to miss the point. When we speak of "the public" in this regard, we do not mean the voting public, still less the flesh-and-blood people you see walking down your road; we mean the cybernetic notion of the electorate which dominates the thinking of political parties and the media. The quark, then, is a symptom of a model of politics which sees people not as individual human beings with problems, outlooks, aspirations, opinions, moods, desires and needs, but as units, atoms and sub-particles in a process which can be approached in the manner of a piece of matter and understood according to laws of quota-controlled representative sampling and statistical probability theory.

It is ironic that those most exercised about political corruption and the untoward relationship between politics and business have always been the most zealous in seeking to extinguish the last sparks of what is pejoratively termed "clientelism". Clientelism had many faults, and was itself prone to abuses and corruption, but these dangers were small indeed when compared to the amorality associated with the politics of the quark. (A further irony is supplied by the fact that, since much of the money given by businessmen to politicians over the years will have ended up paying bills for media advertising, the chances are that the contents of the proverbial brown paper bags will have gone towards paying the salaries of those now seeking to expose such practices.)

As always, you need to dig much deeper to find the true immorality. The original sin besetting modern politics is not brown paper bags but the detachment of politics from the concerns of real people. If this had not occurred, business people would never have been able to gain special favours from politicians, nor would the notion of huge profiteering from a change of land use make any sense. The real immorality resides in the creation of such massive opportunities for the exploitation of the basic needs of human beings, which could not have occurred if politics had remained rooted to the community.

The politics of the quark results in nobody deciding anything, thinking anything or leading anywhere. In pursuit of the quark, the politicians follow the media which follow the consensus of the public view which is itself garnered from opinion polls which are a regurgitation of a debased political discourse laden down with reheated clichés and political correctness. Nobody is in charge, and nobody is contributing anything new, so the whole thing is self-recycling and cannibalistic. The edifice stays upright only in the manner of a bicycle: through forward movement under its own momentum. Irish politics has come to resemble an overused five-pound note: it has been recycled so much, it is unrecognisable as itself. An appropriate symbol all round, when you come to think of it.

(June 2000)

19

REVISITING THE CAMEL AND THE EYE OF THE NEEDLE

WE USED TO BELIEVE THAT POVERTY was a prison but now it seems to be more like an airport. Airports tell you that you are an outsider in a torrent of insiders, but in a sense are defined by their state of constant flux: nearly everyone you meet is passing through. Poverty, according to a survey published last week in the UK, is a little like that.

A pamphlet issued by a British government think-tank suggests that lifelong poverty is exceptional, that being born poor does not mean you will stay poor for life, and that the idea of an underclass is a social policy fallacy. These are new and radical ideas, but they become interesting because the think-tank, Catalyst, is not a right-wing quango but an "Old Labour" body chaired by the former deputy leader of the Labour Party and implacable opponent of Blairism, Roy Hattersley. The Catalyst pamphlet, *Poverty and the Welfare State: Dispelling the Myths*, examines the evidence of British poverty between 1996 and 1999, and claims that sixty per cent of the UK population spent at least one year in poverty as currently defined. The report asserts: "Poverty is generally an experience for part of people's lives, not for all of it."

The report was widely discussed in the UK but hardly at all here, although its findings will broadly translate in this society.

One implication is that our inclination to see poverty as a moral question may no longer be useful. The rhetoric of what has been somewhat snidely dubbed "the poverty industry" would suggest that the poor is a discrete and clearly identifiable social grouping, concerning whose circumstances the rest of society should feel guilt and shame on account of experiencing comparative good fortune. The tone of those who criticise society for its failure to redress its own poverty — i.e. charity organisations, church groups, certain media analysts and left-wing politicians — is that of the fundamentalist preacher informed by the parable of the camel and the eye of the needle. This is true even of left-wing journalists who live in big houses and drive big motor cars. We used to imagine that such moralistic hectoring was essential to promoting some semblance of social solidarity. But if most of us have already been poor and are in some danger of being so again, the notion of an objectified sector of society towards which we are obliged to show sympathy and support is overtaken by the idea that, in tackling what we term poverty, we need to abandon patronising notions of altruism and obligation and perceive this as a technical issue of enlightened self-interest. At least in the context of a modern, essentially market-driven economy, poverty may have but a passing relevance to morality. The proper distribution of resources is a matter of efficiency, and may indeed be inhibited by the emphasis on what we term compassion.

It is strange indeed that the three most visible sources of the current moralistic approach to poverty — religious institutions, the media and various left-wing groupings — all owe the power of their argument to an essentially Christian view of money and wealth, which employs rhetorically inspired guilt as the mainspring of its operation. This philosophical model takes as gospel the idea of a limited cake, and assumes that if one slice is larger, then others must be correspondingly smaller. But this idea has little relevance in a market economy in which the moving frontier of wealth-creation sets no barriers or limits on the bounds of personal enrichment. Indeed, current ideas about poverty may be dividing those with wealth from those without even more than does their actual economic estrangement. For one thing, the established concept of poverty, estimated on the basis of comparison with the relative wealth of an individual, is rapidly being discredited. This definition gives a new meaning to the notion that the poor will always be with us, for if you calculate poverty by comparison with average income and possessions, there will always be a proportion with less than that average. This does not mean they are necessarily suffering from anything remotely definable as poverty.

The Christian metaphor of the camel and the eye of the needle may require updating, since it derives from a time when the divisions between rich and poor were indeed fixed and fairly unbuckable. In ancient societies, riches were generally inherited and came without effort. Likewise, poverty was a life sentence. The poor were therefore, if only by virtue of seeking consolation, far more likely than the rich to focus on the hereafter as the solution to their condition. Today, the converse may be true: the poor, by virtue of the opportunity that exists to escape their condition, are much less likely to turn to God, at least until they have tried money; whereas the rich, having discovered that wealth has not cured their essential unhappiness, have a better chance of seeing the light.

It is a bit of an irony also that, to the extent that inherited or life-long poverty continues to be a problem for some, it generally occurs in a particular type of urban context, the irony arising from the fact that the urban is the, so to speak, traditional repository of left-wing values. Perhaps some of those who accuse society in general are seeking to conceal the poverty of their own thinking.

(September 2002)

20

CARTOON CITY

WAITING FOR INSTALMENTS OF THE charming saga of gangland Limerick, I got to thinking that we have finally obliterated the melodrama of the 1950s and replaced it with a cartoon. In recent decades, much of the intellectual life of this society has been directed at deconstructing the mawkishness, piety, hypocrisy and small-mindedness we had come to associate with 1950s' Ireland. Our neurosis did not allow us care that we were removing also our collective moral tent-pole.

For all the rhetoric to the contrary, the ideology of this society is now broadly leftist, i.e. driven by the belief that everyone has an equal right to material prosperity, and that any deviation from this principle represents a moral failure. This view is held by many commentators and academics, as well as by the clergies of every religion, and has been the formal editorial policy of most of our newspapers for years. Its power derives mainly from the indoctrinated guilt of those who, though materially comfortable, have become convinced that prosperity is less than wholly moral while others are comparatively less well-off.

Criminality is the opening faultline between "haves" and "have-nots". In the much-maligned 1950s, crime was infinitesimal compared to what it is now. We comforted ourselves until recently that crime levels here were much lower than elsewhere, but this becomes less true every statistical year.

Twenty years ago, it was fashionable to equate rising crime straightforwardly with poverty. This analysis was rebuttable on the basis that, even when people were relatively poorer, they were less inclined to plunder and steal. Some analytical refinement was necessary; hence the analysis that crime is the product of alienation, or anomie, arising from increased economic polarisation. This suggests that it is insufficient to eliminate conventional poverty, because any degree of inequality can provide a rationale for those who decide to take what they are not given. Even well-off, intelligent people now accept this.

Another word for anomie might be resentment. Motor repair workshops now experience a windfall in January/February, fixing newly registered cars which have been gratuitously defaced or damaged by passers-by who are, it seems, expressing some deep-set existential grievance at the unfairness of life. In mentioning this phenomenon in polite society, one encounters an ambiguous response: even self-starters whom you would expect to be outraged feel obliged to make pious remarks about our two-tier society.

Whatever the motivations for rationalising the criminality of allegedly disenfranchised elements of Irish society, the result has been the validation of that criminality by dint of the general acquiescence in the belief that such immorality is counterbalanced by the immorality inherent in society's failure to provide equally for all citizens. It is not a coincidence that this was the core philosophy of the late Martin Cahill.

It is well established that, to succeed in life, a human being needs both personal achievement and a high degree of self-motivation to pursue this, and everyday experience tells us that there is no absolute entitlement to benefit to any particular degree from the earth's resources. Animal societies prosper only to the extent that they marshal collective energies. The human experience of socialism demonstrates that attempts to buck these natural laws are doomed.

When I was a boy, the greatest compliment you could pay a man was to call him "a good worker". This accolade disappeared during the 1980s, when high unemployment made it unacceptable to judge someone by criteria which appeared to place his moral status beyond his control. We constructed a society which, while maintaining a core system of motivation for those deemed full members, sought to disperse its self-induced guilt by deviating from this logic in respect of elements considered ill-adjusted for communal wealth-creation. Hence, the welfare society and its inaccurately termed "working-class" ghettoes.

There are those who insist the problem is that we have not pushed the equality agenda far enough. But even by the logic of the polarisation argument, which suggests that the disenfranchised will not become enfranchised until they are driving State-provided top-of-the-range 03 cars, it seems clear there is no exit that way. The nature of a welfare society, which involves effective imprisonment in second-class ghettoes by dint of means-tested benefits which in effect prohibit legitimate self-advancement, ensures that our developing cartoon society is self-consolidating. Although fuelled by a tabloid culture which appends ridiculous cartoon names to murderous thugs, as though to suggest that their victims bounce back from the *Thwack!* of their coshes, this cartoon Ireland is largely the creation of our guilt and delusion.

A cartoon has uniquely distinguishing characteristics — unreality, comedy, violence — but most fundamentally a suspension of empathy with their fellow humans. The denizens of these ghettoes are not, generally speaking, poor in any objective material sense: most of them have modern, warm houses, basic incomes and satellite TV. Their poverty is mental, emotional and spiritual, and largely the consequence of what purported to be their salvation. Despite being victims of the general "compassion" they do not feel, so to speak, "empathised with" by society, and withhold empathy in return. They live their cartoon lives in what appears to be an emotional vacuum, and the rest of us observe in a confusion of dissociated horror and bewildered amusement.

(February 2003)

21

THE GUILT ASSUAGER

T HERE IS A BEGGAR WITH A PITCH close to the entrance to a car
park used by the customers of one of Dublin's more upmarket
department stores, who appears to understand the concept of societal
guilt arising from newly acquired wealth better than any politician or
clergyman. I have been observing him for some time and am lost in
admiration for his ability to manipulate the potential discomfort of
those who have just emerged from a bout of retail therapy and are
headed to stash the goods in the boot of their 03 reg. I sense that he has
not merely seen through all the rhetoric of social concern, altruism and
Christianity that pervades our public discourse on a daily basis, but has
utilised this knowledge to earn himself a living while providing a
multi-dimensional public service — both in the sense of revealing the
reality beneath the humbug of Irish society and alleviating the guilt of
the conspicuous consumer in return for a minor consideration.

He sits a few yards from the entrance to the car park, with a box
in front of him. Knowing he is there, the objective of the less philan-
thropic shopper (i.e. nearly everyone) is to stare fixedly ahead, pretending to be lost in thought. But our man is wide to this tactic, and
waits until the target has crossed over an imaginary line beyond
which it is all but impossible to find the grace to relent and pay up. At
this moment, he cries out, along the lines of: "Have a nice evening,
Madam!" This ejaculation is devoid of aggression or obvious malice,
but suffused with a regretful irony, which says: "You have missed an
opportunity to be Christian! Woe!"

What tends to happen next is infinitely interesting. It seems by then to be too late for the uninitiated shopper to repent and make good. Already, he or she is headed for the slot machine inside the car park foyer. The shopping bag has acquired a new heaviness, the endorphin-releasing benefits of its contents being diminished by the second. To turn now and put an offering in the box would require acting of Oscar-nomination accomplishment. While the point of the determined stride towards the car park has been the pretence of unawareness of the beggar's presence, and his vocal intervention has rendered this futile, it is not easy to suddenly stop, turn around and convey by an act of generosity that one would have done so earlier had one not been preoccupied by some urgent matter. In any event, the momentum of the determined stride is carrying the now fruitlessly repentant shopaholic relentlessly towards the car park doorway. It seems, for the moment at least, that the beggar's outburst of apparently soulful benevolence has been entirely gratuitous and in vain. At best, one might suppose, he has made a mark for the future, teaching his subject a lesson to be remembered. He has tapped the buttons of modern Ireland's guilt-based inability to unabashedly wave its wad in the face of the also-rans.

But lo, a remarkable thing then tends to occur. The shopper sheepishly escapes through the doorway and heads for the slot machines. He or she shuffles through purse or pocket, and selects a higher-denomination note and feeds it into the slot machine. In a moment or two, the change comes jangling down. As though by some unspoken conspiracy, these machines never seem to have any notes to give in change, so that what emerges is a pocket-bursting weight of coin. This, the noise it makes and the moment of grace supplied by the slight delay, offers the shopper an opportunity of redemption. He is struck by an inspiration and, at the same moment, his acting skills have kicked in. He pockets a handful of the coins and, taking the rest in his hand, returns to the street and drops them in the beggar's box. His air is not one of confession or repentance, but perhaps of a slightly injured innocence: "You see," he seems to say, "it was simply that I had no change! Surely you did not think I was forgetting you? In fact, my hurry was inspired not by a desire to ignore you, but so as the quicker to come to your aid!"

The beggar smiles the smile of a shopkeeper who has just dispensed a good or service to a paying customer, which, of course, is precisely what he has done in granting the conspicuous consumer licence to nose his 03 Mercedes onto the road without compunction or guilt. "Thank you, sir," he intones, his irony melted away. "Have a nice evening now."

(June 2003)

22

THE MALADY OF INFINITE ASPIRATION

THE CALL FROM THE WESTERN HEALTH Board for fines to be imposed on those presenting to hospital accident and emergency
departments as a result of over-indulgence in alcohol is radical and
interesting, but ultimately wrong-headed. It fundamentally misunder-
stands the nature of alcohol abuse, both in the individual and collective dimensions of the problem.

The misapprehension is captured sublimely in Councillor Des
Bruen's assertion: "People who are seriously ill are being kept on trol-
leys in A&E because of all the services being used by people who are
under the influence, [which is] self-inflicted." The misapprehension
arises from the fact that the vast majority of those presenting for treatment at A&E departments on account of injuries arising from the abuse
of alcohol are, in fact, seriously ill. They suffer from the disease of alcoholism.

We tend to relate alcoholism only to the tramp guzzling cheap
plonk in the gutter, but that is only one of its many manifestations.
Someone who drinks so much and in such a way that he or she ends
up in an A&E department is almost certainly an alcoholic. Non-
alcoholics, people who can drink normally, do not find themselves in
this situation.

Our cultural attitude to alcohol tends to oscillate between two dia-
metrically removed points. On the one hand, we tend to be tolerant beyond prudence of those who over-indulge. In this part of our collective

brain, we imagine that a tendency towards drunkenness is, if a flaw at all, a flaw to be indulged. But occasionally, when things get out of hand, we lurch off into total intolerance, demanding that those who appear to take our first response too literally be brought to account for their conduct. The two responses might be called half-full and half-empty manifestations of the same misunderstanding, which itself results from a misdiagnosis of the problem.

Either alcoholism is a disease or it is not.

More than six decades ago, William D. Silkworth, a medical doctor consulted by the embryonic Alcoholics Anonymous, defined two of the key symptoms of alcoholism as physical allergy and mental compulsion. This means that (a) the body of an alcoholic is not the same as the body of a non-alcoholic; and (b) those who drink abusively are drinking to overcome a craving beyond their mental control. The only hope of recovery, Dr Silkworth asserted, is "an entire psychic change".

If this is true — and six decades of experience tells us it is — then punitive methods against those suffering from alcoholism are, firstly, doomed to failure; secondly, liable to wrongly exculpate society in an unhelpful way; and, thirdly, likely to short-circuit the learning process at both individual and collective levels.

If alcoholism is a disease besetting the individual, then it is reasonable to conclude that disproportionate consumption of alcohol in the collective dimension amounts to a national pathology. Already, in the belated responses to this well-established crisis, we observe our own desire to obfuscate and deny this possibility. The standard analysis is that alcohol consumption, even to considerable excess, is a symptom primarily of enjoyment, with a few debauched individuals contriving to spoil the party for everyone else. This viewpoint would seek, up to a very stretched point, to interpret the massively increased consumption levels of recent years as evidence of a somewhat unabashed celebration of national prosperity. But the statistics suggest that the relationship between the consumption of alcohol and increased wealth is not so straightforward. Over the past decade or so, more affluent households and individuals have consumed more alcohol than before, but the most significant increases in spending on alcohol have tended to be in the lower socio-economic groupings, which manifest a more increased relative spend on drink than the more comfortable classes. The sole exception to this pattern is among small farmers and agricultural workers, whose drinking patterns have not altered significantly.

A crude analysis of this might go as follows: that the increased consumption of alcohol in Irish society, and the epidemic of alcoholism which accompanies it, are the symptoms not so much of increased prosperity as of increased alienation from the society which prosperity has delivered. We need a new word for this, since "alienation" has been rendered meaningless by the dead-hand of Marx, and another alternative, "anomie", is too opaque and pretentious to be of any use in the project of collective enlightenment.

Identified by the French sociologist Emile Durkheim, "anomie" is a condition afflicting societies where the normative regulation of relationships by rules and values has collapsed, resulting in individual feelings of despair, isolation and meaninglessness, which surface in the form of various social disorders such as now beset this Republic. There can be little doubt that the national alcohol problem is one such symptom. The physical and mental symptoms of the disease of alcoholism are, in the individual, the manifestation of the spiritual paraplegia besetting the collective to which he or she belongs. Durkheim called it "the malady of infinite aspiration", the condition of wanting more and more of what fails to answer your questions.

It is a strange irony that, even in seeking to redress this malady's more acute symptoms, we think immediately in terms of money.

(December 2002)

23

THE GOD-SHAPED HOLE

I WAS INTERESTED IN THE ANALYSIS advanced on the Letters page last Tuesday by Dermot Stokes concerning drinking and young people. He was responding to a previous letter by Dr Michael Loftus of County Mayo, who has long warned about the dangers of alcohol abuse in Ireland.

Dr Loftus had criticised the endorsement of the Taoiseach and the Minister for Sport of the announcement that Diageo, the parent company of the drinks company Guinness, is to sponsor the joint bid by Ireland and Scotland to host the 2008 European Championship. He complained in the context of what he described as the "startling" facts about alcohol abuse contained in the interim report of the Strategic Task Force on Alcohol, which revealed that Irish consumption rose by forty-one per cent between 1983 and 1999.

Mr Stokes pointed to a more hopeful trend. Essentially, he was arguing that, since the vast bulk of the increase in consumption has occurred in the 18–34 age-group, Irish demographic patterns do not necessarily lend themselves to Doomsday comparisons with other countries. He argued that the fact that the proportion of our population in the 18–34 range is vastly higher than in other countries in Europe goes a long way towards explaining why alcohol consumption has risen dramatically here while declining elsewhere. "Over the past decade and a half," he wrote, "a massive population bulge has moved into this heavy-drinking age range. . . . Dr Loftus might take some comfort from the fact that our population bulge is now beginning to leave the heavy-drinking age range." This "should lead to a move from the dangerous heavy drinking and bingeing pattern characteristic of the 18–24 and 25–34 age-groups towards the safer, regular and moderate drinking characteristic of an older population".

In statistical terms the picture is precisely as outlined. But the analysis rests on the assumption that excessive drinking, because it has manifested itself primarily in the younger age-groups, is a kind of lifestyle option, a phase the young are going through. It emphasises the circumstantial patterns while overlooking why people drink to excess.

There is, of course, a considerable social phenomenon of moderate alcohol-intake, but this is not the issue. Alcohol abuse occurs in conditions exhibiting fairly clear-cut common characteristics and symptoms. For its abusers, alcohol becomes not a social lubricant or an enhancer of enjoyment but an analgesic and substitute for meaning in their lives. Alcoholism, it has long been established, is essentially a disease of the spirit. This sounds abstract, but is remarkably concrete.

Modern society, by virtue of its rational mindsets and pursuit of technological solutions to publicly visible problems, has caused us to forget how relatively powerless the individual is to deal with issues which the society at large feels it has all the answers to. In the past, such feelings of impotence were offset by a belief in God, but this is no longer an option for many. The result is that, without anyone, least of all the individual, being especially conscious of this, human beings have been burdened with bellyfuls of fear, anxiety and sadness concerning things our antecedents regarded as the will and the responsibility of God. Drugs and alcohol are the most readily available non-spiritual antidote to these feelings. People who abuse drink or drugs invariably do so because they are seeking to fill what Salman Rushdie called the "God-shaped hole" in their psyches.

What evidence we have concerning the collapse of belief in God in Irish society displays enormous circumstantial conformity with the increasing abuse of alcohol and drugs.

A survey of third-level educated young adults between the ages of twenty and thirty-five, conducted by Desmond O'Donnell OMI, and published in the January 2002 edition of *Doctrine and Life*, presented a fascinating sketch of the spiritual outlook of the young. In general terms, about two in five respondents appeared to have no belief in a spiritual dimension. Of these, a significant majority were male, with younger males being much more likely to lack such belief. For example, five per cent of males, but only three per cent of females, declared an outright denial of life after death, and those between twenty and twenty-five were four times more prone to such a view than those aged between thirty and thirty-five. Asked to choose between twelve possible descriptions of their experience of God, the respondents displayed a similar pattern, with the twenty to thirty age-group being less likely to accept descriptions like "peace", "trust", and "being loved". Negative experiences of God were more common among males, with eight per cent of males as against three per cent of females agreeing to the term "nothing" as a description of their relationship with God.

In general, the worst abuses of alcohol occur among males in their early twenties, the cohort in which belief in a spiritual dimension is most lacking. This is not a coincidence. And since such unbelief is a relatively new and growing problem, and since alcohol abusers do not suddenly convert to moderate consumption on reaching a certain age, and since experience tells us that God is not miraculously restored to the lives of adults without some profound spiritual transformation occurring, it is likely that, far from dissipating when the present demographic bulge passes into middle-age, our national alcohol problem will continue to grow and grow.

(August 2002)

24

A USEFUL GOD

BECAUSE THE CATHOLIC CHURCH IS by its nature authoritarian, and the Irish church especially so, every word uttered about God is interpreted within an established mode of thought which is difficult to circumnavigate. We see God as a kind of establishment presence, a forbidding force demanding obedience, respect and adoration. Thus, any attempt to invoke His name invites a backlash from those who have set their caps against either God or the very possibility of God, by which I mean not just atheists and agnostics but also those who believe in God but who just don't like Him very much. It is assumed that, by invoking God, you are trying to persuade people to re-submit themselves to an authority they have either dismissed or repudiated.

Catholic clerics invariably suggest that faith in God must be unconditional and unquestioning. But I often think that such notions of faith, religion or spirituality are counter-productive. Catholicism teaches us to think in terms of our duties towards God, forgetting that what defines our relationship with Him is the knowledge of what He can do for us that we cannot do for ourselves. His most vital role in the lives of human beings is in relieving them of the responsibility to take on the role of God themselves. The important thing is not whether I am sufficiently devout or God sufficiently happy with my piety, but my awareness of the fact that I myself am not God.

I did not make the world and know relatively little or nothing about its nature and workings. If I cease to believe in God, I am immediately burdened with a responsibility to explain and control, to make the world fall into line with my thinking. Having declared God dead or non-existent, a vacancy appears on the throne of power, and I am impelled to fill it. Only the constant consciousness that the world is mainly outside my control absolves me from this burden.

And so, if God does not exist, I have an urgent need, in my own interest, to invent him. In the knowledge of God I sleep tightly at night, like a child who knows his parents are asleep in the next room. Without Him, I lie awake planning how I might manage the world tomorrow.

This is the point I was trying to make a fortnight ago when I wrote about the relationship between declining faith and the growing abuse of alcohol. Some readers wrote in to take issue with what they imagined I meant. They appeared to assume my point to be essentially along the lines of the old-school religious objections to alcohol — mainly grounded in the alleged sinfulness of abuse, and the consequent absence of piety to be expected in the abuser. These are secondary, if not irrelevant, factors, except in so far as that, in the fundamentalist disapproval of excessive consumption, there may well be a logic concerning the fundamental problem presented by drugs and alcohol, which has been buried under centuries of false piety and pseudo-moralism.

This fundamental problem is that drugs and alcohol enable me to feel, falsely and temporarily, that my becoming God may not be such a preposterous idea after all. By dulling my sense of personal impotence, they lull me into a feeling of omnipotence, which remains for as long as the drug is working and available. A human being whose existence is driven by such substances is a potential danger to himself and the world, not just in the more obvious ways, but in the sense that he becomes immune to the idea that he is just a minor DNA variation on the first forms of life to emerge from the swamp.

One reader from Dalkey wrote that "to suggest that religious people are by definition not capable of alcohol abuse [is] obviously absurd". It may be, but I did not suggest it. The connection between religion and faith is in my experience like the connection between banks and money: having an account does not make you rich. He went on: "One of the most deeply religious people I have known was a devout Catholic priest whose love of the spirit extended to several bottles of it a day." I don't doubt that this priest was indeed a devout Catholic. Nevertheless, he couldn't possibly have had a true belief in God, because someone who truly believes will have no use for crutches. I have known many priests who successfully did battle with the bottle, and all of them were prepared to acknowledge that, prior to coming to grips with their dependency, their faith in God, for all their ostensible devotion, had been illusory.

It is interesting that the Pope, speaking recently in Krakow, spelt out the problem of evil in precisely the terms in which I attempted to present the alcohol problem. Identifying the core malfunction in human society as mankind's attempts to usurp God's role as the creator of life, he condemned man's attempts to "establish the limit of death". But by confining his remarks to abortion, euthanasia and the cloning of human cells, the Pope possibly short-circuited his own message, causing it to be read as a repetition of the standard Catholic ideology.

The insight transcends all such matters, however important. Every attempt to assert that mankind is self-sufficient has disastrous consequences, mainly for mankind. Man is not God, and never will be, and our only hope of peace, either personally or collectively, resides in acknowledging this reality.

(August 2002)

25

THE NECESSARY ILLUSIONS

JOINED-UP HOUSING DAMAGES YOUR health. Modesty forbids me to say I told you so, but the national health and lifestyle surveys 2003, published last week, leave no room for doubt. People in the east are fatter, drunker, smokier and druggier than the rest.

There are other broad-brush findings, like that women are healthier than men, which we already knew; or that single people are healthier than those who are married, cohabiting, widowed, separated or divorced — unsurprising when you think about it. But these distinctions are minimised by the regional factor, which clearly relates to urbanisation. The figures are an indictment of official policy and ideology over four decades of enabling the drift of human capital to the vortex of centrifugal forces. The destruction of de Valera's "rural idyll" has ended in the tears of the obese, the cancerous and the alcoholic.

It is vital that we not succumb to efforts by the same ideological forces that brought us here to spin the figures back into harmony with their discredited paradigm. Already there is talk about the alleged links between, for example, obesity and what they call "deprivation". Now they expect us to swallow the idea that poverty, once associated with emaciation, is synonymous with being overweight.

Behind the figures is a blacker picture. Fundamentally, the statistics reflect something deeper than public policy, or education, or even ideology — the grip of addictions on a psyche whose spiritual pilot-light has gone out, a nation suffering a creeping spiritual death.

The late, great Dr Bartley Sheehan, being a coroner as well as a GP, had a doctor's wisdom about death and a coroner's wisdom about life. My journalistic questions, he told me one day as he groped my windpipe, were upside down. The puzzle, he said, is not why some people kill themselves but why the rest of us don't. The reason we don't is that we have hope. Robbed of hope, we will find any number of exotic and roundabout ways of doing away with ourselves.

Hope is either material or spiritual, and, if the latter, becomes faith. Life without faith is a trial made bearable only by comfort, sensation and illusion. Although the material world and its manifold mouthpieces try hard to conceal this from us, life of itself is going nowhere fast. Without belief in something beyond, life is a headlong journey to the grave, punctuated by episodes of indulgence which are themselves part of an infrastructure of necessary illusion. We all need illusions, and perhaps if I wished to indulge the unbelieving with a view to sucking them in, I might agree that the greatest illusion of all is that there is something beyond. But I would have to add that this is the one that, to say the least, damages us least.

Without that ultimate, if you like, illusion, a mortal life becomes grounded in idolatry — of money, sex, nicotine, sugar, dope, carbohydrates or big cars. And though we have spent the past forty years — when we weren't busy constructing urban jungles — trying to paint God as the biggest illusion of all, in truth He is the safest, perhaps especially if He doesn't exist.

You need but to glance through last week's figures to see that somewhere in the logic flowing from Dr Sheehan's thesis lurks the explanation for everything. If we see obesity, drunkenness and addiction as expressions of unhope arising from a confusion as to what life is — we perceive that the people in the most pain are those with the fewest choices, in this world or, in a sense, the next.

The only poverty that need concern us is poverty of spirit. The people suffering maximum pain are those who have been crammed into factory-farm estates devoid of either factories or farms, had their banks of hope and imagination burgled by bad planning and ignorant ideologies, and had cavity-block walls flung between them and the possibility of illusion. And unlike the rural poor, they also had their God confiscated by supposedly smarter minds intent upon denying them their opium in order to prove a point. They didn't quite say, "Let 'em shoot heroin!" — but they may as well have.

Human beings need to be near to nature, as close as we get to knowledge of God. It is possible to live in the city and retain enough hope to avoid drinking, drugging or eating yourself to death, but only if you have the means to create your own illusions, worldly or otherwise: space, a country cottage, enough money to create enough dreams to keep at bay the sense that it is all ultimately going nowhere. Or maybe a comfortable prayer-mat stashed discreetly in the downstairs toilet.

And that's why the best arguments for decentralisation are irrational ones.

(December 2003)

26

SPECTATORS AT THE CARNIVAL OF BELIEF

ONE OF THE THINGS YOU LEARN from observing what is termed "modern society" is that, by virtue of being discussed at all, certain ideas and agendas move willy-nilly closer to realisation. Thus, it can be said with some certainty that, one of these days, the intermittent public campaigns to remove the Angelus from RTÉ radio and television will finally achieve their objective. The most recent efforts appear to have fizzled out for the moment, but it is only a matter of time before the project is resumed, and each new wave will have an even more urgent impetus. Like everything else, it is a question of modernisation: the Angelus is "out of tune" with modern society.

The main argument for this assertion is that the Angelus is "sectarian". Because it is a ritual belonging to a specific religion, i.e. the majority religion, it is deemed not merely to exclude others but even perhaps to be insulting to them. The time has come, we are told, to replace it with a more "inclusive" ritual. The trouble with those who make such suggestions is that what they mean by an "inclusive" ritual is one that is equally meaningless to everyone.

To avoid the usual neurotic attacks, I should point out to readers that I am not, in fact, on the Papal Nuncio's Christmas card list. In fact, although I was certainly brought up as one, I don't really feel entitled to describe myself as a Catholic at all. Having been steeped in Catholicism for more than twenty years, and having spent even longer trying to recover from the experience, I might be expected both to understand the objections to the Angelus and even to agree with them. But it is precisely because I understand them that I find myself in disagreement.

When I was an innocent young altar boy, the ringing of the Angelus was perhaps the most sacred of the roles which could be performed by those without benefit of ordination. The sacristan who was responsible for this task on a daily basis at home in Castlerea was Jack Cassidy, a man of the utmost punctiliousness and, indeed, punctuality. I never knew Jack to be more than a couple of seconds late with the first ring. No matter where you were, within as much as five miles of town, it was certain that at noon and at six you would hear the Angelus ring, and that you would hear it ring on time. Leaving aside the purely Catholic dimension, the Angelus bell was an extraordinary few moments twice every day, if only because Jack Cassidy's almost superhuman exactitude, based on deep reverence and personal faith, reminded us that there was something bigger and more constant than ourselves.

I would miss the Angelus, not just because of its religious significance, but also because of its reassuring cultural content. I would go so far as to say that there are few things on national radio today that give me as little offence.

But let us leave aside the vast cultural resonances of the Angelus bell in Irish society, and confine ourselves to the notion that all that is at stake is a piece of religious symbolism. As such, it has the capacity to draw together, even yet, a majority of Irish people, in prayer and meditation. Of how many other things can such a statement be made? What, in this entire society, is more inclusive than that? And does anybody seriously imagine that, notwithstanding the ubiquity of modern mass media, anything more inclusive will ever again be achieved?

Or do we begin to detect that perhaps inclusiveness is not what is at issue at all? In truth it forms no part of the campaigns to remove the Angelus from Irish radio and television that we might find something to replace it with. In the first place, this would be impossible, and in the second, if by some miracle such a thing were to be discovered, there would be an immediate campaign to remove this as well. For it is precisely because it reminds such people that there is something greater than themselves that so offends those who wish to put an end to the Angelus.

The advocates of such changes invariably come up with all kinds of politically correct stuff about minorities feeling offended by majoritarian practices and rituals. The funny thing is that when you actually talk to the people who are supposed to be mortally offended by such things, they invariably say that they have no difficulty with them at all. Most members of other religions who live in Ireland tend to accept that Catholicism is the majority religion, at least in a nominal sense, and if anything are quite pleased to see evidence of any form of spiritual practice around them. Indeed, only last week, the Protestant Archbishop of Dublin, the Most Rev Walton Empey, said precisely as much, when he remarked that he actually welcomed the Angelus bell "as a reminder to us all, even if we don't use this particular prayer, to use our own prayer".

To see other people practice their culture or religion does nothing to damage or offend people who have strong identities and beliefs of their own. And here we reach the nub of the issue: in truth, the Angelus does not exclude anyone other than those who were born and raised as Irish Catholics and who have rejected this faith of their fathers. They speak of liberalism, inclusiveness and tolerance, but they are really in the business of venting their disgruntlement with the Catholic Church.

The very idea of a ritual that would deliberately include everyone is a nonsense. The point of rituals is that they are evocative of specific experiences. But one authentic and profound ritual — even one that is fully accessible to only a minority — can be infinitely more powerful that a host of tokenistic rituals carried out in the interests of political correctness. Last year's inauguration of President McAleese provided a perfect example: the succession of rituals representing various religions was manifestly designed to minimise the role of the majority religion, and ended up with the spiritual content of the Academy Awards.

There is a paradox about faith and pluralism that liberals are utterly unable to perceive. The notion of "choice", which liberals are big on, is capable of bestowing benefits on only a single generation. It cannot be handed on. The present generation of neurotic Catholics, who run everything worth talking about in this society, are capable of making a "choice" about their religious practice (in most cases choosing not to practise) only because they were handed a ready-made faith in the first place. Many of them think of themselves as atheists, agnostics or whatever, but they are really lapsed Catholics who keep their options open and their eyes peeled for signs of the final furlong. They think of themselves as secular citizens, but in reality their heads are choc-a-bloc with Catholic indoctrination and dogma. Their endless battling with the religion of their youth means that they have deeply fulfilling spiritual lives. But post-Catholic neurosis, unlike Catholicism itself, cannot be handed on. It is reactive, and therefore prone to sudden death. Moreover, since their own neurosis leads them to hand on to their children not the faith which has given them the luxury of lifelong dissent but "a wide-ranging tolerance and respect for all cultures and religions", they have ensured that the next generation will not just have nothing to believe in but also nothing to refuse to believe in. Faith, like culture, is not genetic. You cannot pass on a vacuum. Other people's eyes may be deserving of respect and recognition, but they do not allow me to see.

This is the paradox of pluralism: it champions everything except existing reality. It is in favour of everything that exists someplace else, and believes that what exists in the here and now should move over and make space for what might or should be. This is why it leads not to diversity but to nothingness.

Faith is specific, immediate and particular. Faith requires that you believe in something yourself, here and now — not that you believe in the right of someone else to believe something. In an effort to counter past or present intolerance, there is a strong strain in our present culture seeking to tolerate everything except that which is not "other". Those minorities who present themselves, believing what they may, are to be respected, tolerated, cherished, celebrated, but the majority get to believe in nothing except that everyone else is entitled to believe in what they choose. And what then do the children of the majority become but spectators at the carnival of belief, which we have promoted, tolerated, affirmed, but declined to participate in? There is not much point in my being in favour of other people believing things if I do not believe in anything myself. Moreover, far from reassuring those with strong other beliefs, my lack of belief makes them uneasy and my supposed tolerance seems more like condescension. This will leave nothing but an empty shell looking benignly out on a teeming ferment of belief in which it has no part to play other than that of patronising observer. We will tolerate everything, but be nothing.

There is what I would characterise as the multicultural theory of postcolonial Ireland, which goes something like this: because we now have growing numbers of different faiths and traditions living among us, we cannot any longer imbue Catholic children with a sense that the Catholic religion is central or uniquely truthful. This sounds wonderfully tolerant, magnanimous and pluralist, until you consider what would happen if Catholics were to suggest to Muslims that they are not permitted to see Islam as central or uniquely truthful. If you are a Catholic, then it is entirely natural to believe that Catholicism teaches the truth, and this in no way interferes with the right of others to believe the same of their own faith.

I do not suggest that Catholics should disrespect the beliefs of others; what I say is that it is wrong to expect Catholics to dilute their beliefs in case someone might take offence at the suggestion that Catholicism is closer to the truth than any other tradition. If Catholics do not believe this, why be a Catholic?

It is as though we wish to educate our children to the point of scepticism we ourselves have reached after several decades of intense struggle with the Catholic Church. Much of our thinking on these matters is what I would term parasitic, which is to say that it rests on the assumption that everything we have come to know, understand and believe can be taken for granted, that it always existed and will remain in spite of all. This is folly, because scepticism is the luxury of those who already have beliefs on which to exercise their doubts. But you cannot begin the comprehension of the mysteries of existence from a position of doubt. The transmission of beliefs requires to be informed by the concrete before it can afford to be infected by confusion.

If my six-year-old child asks me a theological question, I do not burden her with the crypto-agnostic angst of my forty-seven-year-old paradox-ridden head. When she asked, "Daddy, is heaven before or after outer space?", I did not tell her that heaven may be a product of man's inability to accept the nothingness of existence, which is what I might have said if I was being interviewed by the religious corre- spondent of *The Irish Times*. Instead, I said, "After." And she said, "So, first you have the clouds, then you have the sky, then you have outer space, and then you have heaven. Right, Daddy?" And I said, "Right." Before you can learn to doubt, you must find something to have doubts about.

Diversity is essential to the health of public culture. But in faith as in economics, public virtues can be private vices, especially since radical personal belief-systems are obtained by picking and mixing from the public buffet. The diversity of a culture depends on the indi- vidual vigour of its singularities. If you destroy the particularities that create the discrete entities of a culture, what is transmitted to the indi- vidual is not an interesting postmodern comprehension of paradoxical realities, but a sense that truth is a mirage.

Like place, faith has no scope for generalisation. What is here is here, and what is true is true. It never ceases to amaze me that those who are most assiduous in asserting the rights of (certain, selectively ordained) minorities to exist and prosper are almost invariably the same people who contend that political and economic virtue resides in large entities like the European Union rather than small ones like, for example, the Irish nation. Big is okay, it seems, in matters political and economic, but not when it comes to religion: Single Market good, One True Faith bad. It is fashionable, in the modern world, to be a citizen of large entities, like Europe and the world, but not to belong to small, singular places like Tulsk or Manorhamilton. But without the particular there is no general, and without a belief in something there is nothing to tolerate. Moreover, faith is always inspirational: to be in the presence of one human being who believes in something is better than to be in a vast crowd of people who are committed to tolerance and mutual respect but have not a single belief between them.

The attacks on faith and on place tend to come from the same quarters and for the same reasons. Materialism suspects, above all, those who believe, because they tend not to need to buy things. You cannot build a strong industrial and service-oriented society where there are strong beliefs, because instead of requiring the services of lawyers, counsellors and architects, people have recourse to "traditional" entities like families and communities. In the "modern" world, it is fine to be dependent on aromatherapists, but not on priests; it is okay to believe in opinion polling, but not in transubstantiation, even though the evidence in either instance may be equally circumstantial.

Secular-liberalism or whatever we may call the present babble of unbeliefs that rule our public days and nights, is deeply suspicious of any form of belief, precisely because faith is always specific.

The least tolerant people in Irish society are not, after all, those with a strong belief in Catholicism, but those campaigning to remove Catholic rituals from the sight of Irish society. The attempt by such people to pass themselves off as liberal is taken seriously by nobody but themselves. The real test of liberalism is not the capacity to tolerate other people's beliefs but the capacity to tolerate in others the beliefs that you have rejected for yourself.

(This essay is an amalgam of two columns which appeared in The Irish Times *in February 1998 and August 2002)*

27

WHEN THE FEMINIST AND THE FASCIST CAN BE FRIENDS

(A response to the banning by the French government of religious dress and symbols in state schools)

THE HIJAB CONTROVERSY BRINGS liberalism and multiculturalism to the limits of coherent coexistence. Hitherto they seemed natural bedfellows, bestowing tolerance and piety in all directions in the manner of a John and Yoko bed-in. But this bursts the hot-water bottle, and no mistake.

For here is an issue on which the feminist and the fascist can be friends — the one because, you know, those Muslims are so oppressive of their womenfolk; the other because the darkies must be kept down. Liberalism suddenly finds itself abed with the previously anathematised — the racist, the bigot, the xenophobe and those branded with these labels for trying to draw attention to the inevitability of our ending up where we are. The usually monolithic liberal-left constituency is divided between those who say that diversity is the pre-eminent value of pluralist society, and those who have suddenly decided that equality is more so.

This might seem either an exceptionally complex issue or an aberration that defies the logic of tolerance we had so come to trust. It is neither. Although liberals strain to create a new equation to explain the inconsistencies in a nice liberal way, the truth is that we have hit philosophical bedrock. The hijab issue provides a convex-mirror image of the advanced inconsistency arising from liberalism's belief in the unlimited reach of a coreless diversity policed by rigid notions of equality. Such diversity is as unworkable as equality is impossible.

Any notion that the French decision to ban the hijab in state schools was motivated by concern for Islamic females is humbug. Similarly, combining the ban with a prohibition on other religious symbols, thus presenting it as an attempt to achieve separation of the religious from the civic, is a fig leaf. This is an attempt to curtail the devotional influence of Islam, which now threatens to swamp a Europe rendered faithless by materialism and hubris.

In the equal treatment of the iconography of indigenous and external belief systems can be found the seed of Europe's undoing. It is precisely the equation of Christianity with other religions that brought Europe to its present point of vulnerability. The idea that we can arrest the influence of Islam by limiting further the instruments of our own salvation is to propose treating the condition with the virus that caused it.

Liberal Europe is in philosophical disarray, because its logic has worked too well. The idea of Europe is based on frontierless European superiority: people from all over the world would come here — as needed, of course — to be tolerated and patronised, and would forever be so grateful to, and overawed by, European pluralism and liberalism that they would never seek any kind of autonomy, never mind dominance. To make our tolerance more manifest, we would suppress our own cultural and religious character, lest the visitors become offended.

But instead of sitting demurely in their immigrant corner, some visitors took European tolerance at its word. Eschewing integration with the wider community, they looked to themselves, and began building their own citadels of faith and identity on the foundations provided by modern Europe's parasitic indifference to its own culture and traditions. Then, gaining confidence, they began to agitate and self-promote, to limit modesty to transactions with their Creator, to shout their beliefs from the rooftops and, finally, to observe how wanting they found the host culture in matters of morality and belief.

They were, of course, correct. The host culture had, in the complacency of self-belief, all but deconstructed itself. It no longer believed in anything other than the right of people to believe whatever they pleased. Up to a point, which we have now reached.

The fatal flaw in multiculturalism is its denial of a need for particularity at the centre. To be easy with the beliefs of others, we must first be secure in our own. The problem we face is not the vibrancy of particularisms in Islam, but the weakness of them in our own culture. Secularists always claim that the worst they feel towards intense belief is impatience with its alleged superstition; in fact, they are terrified by its seemingly irrational power. European liberalism shifted the weight of its culture from God to State, and now, finding itself invaded by Islam at full throttle, is unable to match it in kind.

Those who argue that Muslims have a right to dress their children as faith and tradition prescribe are absolutely right. The expression of spiritual belief is a fundamental right, encompassing, among others, the right to bear witness; the right to assert humility before a Superior Being; the right to nurture a collective religious culture.

Europe will soon find that the trite ragbag of orthodoxies — rights, equality, political correctness — with which it has supplanted its traditional values will prove an inadequate defence against the austere rage of those who will now see the blurring of its condescension into totalitarianism as further proof of Europe's intrinsic degeneracy.

(January 2004)

28

SMALL-TOWN GOBSHITERY
AND THE N-WORD

I was in Claremorris a week ago saying a few words at the opening of the annual Claremorris Open Exhibition, a community-inspired art event with global ambitions, entitled this year "Speak to Me". The idea is to invite leading artists to submit works to be exhibited at various locations in the town — shops, an alleyway, the library, the town hall. For its three-week run the exhibition will, in a sense, subvert the smallness of Claremorris by pushing at the boundaries of what is thought of as everyday. One exhibit, for example, is "Knock Knock" a startling piece by Mick O'Shea, which has blow-up latex figures of Christ and the Virgin Mary being prodded at precise intervals by a mechanical contraption. Not long ago, such an exhibit would have created ructions on a national basis, causing devout citizens to take turns to recite decades of the Rosary outside Mr Fix It's shop on Mount Street. Nowadays nobody bats an eyelid, because people have a sense that one of the "purposes" of art is to stretch perception, to challenge and undermine the clichéd and restrictive ways a public language can set limits on the interior, personal voices.

I have been wondering if Enda Kenny perhaps had the misfortune to stop off at Claremorris on his way to Dublin, in advance of making That Speech. Perhaps Mr Kenny, intoxicated by the artistic and intellectual breadth of the works on display, got carried away with the idea that freedom of expression is still permissible. This would explain why he left himself open to a journalistic mauling the weekend before last, by telling, in front of journalists, a fairly unexceptionable story involving use of the word "nigger".

The anecdote concerned an incident in Portugal some years ago in which a Moroccan barman, in the hearing of Mr Kenny and two other Fine Gael politicians, described the late Patrice Lumumba as a "nigger". As a result, Mr Kenny was subjected to an outpouring of sanctity in the Sunday newspapers. Was he a racist? Had he expressed racist views? If not, had he at least "cheapened the debate" about racism, by using an "abusive racial epithet"? Various worthies from the anti-racism industry were trotted out to tut-tut, and Mr Kenny himself was quoted as abjectly apologising for any offence. There was much fretting about whether, in a "multicultural society", Mr Kenny made a suitable Taoiseach-in-waiting. One commentator described Mr Kenny as "a stupid man who should resign but won't".

It is difficult to divine from the reporting what the precise intention or meaning of Mr Kenny's anecdote may have been, but I gather it had something to do with the irony of one black man describing another as a "nigger". Perhaps Mr Kenny was making some point about the naïveté of himself and the couple of political chums who were with him at the time. Perhaps his point had to do with the pointedness of the Moroccan's irony in saying this in front of three white Europeans. I don't know, because the reportage of the episode was so intent on screwing Enda Kenny for the crime of uttering a six-letter word that it did no more than sketch in the context in the rush to nail its victim. Perhaps the anecdote was entirely pointless, rendering Mr Kenny open to the charge that he is a purveyor of meaningless stories, a serious matter but not as serious as racism.

There is stupidity to be found in this episode but it does not reside with Enda Kenny. For here we have a journalism which seeks to construct a story where there is none by pretending a level of stupidity way in excess of what it is possible for any reasonably educated or sophisticated adult to exhibit. We live in a society that claims an interest in openness and tolerance, with journalism arrogating to itself a large part of the credit for nurturing these qualities. Journalists would be the first to pour ridicule on anyone who objected to Mick O'Shea's installation in Claremorris. And yet, such journalists, who in one arena would claim the right to push boundaries in multiple directions, in another insist they have the right to ban outright the use of a particular word, regardless of context — to say, "In future no adult shall utter this word, under any circumstances, without inviting serious consequences." (Surely, if it was wrong of Mr Kenny to use the word in relating his anecdote, it was equally wrong of journalists to use the word in reporting the story?) To call this political correctness would be a gross understatement. It is small-town gobshitery of the lowest order. It is also far closer to racism than Mr Kenny's anecdote, for it ascribes to black people a level of intelligence so low as to render them incapable of distinguishing real racism when it occurs.

What next? A ban on all books, records, films and TV programmes in which the word "nigger" is used? A prohibition on references to culchies, Paddies, Micks, Prods, Kerrymen, pygmies and mothers-in-law?

Or perhaps we should just have a ban on the use of the word "infantile", so such journalism can no longer be named for what it is.

(September 2002)

29

BALLYHAUNIS: THE ACTUALLY EXISTING FUTURE?

INSECURITY RATHER THAN INSULARITY is the issue with regard to what we — or at least those who channel our common discourse — are insisting upon describing as racism.

Sometimes, fear of change and disruption of the familiar can express itself as opposition to the outsider, and even as what seems to be dislike for those who are different. People of a different race or colour offer a simple representation of a complex social condition, and what we call racism, in this context, is simply the public expression of the fear arising from uncertainty and change. Jeering at black people in the street is an ignorant expression of an inchoate fear. It is the fear, rather than its expression, that we should usefully focus on.

There is racism in Ireland, as in all European countries. Europe is the architect of racism in the world, and, since we Irish spent most of the last millennium under the boot of the most racist power on earth, it would be surprising if it were otherwise. Racism is not, as is often alleged, the expression of superiority. On the contrary, it is the expression of a deep sense of inferiority. In the science, yes, of colonialism, racism is the primary catalyst of civilisation, existing in direct proportion to the extent of colonial oppression, and reflecting the success of the coloniser in implanting in the native a sense of his master's superiority in all things.

But this has not yet manifested itself here as a widespread intrinsic dislike of black people or Romanians or Jews. We have had such people here in small numbers for many years, and, apart from the occasional outbursts of ignorance, usually drink-related, have not treated them any differently from how we treat each other. There is some evidence of incipient racism in Irish cities, particularly Dublin, and this is something we have to look at. Perhaps Dublin, having been the centre of colonial rule, is more prone to this condition than other places.

I was most interested in my colleague Fintan O'Toole's column on Tuesday last, in which he proposed that the fact that Muslims have been welcomed in the County Mayo town of Ballyhaunis is entirely a matter of local self-interest. I disagree.

As it happens, I was the editor of *Magill* who, in 1988, commissioned Fintan to write an article about Ballyhaunis. I grew up in Castlerea, a slightly bigger town about twelve miles to the east, across the Roscommon border. As a teenager, I went dancing in Ballyhaunis on Saturday nights. Thin Lizzy played there once, and a friend of mine hitched a lift home from a late-lamented black neighbour of Fintan's, Mr Philip Lynott.

The reason I commissioned Fintan to write about Ballyhaunis was that I was fascinated by the extraordinary juxtaposition of a Muslim culture and what might be perceived as a "country and western" sensibility. Ballyhaunis was by then, in the late 1980s, the location of the unprecedented phenomenon of a pirate radio station which broadcast, weekly from a local nightclub, a version of The Price is Right, presented by another old pal of mine, the peerless Paul Claffey. Several other friends worked in the Halal factory by day and went to the Midas Club at the weekend. It seemed to me that this story unsettled the conventional notions about small-town Ireland and I was intrigued to see what Fintan would make of it. He wrote an exquisite piece, full of compassion and insight. Perhaps it was easier to be compassionate about Ireland then.

It is not the case that Ballyhaunis welcomed the Muslim community only because of the benefits to the local economy. This perspective is easy to adopt in retrospect, but the truth is a good deal more complicated. In the first place, when Sher Rafique first came to town in the mid-1970s, he did not bring with him the approximately 200 Muslims who live in Ballyhaunis now, some of them playing GAA and attending meetings of the local Fianna Fáil cumann. He brought his family and a small number of workers. The impact on the local economy was at first negligible.

In the second place, it is not the case that there was no resistance to the Halal operation. There were public meetings and objections in the Ballyhaunis of the mid-1970s, just as there are public meetings now in Wexford and Kildare and Waterford. I'm sure racist things were said at those meetings, but their occurrence was not in itself racist. The main objections were to the location of the Halal slaughter-house — on the edge of Ballyhaunis on the Claremorris road — and people were concerned about health issues and the smell. In other words, the development was scrutinised and considered by the local community in a democratic and open manner, and ultimately welcomed and approved. And the main reason it was approved was that people could see that the newcomers were decent people, anxious to make a living, who would keep themselves to themselves and not represent a threat to the local community.

In other words, it's not the economy, stupid, but the equilibrium of the community, part of which relates to the capacity of newcomers to pay their way, integrate to a reasonable extent and contribute to the general prosperity. If these considerations could be met in relation to the introduction of refugees and asylum-seekers to any community in Ireland, there would not be a negative response, never mind a racist one. Ballyhaunis, allegedly in the most conservative part of Ireland, with its mosque and vibrant Muslim community, and its contingents of Turks, Syrians, Pakistanis and Egyptians, stands as a challenge to the glib, sanctimonious media sermonising about the nature of Irish racism.

But if you propose sending 400 extra people of any kind into a closely knit community of 1,200 or 1,500 people, and do not expect those people to complain, then there is something wrong with your brain. Most communities would object if their numbers were overnight to be swollen by 10, 15 or 20 per cent. It wouldn't matter if the newcomers were Romanians, Jews, Dutchmen, Red Indians, or brown-eyed octogenarian dart-players — people would have genuine reasons for concern about the sudden change in their way of life. To call this racism is asinine.

(May 2000)

30

THE RACISM OF CONDESCENSION

(A response to a billboard advertising campaign by Amnesty International, featuring photographs of individual government ministers and a slogan, commenting on public policy towards immigrants and asylum-seekers: "Some say they're involved in racism. Others say they're doing nothing about it.")

IN ALL THE EXCITEMENT ABOUT THE offensive nature of the recent Amnesty International campaign against racism, I have not heard it said that both the campaign and the survey conducted in conjunction with it exhibited symptoms of the very condition they were ostensibly designed to expose.

This survey, listing a number of ethnic groups, as well as several religious denominations, asked: "Which of the following groups would you be reluctant to welcome as residents in your local area?" Has it occurred to anyone inside or outside Amnesty International that this is a racist question? Surely, if the term "racism" has any meaning at all, any list of ethnic groupings offering the option of placing such groupings in an order of "preference" must itself suggest the possibility of a hierarchy of ethnicity, and therefore qualify as racism?

I am reminded of the observation of the French philosopher Jean Baudrillard: "Racism is desperately seeking the other in the form of an evil to be combated. The humanitarian sees the other just as desperately in the form of victims to aid. . . . The scapegoat is no longer the person you hound, but the one whose lot you lament. But he is still a scapegoat. And it is still the same person."

Racism is a precise form of scapegoating, and is just as unpleasant when resulting from condescension as from contempt. How ironic, then, that in supposedly seeking to highlight the issue of racism in Ireland, the hitherto unimpeachable Amnesty International should resort to scapegoating the Taoiseach, Tánaiste and Minister for Justice in respect of an issue which is a collective rather than an executive responsibility.

There is racism in Ireland, but it is neither as prevalent nor as widespread as Amnesty suggests. To place Travellers in the "racism" equation is a mistake to begin with, since Travellers are not an ethnic group, and so not even the most extreme public sentiments against them could remotely be described as racist. According to the Amnesty survey, forty per cent of Irish people would be reluctant to welcome Travellers into their area. Two things strike me about this: (1) it is a ludicrous underestimate of the hostility towards Travellers; and (2) the question implies, against massive evidence, that objections to having Travellers as neighbours could result only from prejudice. Many of those who object to Travellers can point to overwhelming evidence in support of their objections.

Secondly, the use in the question of the term "groups" creates a confusion which in effect neutralises this question altogether. There is an enormous difference between objecting to the presence of an individual or a family belonging to a particular ethnic or other grouping and objecting to the arrival of a "group" *per se*. The sudden arrival of a "group" of any kind might be likely to cause upset or anxiety in any community. One way of offsetting the negation of this question might have been too include in the survey a question about attitudes to the arrival of a "group" of Aryan nudists, which might have provided some perspective on the responses to the other categories. As it is, what is revealed may not be racism, but respondents' entirely legitimate regard for the integrity of their existing communities.

Beyond its individual manifestation, racism is a collective syndrome, born of the desire to feel superior. This desire is itself, paradoxically, born of the fear of acknowledging the darkness within oneself. The "psychodynamic" explanation for racism is in terms of a desire to project the "bad bits" of yourself on to another person or group, thereby allowing you to become cleansed of venality and imperfection and correspondingly superior to those you seek to disparage. The most obvious context for this condition in the geopolitical arena is colonialism, whereby whole peoples were scapegoated by a small number of powers craving territory and dominion over others. It was this process which rendered racism a global phenomenon, and moreover associated it primarily with the dominion of white over black.

But, of course, the Irish experience of racism is primarily from the receiving end, by virtue of our relationship with England, the most racist power on earth, and this experience was of white-on-white. One of the effects of enduring racism is the desire to offload the received feeling of inferiority on to some new scapegoat, and in this sense it is somewhat surprising that the evidence of racism in modern Ireland is not a great deal more prevalent than it is.

It is odd, then, that, in purporting to confront the incidence of scapegoating of particular categories of newcomers to this country, Amnesty International should suggest an "involvement" in racism by elected representatives who have done no more than carry out their responsibilities in relation to immigration and asylum-seekers. This is utterly in keeping with the notion of scapegoating as a way of offloading negative qualities on to some third party. There emerges, in this society now, a disquieting, even sickening, attempt by certain sections to present themselves as superior to the majority by virtue of their self-advertised "tolerance" of immigrants and asylum-seekers. In most instances, this "tolerance" remains untested in real life, but remains in the realm of rhetoric and priggish denunciation of others, which is itself a precise encapsulation of the essential racist impulse. It is a pity that Amnesty International has sullied its exemplary record on behalf of the world's downtrodden and dispossessed by offering itself as a cheerleader for this tendency.

(May 2001)

31

THE QUANTIFICATION OF HYPOCRISY

ON INITIAL SCRUTINY, THE MOST informative aspect of last week's *Irish Times*/MRBI poll on public attitudes to immigrants was its revealing snapshot of public hypocrisy. On the one hand, it revealed that, whereas sixty per cent of those surveyed believe we should take a more generous approach than at present to refugees and immigrants "in view of our own history of emigration and our current prosperity", a considerably greater proportion, seventy-four per cent, think the numbers of refugees should be "strictly limited". Nearly half of those surveyed, forty-two per cent, believe that only refugees qualified to fill specific job vacancies should be admitted, with forty-nine per cent disagreeing with this.

This invites a question: what form of "generosity" do those people have in mind who answered the first question in a manner "sympathetic" to "refugees and immigrants" while simultaneously believing that numbers should be "strictly limited"? Perhaps, one is tempted to observe, they were thinking of more comfortable holding cells, or first-class travel for refugees on their journey back home.

But such glib observations do nothing to come to grips with what appears to be a fairly significant degree of genuine public confusion. In truth, the poll tells us very little, as the confusion of terms like "immigrant" and "refugee" of itself negates the claim in the headline: "Seventy-four per cent want strict limits on refugee numbers." But I believe the poll does actually tell us a great deal about the nature of our discussion about immigrants and refugees.

This issue is now threatening to overtake unwanted pregnancy as the great liberal bullworker of "modern" Ireland. Few issues of the present time have the same capacity to allow liberals to flex their morally superior muscles, to pretend compassion and concern for humanity while inviting not an iota of responsibility for the consequences of their stated beliefs. As Ivor Callely has discovered, to give voice to the undoubtedly widespread public fears on this issue is to volunteer to become a liberal whipping-boy, enabling commentators and politicians to present themselves in a gracing light by attacking those who are prepared to express an honest perspective. (Note that it is never necessary for the liberal Don Quixote demonstrably to hold views which might be identified as antithetical to those he attacks, still less to have alternative perspectives or solutions to offer; all that is necessary is that he be convincing in his piety and "right-thinking".)

We have travelled less far than we imagine since the days of giving pennies to the black babies. The mirror-image of the bigotry of those who seek to exclude because of skin-colour or origin is the pseudo-humanitarianism of those who seek to consign immigrants and asylum-seekers to the role of objects of alleged liberal compassion. This too is racism, because it dehumanises immigrants by turning them into ciphers on to which we project our alleged sympathy and pity, creating scapegoats for our bogus compassion as well as our contempt.

Last week's poll exhibited this syndrome in a most eloquent manner. The question as to whether or not we should "take a more generous approach than at present to refugees and immigrants in view of our own history of emigration and our current prosperity" is a classic example of liberal piety — a have-you-stopped-beating-your-Filipino-maid? type of question. The phrase "more generous" is heavily loaded in a moral — or rather a pseudo-moral — sense, as is the placing of our obligations to immigrants in the contexts of our own historical experience and *our* (my italics: everyone's?) "current prosperity". This contrasts strongly with the decidedly rawer, factual nature of the questions about whether or not only those with appropriate qualifications should be admitted and whether or not numbers should be "strictly limited".

All polls are subject to this kind of tendentious question-framing, but here it appears to have been governed by a revealing woolliness rather than by any desire to achieve a particular result. An interesting aspect of the result was that supporters of Fianna Fáil were significantly more "liberal" in their responses than supporters of Labour or the Progressive Democrats; this is because Fianna Fáilers, by virtue of being stigmatised as reactionary by definition, are now in the position of having to advertise their modernity at every opportunity, whereas followers of the other parties feel confident that their liberal credentials will be accepted at face value.

What does "strictly limited" mean, anyway? Is it different to "limited"? Far from being a facetious question, this underlines the true nature of liberal hypocrisy on this issue.

We do not have a multiplicity of possibilities as to how we deal with immigration. I believe we have three: declare Fortress Ireland; throw open our doors to all-comers; or formulate a policy based on absolute numbers of immigrants. (We do not have the option of placing limits on the number of asylum-seekers who come here.) Virtually nobody is proposing either of the first two approaches; so the solution, by general agreement, resides in deciding roughly how many people we are ultimately prepared to accommodate. But this is the one aspect which liberals are not prepared to confront.

It shouldn't be all that difficult. Are we prepared to admit, say, half-a-million people under various categories? "Oh, don't be ridiculous," comes back the liberal riposte. All right then: five. "Sorry?" Five immigrants. "Oh, now you're being facetious again." No, I'm not, but at least we've established that you believe the final figure should be somewhere between five and 500,000. Okay, how about splitting the difference: 250,003? Is that still ridiculous? And so on, hopefully to some kind of conclusion. This approach, I guarantee, will either very quickly bring us to an approximate idea of how many immigrants we believe we should take, or just as rapidly reveal the extent of our hypocrisy.

Exercising the standard liberal irresponsibility, I might suggest that, if we want to make this into a "moral" argument, we have no option other than an open-door policy. In a sense, there is no other way of dealing morally with the issues raised by immigration in the context of our own history and our alleged present prosperity. But those who say that the consequences of this for the character of our society would be enormous are absolutely right, and such a choice would need to be preceded by a truthful and comprehensive public debate, free of bullying by those of either pluralist or purist complexions. (I do not believe, incidentally, that it would turn Ireland into a "multicultural society"; the nearest example of a society like this is in Britain, where the alleged "multicultural coexistence" is achieved largely by the avoidance of eye-contact.)

Even if it were not already too late, Fortress Ireland is not a moral solution, although it would certainly be more principled than the notion of an upper limit. At least those who advocate this option have the courage of their convictions.

If we opt for a limit, "strict" or otherwise, on the number of people who should be entitled to come and live here, I think we should keep the moralising to a minimum and confine ourselves to pragmatic discussion of the practical issues.

(February 2000)

32

THE GREAT PRETENDER

ONCE UPON A TIME, THERE WAS this island nation, which for a considerable period had been ruled or run by those who fought in its revolution of some decades before. And at the moment when the torch of power was to be handed for the first time to a generation once removed from the scorched earth of civil war, there emerged one man who, though short in physical stature, in another sense stood trunk and torso above all others with pretensions to lead. This man was widely regarded as the most brilliant, the most charismatic, the most visionary of his generation, the ideal instrument of the next phase of national development. Gradually, the people too came to see this. But in the hearts of the mediocrities all around him, there remained a reluctance to face reality. Though lesser men all, emanating from a higher stratum of the society than the Great Pretender, they felt superior to this man of lowly origins. And so, although lacking any remotely comparable qualities or abilities, they nurtured ambitions to lead instead of him.

An opportunity arose. The conflict which had abated in the State some decades previously had continued intermittently in another, still-occupied part of the national territory, and now had broken out again. The escalating conflagration threatened to spill over and engulf the fledgling Republic. This fear, however, was for most of the people much less important than a sense that help must be extended to their brethren in the occupied territories to the north. The mediocrities saw in this situation the opportunity to dispose of the Great Pretender once and for all, and a trap was set in place, whereby they were able to seize power, banish the Great Pretender and present the coup as a successful attempt to preserve the State from civil war. The would-be leader of his people was dragged before the courts and, although acquitted, remained overcast by the cloud of suspicion which had been insinuated around him.

The Great Pretender, however, did not shrink away to his lair to lick his wounds. Instead, he mounted his chariot and headed to the country, where he began to nourish and rekindle the embers of his popular appeal. Denied his rightful place as leader by the usurpation of the State's authority, he sought to open up an alternative route back to glory. Very quickly, however, he came to realise that this would not be an easy or an overnight task. He was a man of relatively modest means, who had sacrificed his own capacity for significant self-enrichment by virtue of his vocation as leader of his people. But help was at hand. A number of wealthy merchant princes, outraged by the treatment of the Great Pretender at the hands of the infidels of mediocrity, came to his aid, bestowing riches and favours upon him so that he could be free to continue with his mission of self-rehabilitation. Meanwhile, owing to the incompetence of the mediocrities, the fortunes of the people went into dramatic decline. A nation which had a short time earlier appeared to be on the brink of prosperity, now, in the hands of the mediocrities, plunged into the mire of economic depression. The merchant princes, seeing their nation and its economy going down the drain, dug deep into their pockets once again.

It was to take many years of the frequently indigestible hospitality of his people before the Great Pretender reclaimed his rightful place as leader. Oh joy! The mediocrities fumed and spluttered, but to no avail.

But alas, our tale is not destined to have a happy ending. The years spent cast out in the desert had hardened our hero's heart. No longer was he the warm, fun-loving rascal of old, but embittered by his experiences to the extent of being mistrustful of all but his most intimate allies. Throughout the early years of his resumed leadership, he remained fearful of challengers to his position, particularly so of a number of individuals from far-flung regions, who spoke in impenetrable singsong accents, and whom he suspected had been key players in the conspiracy against him. In due course, he banished them from his presence and surrounded himself with men from a different province, whose hearts still burned with the spirit of revolution.

But his enemies did not rest. Instead, they plotted and conspired against him, frustrating his every attempt to consolidate his leadership and turn the fortunes of his people around once more. But then, at last, he began to succeed. A little progress was made. Then, seeing their opportunity, his jealous rivals took advantage of an opportunity to return to the warm embrace of the Great Pretender. For a while it looked as though a momentous reconciliation has been achieved. But woe, very soon it transpired that the mediocrities have simply taken advantage of the Pretender's temporary weakness to undermine him from within. Soon they would banish him permanently, but, not content with this, immediately set in place a number of Inquisitions by which to finally destroy his image in the eyes of his people. These Inquisitions inquired into everything which might even remotely offer up the prospect of finally discrediting the Great Pretender, but ignored all the matters — including the manner in which the resources of the State had been marshalled against this one man — which might have thrown light upon his own motivations or those of the merchant princes who had supported him. By now, with the fortunes of the nation restored to rude good health, the Great Pretender was no longer necessary, and could be disposed of for good.

(May 2001)

33

THE TRIAL OF THE WITCHDOCTOR

(On the appearance of Charles Haughey in court on criminal charges arising from his evidence to the McCracken tribunal)

THINKING UP SUITABLE PUNISHMENTS for Charles J. Haughey has become something of a national pastime. I met a man recently who thought the best way of dealing with the former Taoiseach was to make him live out the rest of his life in a two-bedroom, semi-detached council house. It was on the tip of my tongue to ask him if he thought Mr Haughey should be entitled to a medical card, but something about the quiver of his jaw told me that such jokes would not be regarded as matching the height and tone of his dudgeon.

Had I been of the informing breed, I would have immediately reported this man to the Revenue Commissioners, on the grounds that his annoyance about Mr Haughey's skilful evasion of the business of rendering unto Caesar seemed to present a *prima facie* case that he had one or two fiscal secrets of his own. Accusation, as is recognised in certain psychotherapeutic circles, is another form of confession.

The great difficulty with attempting to analyse the subtexts of these events in any even-handed, compassionate and therefore truthful manner, is that it will be assumed by those who wish perceptions to remain precisely as they are that such explorations arise from a simple desire to get the present accused off the hook. I could go into a long rigmarole about my personal views of Mr Haughey, but I have long since found that there is no point in trying to undermine such perspectives, since they exist in the first place as an alternative to thinking; and, since any initiative to deconstruct them would invite at least a modicum of thought, it is clear that all such efforts are utterly pointless.

I would, however, like to point out one or two of the ironies that surround Mr Haughey's imminent appearance in court.

Mr Haughey stands accused of getting handouts from business people and of failing to pay tax on such income. At the cultural level, there is the secondary charge that, by allowing himself to become dependent on such largesse at a time when he was — as is inevitably added with great piety — "Taoiseach of this country", he brought his nation, office and people into disrepute.

I just think it should be recalled that, at the time when all this was occurring, it was the policy of this State to seek and obtain hand-outs from any consenting quarter, and that this approach rarely met with anything but the maximum public approval. During the period when Mr Haughey is said to have had his hand in Ben Dunne's wallet, virtually the entire political discussion of the day was to do with cohesion and structural funding, and the imperative to "draw down" as much from such sources as was conceivably possible. Politicians of the time ballyragged each other on a daily basis about alleged failures to place a sufficiently efficient tap on the resources of our "partners" in "Europe". This policy was successful to the point where nearly ten per cent of GDP over the past decade was obtained from such sources.

In truth, the greater part of Mr Haughey's job as Taoiseach involved the art of sticking out his hand, on behalf of this State and its citizens, in any direction wherein he imagined it might be crossed with any form of coin or currency. On this basis, might it not be argued — in the same manner as it is argued that Mr Haughey contributed to the "turnaround" in Irish economic fortunes since 1987 by virtue of his "management of the public finances" — that his unique talent for begging was the true engine of the Celtic Tiger?

Let us be frank about Charlie. There is hardly a truthful adult alive in this country today who will not admit to having wondered at some time or other how it was he got to be so rich. But only a few gave voice to their wonderment and nobody did anything. Most of us were happy to shrug it off with some vague notion of "shrewd investments" or woolly ideas about the astute riding of the rising tide. Charlie was the Fat Chieftain who, because he had so demonstrably catered to the needs of his own table, might enable some occasional scraps to stray in our direction. On this basis, we elected him in 1987 and again, albeit more grudgingly, in 1989.

At least on his and our stated terms — Charles Haughey did not let us down. In those few years in office, he created the foundations for a society forged in the image of his own housekeeping practice. Today, we have an economy set in the quicksand of multinational caprice, buttressed by tax-dodgers and pebble-dashed with EU structural and cohesion funding.

For many years now, our economic administrators have been operating a policy of enticement based on the use of low tax rates to tempt tax-avoiding multinationals in our direction. The most "attractive" attributes of Ireland's economy are its high tolerance of such exotic practices as tax-dumping, phantom calculus, creative accountancy and fiscal blind eyes. Even as we set up tribunals to investigate the tax affairs of those who have created this economy, we have been acquiring a worldwide reputation as the industrial equivalent of the Cayman Islands. We have, moreover, been more than happy to live with such contradictions. Our entire industrial policy is based on a series of scams that put Charles Haughey and all his works and pomps in the ha'penny place, and yet we feel entitled to parade our virtue as though Mr Haughey had dropped a used betting slip in the Garden of Eden.

It is a fascinating thought that we now have the same sense of mystery and bemusement about our own alleged economic good fortune as we once had about Mr Haughey's, but seem unwilling to follow the same logical route in order to arrive at the same kind of prosaic conclusion about the national picture as we have now arrived at about Charles J.

I recommend to all readers of this newspaper, and especially those who are consumed with the present investigations and therefore looking forward to the spectacle of Mr Haughey in the dock this week, that this might be a good time to buy and read the script of Arthur Miller's wonderful play *The Crucible*. Act One of the published script of the play, based on the witch trials of Salem in 1692, is punctuated by occasional notes by the author about the social and spiritual context in which these terrible events occurred. Miller wrote in one of these notes:

> When one rises above the individual villainy displayed, one can only pity them all, just as we will be pitied one day. . . .The witch-hunt was not . . . a mere repression. It was also, and as importantly, a long overdue opportunity for everyone so inclined to express publicly his guilt and sins, under the cover of accusations against the victims.

For the people of Salem in 1692, just as for the people of the Republic of Ireland in 1998, there was much beneath the surface sanctity, and much that emerged that was other than it seemed. Arthur Miller went on:

> Long-held hatreds of neighbours could now be openly expressed, and vengeance taken, despite the Bible's charitable injunctions. Land-lust which had been expressed before by constant bickering over boundaries and deeds, could now be elevated to the arena of morality; one could cry witch against one's neighbour and feel perfectly justified in the bargain. Old scores could be settled on a plane of heavenly combat between Lucifer and the Lord; suspicions and the envy of the miserable could and did burst out in the general revenge.

(August 1999)

34

TWELVE REASONS TO FORGIVE THE FAT CHIEFTAIN

I AM TAKEN ABACK BY BOTH THE cynicism concerning Charles Haughey's state of health and the obvious unwillingness to forgive him "just" because he might die soon. It's not that I truly believed we were "still" a Christian people or anything like that, rather that I am surprised at our willingness to hold out for so long before stopping in our tracks, turning around and neurotically charging in the opposite moral direction. In order to be of assistance to the national conscience, I would therefore like to offer the following twelve reasons why we should forgive Charlie Haughey.

1. We created him. I don't mean in the sense that we elected him, but that we imagined him into what he became. Everything he did was done in his role as Fat Chieftain, a role imposed on him by us. Being poor and hungry, we desperately needed to believe that this man, with his aura of riches and mystery, could make us plump and happy. More than anything else, he did not want to disappoint us.

2. The main reason we are mad at him is because we have discovered that there was no magic, that he accumulated his own riches not by wizardry but by supplicancy. The truth, of course, rendered us disappointed about him, but more fundamentally about the illusion he had helped us create concerning the possibility of material acquisition in general. This, however, was a necessary

lesson, and in a sense Charles Haughey has spared us having to learn it in a more difficult way.

3. There is considerable circumstantial evidence that Charles Haughey delivered on the contract he made with us. When Mr Haughey walked into Government Buildings thirteen years ago, this State was on the verge of bankruptcy. Today our economy is, as we keep being told, the envy of Europe. This turnaround in the national fortunes has much more in common with the manner of Charles Haughey's own enrichment than with the careful, muddling husbandry of his political rivals.

4. Most of the reasons we advance for seeking vengeance on Charles Haughey do not stand up. There is no evidence, for example, that any of his benefactors received anything tangible in return for money, or indeed that they sought favours from him. Like many of us, the merchant princes who supported him seem to have been simply infatuated with the aura of majesty and power around "Charles J. Haughey".

5. More than any other leader or public figure since de Valera, Charles Haughey defined his time, his country and his people. This is not necessarily a compliment to Mr Haughey or his people, but it is true nonetheless. The imagination of a nation cannot survive without epic characters, and Charles Haughey was, for more than thirty years, the central character in the national drama. He was our Hamlet, our King Lear, our J.R. and our Mike Baldwin.

6. He was a star, and we have decided in other spheres of endeavour that stars deserve to be paid vast sums of money just for being stars. Pop singers, TV presenters and actors "earn" much more than Charlie managed to stroke over the years, and we do not think this in the least bit odd. Haughey made them all look like extras, and yet we expected him to be star, chieftain, hero and villain, while surviving on a TD's salary. And he was running the country as well.

7. Although it is true that he did not serve his people as well as he might have — more in the sense of failing to do things that were necessary and possible than in that of stroking left, right and centre — Charles Haughey still did more good than most of his peers. It is remarkable that, in my own lifetime, only Mr Haughey's great friend, Donogh O'Malley, and his arch-enemy Noel Browne, were comparable when it came to implementing changes for the public good.

8. Charles Haughey had occasional flashes of deep principle, as in his response to the murderous sinking of the *Belgrano* in 1992.

9. He gave us lots of laughs. Any Taoiseach who presents a British prime minister with a teapot has got to be a national treasure.

10. Even at the worst construction, Charles Haughey was infinitely preferable to some of the loathsome creeps who have spent their working lives attacking him. For example, consider the fact that several of those who have done little except snipe at the Fat Chieftain have themselves made strenuous efforts to avail of his provision of tax-free status for creative artists, not for books, symphonies or paintings, but for the articles they wrote attacking Charles Haughey. Get this: these fellows, who could see no good in Mr Haughey otherwise, were prepared to acknowledge that this provision was actually admirable, provided, of course, that they were given the benefit of it in a manner for which it had never been intended. I know of one journalist who approached a leading poet requesting him to write a reference asserting that his venomous attacks on Mr Haughey were actually pure poetry. To his credit, the poet declined. And to the credit of the Revenue Commissioners, let it be noted that none of these applications was successful: these creeps still pay tax.

11. Anyone who can go out into the storm of hatred that Charles Haughey has evoked, and still walk like Napoleon, has something

we need to pause and look at. Mr Haughey, for all his faults, has grace and dignity, as he showed at Jack Lynch's funeral last year.

12. If he dies without forgiveness, our initial pangs of regret will rapidly turn to guilt and ferment into a profound self-loathing. The emotions we have about Charles Haughey, unlike those we feel towards other public figures — with the possible exception of Gay Byrne — are comparable to the emotions existing in a family situation. Hate is matched with love, scorn with compassion, and frustration with admiration. The bitterness that is felt now will soon pass, to be replaced by nostalgia, sadness and regret.

Forgiveness would therefore also be a selfish act, albeit a graceful one. If we don't forgive Charles Haughey, we will never forgive ourselves.

(October 2000)

III

John Waters is Unwell:
Sex, Spuds and Rock 'n' Roll

I

THE SECRET HISTORY OF THE PAST

I GREW UP IN A PLACE HALFWAY between nostalgia and prejudice. Others know it as Castlerea, County Roscommon, but that name comes, as does the name of any place, with other people's understandings, and these have nothing to do with the place I know. It is mine alone.

Thirteen years ago, when I began writing for *The Irish Times*, I embarked on what I now recognise as a fruitless exercise in explanation and justification of the place whence I came. I was reacting to the shocking level of ignorance around me, a risible set of perceptions that placed my home territory, and others, beyond a boundary separating sub-modernity from someplace called The Present. This landscape of prejudice was dotted with icons of a lately proscribed Ireland: smoke-filled thatched cottages, Marian statues, country 'n' western, cute hoors with facial tics, and the occasional skeleton of a Morris Minor. Describing what my "home" was actually like, in the face of such prejudice, was impossible, not least because the landscape did include all the things the prejudiced descriptions asserted. Yes, there were Marian statues, and Big Tom was indeed the King: but these phenomena had quite different meanings to those attributed by outsiders, which had removed from them all irony, mischief, wit and subversion.

I used to think I could explain home by describing, for example, how, when you walked out the back door you were in the country, and if you left by the front you entered the city. Painting pictures of a walk up Main Street, stopping at the Fair Green for a chat with a

Gortaganny sheep farmer about the price of lambs or drink, and then on to the Roma Café, where you might get into an argument about what Brian Eno meant when he said that lyrics can obscure the meaning of a song, I would explain how this represented a walk through three centuries, none of which prevailed. But it was a waste of time, because you can never explain things to people who aren't listening.

When I contemplate Castlerea today, it strikes me that what might be called the objective essentials haven't changed much. For all the talk about progress, apart from laptop computers and mobile phones, the changes to Irish life in my lifetime have been mainly superficial. Twenty-odd years ago, when I first wrote for *Hot Press*, I had to forage around town collecting fivepenny pieces to ring Dublin from a callbox, in the usually doomed hope of getting Niall Stokes on the line. Now I can plug in my computer and blah blah. Otherwise, there is nothing significantly different about the town, except the prison, which is what outsiders think of when they hear the name Castlerea.

And yet the place I grew up in has gone, mainly because it existed in my head, an improvisation on reality that transformed a small western town into the centre of the galaxy.

It is possible to talk about Roscommon by drawing on its rich history, important landmarks and scenic spots. You could write about Douglas Hyde and Sir William Wilde, give a mention to Rockingham and Rathcroghan, enthuse about the beauty of Lough Key and the unfathomableness of Lough Allen. But this would mean little to most who grew up there in the past forty years. From the moment that Elvis wriggled his pelvis and Brendan Bowyer came to the Casino Ballroom purveying a passable imitation, the significance of the location changed forever in the minds of its young. Then it became a backdrop to lives lived at the centre of the universe, in which everything was invigorated by the connections with the universal that invaded every young mind and heart. Alongside the Casino, the venerable River Francis still followed its ancient course to the Suck, and the statue in the Marian shrine on the bridge still smiled benevolently on the one-night-standers who walked hand-in-hand to the lovers' lane that was the Riverside Walk,

set discreetly behind her back. But nothing of this could be taken literally any more. You "squared" a woman, or, I suppose, a man; you
bought, or had bought for you, a mineral; you danced a little, if you
could, and parodied if you could not; you took the hand of your one-
night beloved and strolled 'neath the moon's gentle beam, down the
drive by the murmuring river, across the old rustic bridge and warily
past the statue to where unmentionable things were said to happen,
though mostly to other people. The music was ever-present, draped in
an irony that seemed to bypass the intentions of those who made or
craved it. And as you nibbled the forbidden fruit, the voice of the King
could be heard, calling down the river, with a phlegmatic simplicity
that seemed, after all, to be aware of both the joke and the prejudice,
embracing an ambiguity hovering halfway between mawkishness and
blasphemy. Maybe it was just me, but I don't think so:

> Someday when we meet up yonder,
> We'll stroll hand-in-hand again,
> In a land that knows no parting.
> Blue eyes cryin' in the rain.

And somehow this kind of kink of happenstance, or the mood of
mockery or incongruity it generated, was enough to render meaningful
the meaningless, to dignify the undignified, to imbue absurdity with a
certain playful tenderness, to make memorable the banal, and send us
home laughing. That was why, when I got the chance, I conspired with
fate to get Big Tom on the cover of *Hot Press*. There are those, God
help them (and some of them write for national newspapers, God help
us) who consequently filed me under "Country". Although the songs
that colonised our heads were "Lovely Leitrim" and "Old Log Cabin
for Sale", in our hearts echoed "Crosstown Traffic" and "The Bewlay
Brothers". We were no more Country than Gavin Friday.

From this distance, the topography of my youth is distinguished
not by hills or rivers, but by three interconnecting phenomena: soccer,
cars and rock 'n' roll. The connection was that all three represented
windows facing onto the possibility of escape. All three came replete

with heroes — George Best, James Hunt, Rory Gallagher — and enabled the environs of Roscommon to be reconstructed into a fantasy
location which might have been anywhere. But their centrality in our
lives bespoke, ultimately, a desire to leave Roscommon behind. In a
sense, we didn't live in Roscommon at all, but in the shadow of Old
Trafford, within earshot of Silverstone, down the road from Wood-
stock, by the side of a clear crystal fountain, in the field where the
wild flowers grow.

A small patch of commonage at the back of our street became
Wembley or the Azteca Stadium. Hackers Lane FC, the creation of
myself and two friends, was a living organisation, every day for four
or so years between the World Cups of 1966 and 1970. At Hackers
Lane, we learned that magic actually worked, that if you ran out after
watching Brazil, there would be an hour or so of grace when you
seemed to float a foot above the ground, when nothing you tried
could fail, or be frightening, when the ball became attached to your
foot and did precisely what you decided.

Tostao. Rivelino. Jairzinho. Waters. Pelé. I suppose the reason I
lost interest in sport afterwards was that this access to magic seemed
to be the whole point of it, that there was no point in admiring other
people's magic unless you could learn it and do it for yourself.

When I was twenty I had a garageful of sports cars (though no ga-
rage) including an MG Midget, an MGBGT and a Triumph Spitfire. I
inherited a certain mechanical bent from my father, of so we pretended
for a time, and we would have long conversations about fuel mixtures,
compression and brake pedal adjustment, usually when I had made the
mistake of soliciting his mechanical advice with a view to making the
Saturday night dance in Glenamaddy. At twenty past nine, he would be
leaning into the engine, his glasses perched on his forehead, enthusias-
tically proposing stripping down the twin carburettors, a job somewhat
analogous to the work of a planning tribunal, while I looked at my
watch. "Excessive idling," he might pronounce at last, setting me to
pondering if this was a verdict on my character or a hint of insider
knowledge concerning late-night lay-by activity with the engine

running. "Too much idling," he would elaborate pointedly, "brings the plug temperature down, so that the combustion deposits are not burned off." He would pause for a moment to allow me explore the labyrinth of moral speculation triggered by this ambiguity. "Your plugs are dirty," he would translate, and go back in to his newspaper.

The Midget was my favourite. I was in love with her (we could call cars "her" then, without fear of a visit from the Thought Police). She cost me £150, six weeks' wages. I called her Brigid, a name partly inspired by a hit song of the time, and partly by the buxom shape of her wing sections, but, for the avoidance of doubt, in no way connected to the matriarchal goddess from Kildare. Red, with a soft top and a 948cc Morris Minor engine, she had the best vehicle registration number in the history of motor cars: 700 VRA, which read in the subconscious as 700 VRAOOOOM!, and turned into a babe magnet a car that, in truth, had difficulty getting over sixty on a straight road.

She is gone now, having shuffled off her oh-so-mortal high-tension coil. All I have left is the numberplate, which sits in the window of a shed in our back yard at home, begging me to shine it up into an artefact to decorate some twenty-first century mausoleum living room wall. So far, I have resisted, perhaps because the intensity of its innocence would eventually break my heart.

The past is a complicated phenomenon and the human memory is a slippery commodity: we edit and filter as best suits our purposes. Nostalgia and prejudice are equally unhelpful. All we can do, I've finally decided, is say how it was, and if they, whoever they are, decide that we were all in thrall to priests and Big Tom, then let them at it. But that should not prevent us speaking to one another in a language that transcends both prejudice and nostalgia, to create, re-create, the secret history of a time that was not unlike the present, except that it was, because we were younger and travelling the road for the first time, sweeter and more, in a quite literal sense, sensational.

(August 2003)

2

THE LONESOME TOUCH OF MARTIN HAYES

T HE IDEA OF ORIGINALITY IN A PLAYER of traditional music might seem somewhat oxymoronic. There are those who hold — vehemently, in some cases — that the music is there already, that the scope for improvisation and innovation is limited to what is laid down. But this denies the truth that all music develops organically through interaction with external influences. All art is the result of the breath from within coming into contact with the cold pane of external influence to produce the condensation of the work. Thus, notions of "purism" and "authenticity" are misleading and maybe even potentially dangerous.

What we call purism in traditional music circles is emblematic of a condition which has existed also in the wider society, but is now somewhat on the wane: a belief that some "true" and fixed representation of Irishness exists in theoretical form, an outlook that exhibits also a concomitant fear of contamination by alien influences. This might be said to have been the ethic of the founding of the State, and it might indeed be added that it has unleashed a backlash which insists on the opposite: that, in a "modern" world, only external influences have any value. I would argue that the great difficulty we have in attempting to advance by our own lights in this world is in finding a path through these two extremes.

Irish music, in both its traditional and modern incarnations, has a huge capacity for reflection and even prophecy. If you listen to a cross-section of Irish music, for example, on Raidió na Gaeltachta or Raidió Na Life, it is possible to be aware, at some subliminal level, of the reality of Ireland and its recent history, and of the double-binds which emanated from this confusion. For in the music, and how it is treated and played by different people, there exists a series of snapshots of various perspectives on what Ireland is, what it should be, what it might have been and what it could become. In the more purist players, there is an obsessiveness about authenticity, a desire to recreate something deemed to be pre-existing. This, for all its alleged fanaticism, has a profound dignity, arising as much out of love as from "good intentions". Similarly, in some of the more "modern" treatments, it is possible to detect a different kind of obsession, an obsession with reconstruction for its own sake. Both forms are necessary and both have their attractions and appeal. And yet, neither can truly be said to be organic representations of the growth of a tradition through changing times.

In the sleevenote for his latest album, *The Lonesome Touch*, Martin Hayes has written that he believe it a mistake to limit Irish music according to a Hobson's choice of tradition and continuity or change and innovation. The music, he maintains, is capable of containing all these at once: "The real battle is between artistic integrity and the forces that impede creative expression. Traditional Irish music has always experienced change and been enriched by innovation, while at the same time maintaining continuity. The issue that is of utmost importance is that innovation, change, tradition and continuity all be tempered by integrity, humility and understanding. These issues are the issues of all artistic pursuit and are therefore universal, as is the very core of the music itself."

In his sleevenote, too, Martin Hayes lists all those artists who have contributed to the confluence from which his playing emerges: his father P.J. Hayes, John Naughton, Paddy Fahy, Tommy Potts, Tony MacMahon, Paddy O'Brien, Paddy Canny, Junior Crehan, Micho Russell, Martin Rochford, Mary McNamara, Joe Cooley, the Tulla Céilí Band, "and many more". And he also writes that, when he talks about music with his musical partner, Dennis Cahill (who plays guitar accompaniment on Hayes's album and live performances), they are "as likely to be talking about the music of Keith Jarrett, John Coltrane, Miles Davis, U2, Bach, or Beethoven, as we are to discuss the music of Tommy Potts, the rhythm of the great set dancer Willie Keane, or the innovation of the Bothy Band".

Martin Hayes's music is not easy listening. I've had one of his albums, *Under the Moon*, in my possession for two years and have only recently been able to listen to it for extended periods. Such is the depth of the feeling with which he engages that it has often seemed to me that it is only possible to listen to him in an attitude of detachment. To engage with him fully would be to risk a broken heart. I think of Martin Hayes wrestling with his fiddle as I think of a lion-tamer tempting the savage temperament of his charge.

It is difficult to say what it is that Martin Hayes does to Irish music, or what he brings to playing the fiddle. It is tempting to attempt to summarise him by comparison, or to cite certain influences that flicker on the surface of his playing. But what makes Hayes exceptional is that, once you hear him play one tune, you comprehend his musical personality without necessarily being able to describe its elements. This, I think, is because he is uniquely unafraid of the music he plays. Many players, unconsciously or through unquestioning reinterpretation of an evolving approach to playing, avoid the pain at the heart of much Irish music by padding it out with layers of ornamentation. Hayes strips the tunes down to their essential melodies, playing the same notes you would play if you picked up the instrument for the first time and tried to scratch out a tune. But in his mastery of tone and rhythm, Hayes gives the music new meaning, which is perhaps to say that he suggests the scale of its original meaning. His tonality is in itself hugely evocative, like he is playing out of a fog, as though the music is floating in from some slightly distant place. It draws you into the fog, which is where the real source of the pain resides.

The "lonesome touch" is a phrase he remembers from his childhood. "It represents a quality that is difficult to express verbally," he writes:

It is the intangible aspect of music that is both elusive and essential.
The word lonesome expresses a sadness, a blue note, a sour note.
Even though the music bears the trace of struggle and pain, it is also
the means of uplift, transcendence of joy and celebration.

This, of course, is part of our fascination with Irish music: that it con-
tains the echo of all that we have otherwise sought to expunge. Moreover, it now represents perhaps our only means of accessing and embracing the past from which we thought we could escape but could
not. While our only means of entering the fog, it carries also the possibility of redemption. "Meeting and experiencing sadness or tragedy
in art, literature or music," writes Martin Hayes, "is very often the
transformation of that experience to its corresponding opposite, the
release of joy and freedom."

It is very much like keening. The musician, by channelling the
dormant feelings in ways we find bearable, enables us to explore the
host of repressed feelings and denied experience. In *Our Musical
Heritage*, Sean Ó Riada wrote that the most direct means of expression in music is the human singing voice, but that, in Irish music, certain instruments approach the qualities of personal expression of the
human voice, of which the fiddle was the most ideal. This is because
"the player is in direct contact with his instrument; the notes do not
exist until he makes them, and his tone is a completely individual
thing, differing from another fiddle player's tone as much as one
voice differs from another".

As Martin Hayes puts it himself:

> Music is just a language, a means of communicating. It's what it
> conveys that really matters. The music conveys the spirit and soul of
> the people and feelings that sometimes couldn't be expressed in any
> other manner. It's more accurate than any written history because it's
> alive at this very moment.

(September 1997)

3

THE POP PRIESTHOOD

PARTICIPATING IN A RECENT RADIO discussion relating to a book on Irish pop by the promoter Louis Walsh brought home to me that we have yet to even begin the process of comprehending our pop history. Once again, the lines were divided cleanly between those like Louis who venerate showband culture and seek to draw a line of descent between it and the latter-day boyband culture, and those who dismiss this territory out of hand. This, I believe, is a recipe for bad history.

Knocking showbands is an integral part of the ideological mechanism of the entity we now call Modern Ireland. As with Fianna Fáil, the Catholic Church, or the GAA, any attempt to see good in showbands is inevitably interpreted as indicative of sub-modern tendencies. This arises partly from the prejudice of those seeking to denigrate the past cultural life of Ireland so as all the more to valorise their own alleged role in putting it behind. The point of seeking to give the showband era its proper place in history is not to elevate the past by comparison with the present, but to give a more accurate sense of what it was like then, what happened and why it is like it is now.

Showbands were a central element in what we now speak of as the modernisation of Irish life, and the only thing concealing this from us is mindless snobbery. They were far more subversive of this Ireland than any of the institutions — RTÉ, *The Irish Times*, the Well Woman Centre, or the Progressive Democrats — we now think of as the key catalysts of social change.

242

The Ireland into which the showbands exploded was a subdued place, dominated by the Catholic clergy. Sex was forbidden except under licence, otherwise known as marriage, and clergy had the exclusive franchise on this permission. After nearly a century of relentless moral policing, employing judicious use of both the confessional and the ash plant, the church had succeeded in all but curtailing sexual activity outside marriage and done much to ensure that this state entailed the minimum fun. By the 1960s, however, it appears to have occurred to the more inventive members of the clergy that there was more tangible benefit to be derived from other uses of their restraining power on the libido of the nation. It became clear to many of them that their control of sensuality could be utilised to build essential infrastructure, like community halls, churches and so forth.

It was all a matter of supply and demand. Showing an acute grasp of the fundamental laws of economics, the clergy decided to exploit the scarcity they had created by making sexual activity available on a controlled basis to those willing to fork out a nominal sum. By holding out the promise of even minor sexual activity, the priests had, by their own creation, the perfect money-spinner.

The ballroom became, in effect, a place where sex was available under the guise of entertainment, the antithesis of the church, albeit often under the same control. On Sunday morning, the faithful trooped into Mass to be told why they should abstain from company-keeping, self-abuse and mutual gratification, and on Sunday night they handed over their pound notes to the same priest to be allowed into the local Dionysian citadel in the hope of finding a sexual partner for the night. During certain hours, i.e. during and immediately after a properly authorised dance, it became permissible to break the moral code. In the same town, in the same street, in which even a discreet kiss in the open air would at other times be frowned upon, it was possible, under cover of dusk, darkness or dawn, to engage in unabashed fornication, in the open air, in the back seats of Capris, in shoeshop doorways and round the back of the dancehall. Everything was permissible so long as "Show Me the Way to Amarillo" was wafting down the river from the dancehall.

Music was a necessary evil. The clergy looked with deep suspicion on the bands they were forced to engage, treated them as subspecies and paid them as little as possible, awarding themselves special dispensations when it came to stealing money from mere musicians. But they also, unwittingly and unwillingly, gave these musicians an enormous power. For it was to the musician on the stage that the priest devolved the right to sanction and facilitate promiscuity. On Sunday morning, the priest had the power to say "don't", "thou shalt not", or "woe to ye who fornicate". On Sunday night, courtesy of the same priest, the singer or guitarist, or even occasionally the drummer, had the power to suspend this rule and say, "Go for it, boys and girls". Far more than Gay Byrne or Mary Robinson, people like Joe Dolan, Derek Dean, Billy Brown and Brendan Bowyer revolutionised Irish attitudes to sexuality. And it is arguable that Big Tom was more central to the modernisation of Irish society than the First Programme for Economic Expansion.

It is a strange fact of Irish society that the ballrooms have a place in popular cultural memory not unlike that of the Civil War in the memory bank of our political life. Though patently central to our cultural development, they have become unmentionable by virtue of being incompatible with our modern aspirations. This, of course, is not merely unpardonable snobbery, it also self-deceiving and antipathetic to accurate cultural understanding. To seek to trace the genealogy of today's generation of Irish pop superstars, and not factor in the showband phenomenon, is to prohibit comprehension. The standard notion, that the U2-Cranberries generation has roots going back only to Thin Lizzy and Skid Row is fatuous and facile, like leaving Jack Charlton out of the story of Irish soccer.

We forget, you see, what it was really like back then. Recently, I came across an Irish TV guide for the week of Live Aid, in July 1985, boldly promising "15 hours of non-stop pop!" Today, that exclamation mark would strike most youngsters as extremely odd. It is easy to sneer at the notion of showband copyism from the high ground of cultural saturation in the good, bad and ugly of pop, forgetting that, before the advent of RTE Radio 2, there was an average of three or four hours of pop and rock 'n' roll on national radio per week. The only way most people got to hear pop music, let alone live pop music, was in dancehalls. To compare showbands unfavourably, therefore, with anything in the present is — apart from the obvious undertones of present-centred hubris — utterly to miss the point. Until twenty years ago, Irish pop culture was showband culture, and the existence of the ballroom circuit, for all its dubious aspects, resulted in a generation of Irish youth being exposed to an experience that, for all its mediocrity and imitativeness, would not otherwise have been available for another twenty years. Billy Brown, for example, was the first showband musician in the country to wear jeans on stage. Forget your bishop and his nightie — *that* was something.

To attack showbands for lack of creativity is like attacking a baby for being unable to walk. The standard complaint by rock snobs was that showbands lacked originality, being content to purvey cover versions rather than writing their own material. Apart from all the other reasons for this, it is often forgotten that the nature of Irish musical creativity had always been more collective than individual. Irish traditional musicians had always done "covers", interpreting the existing canon and adding to it incrementally in performance. Narrative singing was a collective tradition of creativity, which blurred the functions of author and performer. The notion of one or two people sitting down to "write" a song was alien to an oral tradition holding most of its songs and tunes as an aural commonage.

Showbands, in the beginning of the rock 'n' roll revolution, saw nothing strange about appropriating a range of pre-existing material and interpreting it in their own way. And when you factor in the undoubtedly deeply derivative nature of much of what passed for originality in Irish rock 'n' roll, it occurs that, in their own way, showbands were as creative as anyone. Certainly they were creative of excitement and abandon on a previously undreamed-of scale, and some showband records, like The Royal's version of "The Hucklebuck", and The Freshmen's version of "Papa Oom Mow Mow", can stand with anything in the past fifty years of Irish pop music.

I always think of showbands as the Irish cultural equivalent of potatoes. When confronted by an uncultivated piece of ground, untilled and weed-infested, the best thing to do, as any gardener will tell you, is plant spuds. What potatoes lack in imagination, they make up for by transforming the ground in which they are planted — cleaning it of weeds, opening up its breathing capacity and making it ready for more sensitive crops. Perhaps what some of our self-styled modern anthropologists need is a crash course in crop rotation.

(April 2002)

4

THE QUARTERFINALS MENTALITY

C ULTURE, ACCORDING TO BRIAN ENO, is whatever people do when they don't have to do anything, the instinctual expression of an impulse unrestricted by compulsion. If that is true, then, for the past generation or so, soccer has been more a part of Irish culture than almost anything else, even — and here we have to be sensitive and caring — Gaelic games. It's not just a matter of the World Cup fiesta, which is just the culmination of several decades of cultural gestation. For the best part of fifty years, wherever boys have gathered — at school lunchtime or weekends, in summer holidays, on pieces of waste ground — it was soccer they played. GAA was confined to the structured, supervised, official context of school and the regulatory activities ordained in the community. Given a choice, boys chose to play soccer.

It is possible that the reason is simple: two jumpers thrown on the ground gave you the makings of a soccer pitch, anywhere, anytime, whereas for Gaelic you need a crossbar, which is more difficult to spontaneously recreate. Perhaps, but then again . . . .

A few years ago, in a bid to get a rise out of the nation, Eamon Dunphy said something to the effect that nobody from outside Dublin knew anything about soccer, having never heard of it before Jack Charlton. What was certainly true was that, apart from a handful of clubs, the non-Dublin part of the country made little impact on the League of Ireland. Maybe once in a decade, Sligo Rovers or Athlone Town or Cork Celtic would awake from their slumbers and threaten the Dublin-based dinosaurs in the League or the FAI Cup, and then nod off again.

But soccer in Ireland has never had anything much to do with the League of Ireland, a parallel universe untouched by the Hand of God. Soccer in Ireland, in the sense that we have come to know it, has had two layers: one a fanatical connection with English club football, the other what might be called the spontaneous expression of something essential in the hearts of young males, which manifested itself in the game as played at local level.

Although a few pre-date the introduction of television, most local soccer clubs date from the early-sixties, when *Match of the Day* began to beam into small-town Ireland on Saturdays nights. Many of these clubs started out as acts of subversion, in defiance of the Gaelic pieties of the time and in particular of the GAA ban on foreign games. Many were started by returned emigrants, back from Manchester or Leicester or London, tickling the imaginations of their younger and less-travelled countrymen with the magic of the Beautiful Game. In Castlerea, as in other similar towns, the local soccer club had the status of an illegal organisation. Castlerea Celtic had been founded by a handful of young men, who seemed to meet continuously in James Kennedy's barber shop, in an upstairs room on Main Street. From here they plotted ways of stealing the youth of the town from the clutches of the GAA, or more crucially, debated how to get enough sawdust to line the pitch for Sunday.

Celtic was of course a completely amateur club, playing at local, county and occasionally provincial level. It functioned as the fulcrum of an emerging culture of subversion, providing a goal for the boys of the town to aim towards. It laid The Dream before us. Everybody played soccer all the time, every spare minute of daylight, on every and any available flat surface. As schoolboys, we played initially on Saturday nights in the Fair Green, after an afternoon listening to the English First Division results on the radio, and later at Hackers Lane, the childhood equivalent of turning pro.

And there was Peiler. I don't know if that's how you spell it. It might be Peller, or Pellar, or just Peler. Anyway, that's what, as young boys in Castlerea, we called John Egan, the kind of exceptional football talent nearly everyone will have encountered in their own place at some time — kids they know for certain would, with a different throw of the dice, have been recognised as world class. Although I can't remember precisely why or when or by whom he was given the name, I know it was in recognition of his skills on the soccer pitch, where he stood out like a young Pelé on a Brazilian beach, or a boy Georgie Best on a backstreet of Belfast. I spell it Peiler because I believe it was intended to mark him as an Irish Pelé, and that is what he was.

There were four or five such lads at home who most of us were certain were as good as anyone we ever saw, before or since, and Peiler was one of them. Among the others were Padraig Shallow, who never missed a free kick within thirty yards of the goal; Matt Gannon, who was the best header of a ball I ever saw; and Dermo Carroll, whose ball control was in the same league as Georgie's. And I have frequently, watching Ireland play badly against weak opposition, thought they might do worse than put Dene Lane in the box where he seemed to score more goals, against any opposition, than anyone for anyone.

Peiler had that quality which players like John Giles and Bobby Charlton had also — the ability to control a game, to infuse it with intelligence, to provide reassurance almost to the point of rendering his team invincible. The only problem was his health. He wheezed something terrible and had a mild form of epilepsy, both of which conditions meant that he remained a defender rather than getting to use his formidable skills up front. Peiler played for Castlerea Celtic when he was little more than fifteen, and nobody had ever done that before.

Celtic, one of the first soccer clubs in the West of Ireland, was a club for men. But Peiler was also a member, and co-founder with myself and Gerry Farrelly, of Hackers Lane FC, a club for the lads of the West End of Main Street.

Peiler was the main inspiration behind the growth of Hackers Lane. He was the leader to whom we all looked up. The rest of us were happy to do the work, while he roared at us from the sidelines or the goalmouth.

It is difficult now to convince people around Castlerea that Hackers Lane ever actually existed other than as legend, or that it was what we say it was. It was a real organisation, a genuine going concern, with real members and assets and a life that carried on every day for perhaps four or five years. Its locus was a patch of waste ground at the back of our house, along the River Suck between the Mill Race and Roddy's Field. The ground had a slight slope but was otherwise level, and on it we made a five-a-side football pitch. Others might have been content to use jumpers for goalposts and argue about scores, but Hackers Lane had real goals, real flags, real markings, and even a clubhouse.

There were no goalies, and a special rule about not being able to enter the semi-circle around the goalmouth unless the ball was in there first. The goals were about three feet high and four feet wide. They were precise miniatures of the goals on any professional soccer pitch, carefully constructed from lengths of timber "borrowed" from my father's shed, with proper joints and bolts to hold them together. The nets were made from onion bags from Egans' shop, sewed together with twine, and these were held in place over bed-ends from Roddy's dump. The posts and crossbars were painted white. The pitch was always marked with sawdust from Connolly Brothers or Beirnes' joinery. The "clubhouse" was an improvised affair made from branches and sheets of corrugated iron, to shelter in when it rained. We erected a sign — white lettering on a brown background — which declared: "Hackers Lane FC", with no apostrophe, like *Finnegans Wake*. It was Bird Featherstone who gave it the name, because every time he played there, he went home with black shins.

The games were timed and broken into halves, just like real matches — except we played fifteen minutes a side. This was a departure from the previous tradition in the town, where games were played on Saturday nights in the Fair Green, between teams of maybe twenty boys a side, until it got dark or everyone had gone home.

These games were played in the big cattle pen, when only the dry cowdung saved you from destruction on the concrete floor.

At Hackers Lane, we played leagues and knock-out competitions between teams as carefully seeded as the pitch. We played "internationals" against Ballindrimley, Knockroe and other tribes from the town. Generally we could beat anyone on our own turf, but we got stuffed when we ventured away from Hackers Lane. This was because we were used to the carefully kept pitch, which we reseeded every few weeks. I remember one time holding Knockroe to a nil-all draw at Hackers Lane and then getting hammered on the pitch beside Gannon's house in Knockroe, which had not a blade of grass from one end to the other. Football boots were banned at Hackers Lane, and anyone wearing them, as Seannie Connell and his team were that day, could run rings round us. That's my excuse anyway and, after thirty years, I'm sticking to it.

The life of Hackers Lane coincided roughly with the interregnum between the World Cups of 1966 and 1970, and then it died away as we became more interested in other things. This is where we spent the best years of our childhoods: Gerry "Gamoudie" Farrelly, Andy "Bing" McGarry, Sean "Bozo" Moran, his brother Tommy, Peiler's brother, Eddie and Seamus ("Babalouie"), Michael "Miko" Raftery, Michael "Bird" Featherstone, Gerry Crawley, Peiler and myself. Peiler would stand in the goalmouth, in total contravention of his own rule, and roar us on. His injunctions, which were most colourful for one who was a paragon of devoutness in other respects, could be heard all over the town.

The appearance of the activity of soccer in such a local context must have been, to the objective outsider, a most unpretty, mud-soaked sight. But this was not how it seemed from inside, where it was animated by the dream represented by Bobby Moore and Georgie Best. Like boys all around Ireland, who played in car parks and imagined themselves not at Milltown but at Wembley, we played at Hackers Lane and imagined ourselves in Rio or Mexico City.

We did not look to Merrion Square. The attitude at the amateur level towards home-grown professional soccer and its administrative organisations was ambivalent, a little suspicious perhaps on account of the hierarchical structure of Irish pro and semi-pro soccer being in some way analogous to the GAA hierarchy, but also a strange kind of contempt arising from a sense that the game as played at local level plugged directly into the international level — that it was to Manchester United rather than Athlone Town you looked for inspiration. What is remarkable in retrospect is the intravenous imaginative connection that existed between this and English club football, connecting us directly to the source of the inspiration, despite or because of the fact that this was external. Every boy who ever kicked a ball dreamed of playing at the highest level, so ending up in Sligo Rovers would be, by definition, a defeat. The players who in recent years have been representing Ireland have, perhaps without exception, gone directly from the amateur local level to the English Premiership. The FAI did not intrude upon the consciousness of a single player who made the leap from fantasy to execution. In a sense, then, the FAI has always seemed to be a kind of interloper in the dream that soccer offered. Like virtually every other level of institutional Ireland, it failed to interpret or nurture the dreams of the people in a way that might be termed remotely useful.

Our attraction to soccer was more than an infatuation; it was subversive. There was a sense for us then that it provided a form of liberation from the weight of authority represented by GAA leaders, clergy and teachers — often the same people. It wasn't that we were actively rebelling against the re-Gaelicisation of our cultural horizons, but rather that this process, for all that we may have supported or engaged with it, could not touch some other part of us that still needed to be nurtured. Of what could that part consist? Perhaps it was the colonised part, the part that remained incapable of reinvention, having already been reinvented in opposition to its own nature.

Whatever about nowadays, the appeal of soccer in those days was certainly no fad. For here was something growing within which was not, at that point anyway, the product of global marketing or the excitement of consumerist appetites. It was hard slog wading through six inches of mud on a February afternoon. But we gravitated voluntarily towards soccer because, perhaps, in descending order: it was an international game, which enabled us to feel connected with the outside world; it was subversive of that which, however much we felt drawn to it in one sense, undoubtedly oppressed us in another; and it belonged to that forbidden place, England, which we were aware, despite all the rhetoric to the contrary, had been imbued upon our imaginations if only as the object of resentment, and which we inhabited on a daily basis through reading *The Hotspur, The Hornet* and Enid Blyton.

In everyday, practical terms, it wasn't an either/or. The GAA ban on its members playing soccer created several categories of player: those who played only soccer, those who played only Gaelic, those who played both on the sly, and those who were so good at both that the GAA turned a blind eye. In all but the occasional instance of unfettered fanaticism, arising equally on both sides, there was a perfectly easy coexistence between the two disciplines, with most youngsters carrying their fervour back and forth without loss. But soccer somehow had the capacity to inspire, even in the midst of a mud-soaked bottom of the table Roscommon League clash in November, a sense of magic which, in the GAA context, attached itself only to unambiguously special occasions.

THE GREAT FAILURES OF POST-INDEPENDENCE IRELAND have been of inspiration and administration. Perhaps this was because the best of our potential leaders were killed off, and we found ourselves being led from the beginning by second-raters, who failed to recognise either the scale or the complexity of the necessary project of national reconstruction, and failed also to identify with the exuberances of the people and so convert them from their crude form into something hard and useful. The main failure in this regard was the inability to grasp the essentially dialectical nature of the relationship between culture and everyday life in a society traumatised by radical interference. This failure expressed itself in the determination to revert to some imagined pre-existing state, of both Irishness and self-sufficiency, refusing to see that the nature of Irishness had been altered by its experience of Englishness and that the ethic of self-sufficiency had been damaged by dependency and fear.

It was probably inevitable that soccer would become a vehicle for the unashamed expression of our post-colonial imagination, a sort of surrendering to that which, in other contexts, the national project of de-Anglicisation sought to eliminate. In a sense, soccer provided a kind of revisionist embrace while Roy Foster was still in short trousers, to the extent that when the revisionists, decades later, began to insist that we must embrace the Other within ourselves, many who had spent a generation sporting a Georgie Best hairstyle wondered what they could possibly be going on about.

Once you've been colonised, invaded, violated, you ever after need two distinct forms of self-expression. One is indigenous, a way of telling yourself who you still are. It needs to be of yourself, for yourself, by yourself, yourself alone. The other needs to be other, of the outside, a means of saying to the rest of the world: I, we, are still human, still living, still here; I, we, can do what you can do (almost just as well, at least not as bad as you would expect). We are not as shite as we have been led to believe! Usually this means of expressing ourselves to the external will have been received from the violator, and will provide a way for the violated to seek the approval of he who has tried to persuade him he is nothing. The two forms, obviously, operate at cross-purposes. The very act of participating in something indigenous, however necessary this may be in one sense, validates the violator's poor opinion in another. And by succeeding at the other, I/we affirm a part of our own dread that we may no longer be fully ourselves. We cannot win, but please don't say it out loud.

This paradox defines the relationship between Gaelic games and soccer in Irish life and society. Gaelic games are the means of affirming ourselves to ourselves, a way of expressing our relief at the departure of the invader and celebrating his banishment. Soccer is the

expression of that part of us that remains colonised, however long the
visitors have departed. The people of Ireland cling to soccer as our
writers cling to Shakespeare, and for the same reason. It is the means
we have unconsciously chosen to say, "Look, there is no need to be
disappointed in our progress! Look, we can be like you after all!
Look, we have not fallen back into barbarism! We are something, in
spite of ourselves!"

But this form of expression is both an integral part of the new culture of the people and the expression of the people's cultural estrangement from themselves. Gaelic games, however satisfying they
might be of themselves, never had the capacity to make us feel truly
whole. Even the existence of perhaps the most effective sporting organisation in the world could not gain for us any more than a passing
nod of approval from a curious outsider. We need also to express our
otherness. The difficulty is that the very urge to demonstrate our ca-
pability in this regard is matched by a defeatism implanted also by the
visitor, which tells us that, no, we cannot ever win. What we craved
more than anything was possible only through soccer, and that, because it belonged to our former abuser, was infected for us with a pathology of losing. The very means we had found to express our desire
to be as good as anyone has an inbuilt mechanism preventing us from
becoming that which we craved to be.

This defeatism, by no means confined to soccer, expressed itself
most fatally of all in an almost absolute inability to organise ourselves
in such a manner as to translate our dreams into actions. In the history
of twentieth-century Ireland, only two projects of national reconstruction stand out as successful: Irish music and Gaelic games. The rest is
failure: the language, the economy, the spiritual condition. All domestic institutions assuming responsibility in these endeavours were, for
most of that century, unmitigated disasters of stewardship. Only a
handful of entities and individuals have managed to transcend the pathology of losing, the wouldn't-it-be-great-to-make-the-quarterfinals
mentality: Ryanair, Tony O'Reilly, U2, *Riverdance* . . . then you're
struggling.

By the end of the 1980s the facts of the matter were plain for even the most devoted advocate of national realisation: we were just plain incapable of doing things properly for ourselves. But the incredible success of the national team under Jack Charlton in the late-1980s and early 1990s reveals itself in retrospect as a portent of the Celtic Tiger economic miracle of the decade that followed. And the two phenomena had much in common. Both were managed, supervised and controlled by foreigners, yes, but more pertinently both were based on a product that might be termed non-indigenous.

There is, then, a remarkable similarity between our responses in the dual communal fields of industry and sport, and soccer tells the story more clearly than other sports. In both soccer and industrial policy, we like to leave it to outsiders. It is not that we lack self-belief — indeed, when someone comes in and takes charge, we find self-belief in open-top busloads. But we are poor self-starters, and we are especially poor in seeing ourselves in a sphere of expression or activity we perceive as coming from somewhere else. Such entities fascinate us, seduce us, yes, but we can go only so far in claiming ownership of them.

The Celtic Tiger took the political and economic establishments by surprise, and it was a year or two before they shined up their brass necks enough to go out and start taking credit for it. In reality, though, it was the culmination not of the planning and visualising of the political class, but of a happy collision between the energies of the people and the needs of multinational industry. Just as, in soccer, the dream jumped across the middle-men of the FAI, the Celtic Tiger leapt across the paltry institutional structures which had sought to in-sinuate themselves as proprietors of national endeavour.

The Celtic Tiger was never, in fact, coterminous with the Irish economy. Rather it was the manifestation of a hugely successful, hugely mobile transnational economy operating on Irish soil, using Irish skills and Irish tax-breaks to do in Ireland what it was doing in different ways elsewhere. In the late 1980s, the Industrial Develop-ment Authority embarked upon a new policy, which, for all that it re-flected credit on its creators, involved a certain amount of defeatism. It acknowledged implicitly that we could not after all do certain things for ourselves, that a more sensible and appropriate strategy was needed. Growth in the 1990s was the consequence of this strategy to attract more than our fair share of investments by transnational corporations, using an educated, English-speaking, relatively cheap workforce and extremely low corporate tax rates as bait. The Celtic Tiger told two distinct and different stories about Irish industrial life, the soaring cuckoo-in-the-nest economy comprising mainly US-owned transnationals, producing computers, electronic engineering and pharmaceuticals, which produced about three-quarters of Irish economic growth in the 1990s, and the still-stagnating indigenous economy represented by Irish firms, which, returning the compliment, provided a perfect metaphor for the official bodies of Irish soccer.

The infrastructure of Irish professional soccer had always been inadequate, unconfident, wired to the moral victory. Its best pose was dogged: we would be glad of a draw, would not be disgraced, would gain friends by our sportsmanship, would let them know they had been in a match. But it could not mobilise the people, could not ever seem to scoop up that reservoir of fantasy, of dreaming, of desire, which jumped whole into the arms of the English Premiership. This had something to do with what we now perceive as the inexorable power of the global market, but that was only a part of the story. There is something fundamental here about the way our history has left us.

Unless, somehow, you can bypass the infrastructure into which the logic of defeatism has imbued itself, unless you can carry the dream intact from the moment of inspiration, through the obstacle course of organisation and infrastructure which, by virtue of the paralysis of self-realisation, is incapable of responding, you cannot win. A Roy Keane, a John Giles, instead of bringing the benefits of their boyhood dreaming to the indigenous infrastructure, jumped fully formed into the arms of Manchester United. Only at international level could they bring the dream back, on loan to their homeland, for one night only.

This, or something like it was, I suspect, at the back of the Roy Keane affair of the 2002 World Cup. I'm sure Roy Keane will remain convinced that what concerned him in Japan was the quality of the facilities. But perhaps what he was really seeking to express was the frustration of someone who had grown to see his own dream come true, wanted to make it available to the country he loved, but was confronted and confounded by the ineluctable pathology of losing. The day Ireland beat Saudi Arabia, I heard someone say, "There goes the Irish economy for the next three months." There was a truth in this, but perhaps a more complex one than was intended. Perhaps Roy Keane was, behind his inarticulateness and petulance, trying to say: "There's no reason why we cannot win!"

Perhaps the Roy Keane saga carried also signifiers of the frustration we feel that the interlopers of national policy and administration always seem to leech off the dream, always hold things back, always seem prepared to settle for the quarter finals. Perhaps Keane's response went far deeper than we imagined: our longing to win, combined with our virtual certainty that we won't, makes us cling to each, to any, small victory as to the idea of salvation, and as though it will never be repeated. Perhaps he was giving vent to some kind of existential roar of frustration at the idea that not only do our dreams always seem to get short-circuited, but the entire edifice we construct around our endeavours seems to make this inevitable.

(This essay is an amalgam of two pieces, one written in 2001 for the Castlerea parish magazine, the other published in Magill *in July 2002)*

5

THE POLITBURO OF THE GROOVE

THIS MONTH MARKS THE TWENTY-FIFTH anniversary of the founding of the Irish music magazine *Hot Press*. It's a nostalgic moment for me, since I got into journalism through *Hot Press* and, given how things were at the time, wouldn't have got in any other way. There are people who will find this a reason to be less than grateful to *Hot Press*, mostly the kind of people who nowadays read or write for the magazine.

It's hard to describe today how vibrant and interesting *Hot Press* was when it emerged in the summer of 1977. At the time there was perhaps a weekly total of three hours of pop music on national radio. Coverage of rock 'n' roll in the newspapers was arid and dull. Showbizzy magazines, making no distinctions as to quality or wit, came and went. But *Hot Press*, principally through the writings of the editor Niall Stokes, Liam Mackey and the late, great Bill Graham, hit the floor dancing to a different backbeat, seeming to comprehend that an obsession with this noise went beyond a need for entertainment or diversion, touching on the vital pulses and impulses of the human state.

Rock 'n' roll is about rebellion, yes, but a cardinal misapprehension among those who listen from outside the loop is that this rebellion is merely adolescent, social or political. Much bad and mediocre music affirms this perception, but the best overrides all such short-circuitry and touches the revolutionary heart in its purest desire: to be existentially free. A great pop song, for instance "A Day in the Life",

259

is like a great novel — it bypasses the intellect, conveying through its lack of weight or particularity a hint of other possibilities.

I remember, among a number of seminal early *Hot Press* pieces, one by Niall Stokes about Graham Parker and the Rumour, three-quarters of which was an attack on the Catholic Church. This sounds lame and predictable today, in a culture in which the church is being attacked from all sides, but then it was genuinely liberating, making a precise connection between the oppression inflicted by the institution and the balm of the music. And this pinpoints the difficulty arising not just with latter-day *Hot Press* but with latter-day Ireland and rock 'n' roll. From the culture of a generation ago, which ignored its young, we have moved into one that lionises everything to do with youth. Countless radio stations play pop and rock around the clock, and the coverage of rock 'n' roll in the national newspapers is now indistinguishable from that of *Hot Press*. The culture has flipped over, and the meaning of the revolution has inverted itself without anyone noticing.

In the old days, it was a little daring to write the word "fuck". Now, it is a matter of complete indifference to virtually everyone. There was a time when talk about homosexuality was shocking; now it is merely boring.

There are people who maintain that *Hot Press* has always been obsessed with sex, and they are probably right. The reason, of course, is that, in the beginning, defiance against the precise nature of actually existing oppression made this an obvious battlefield. But things have moved on and nowadays there is nothing revolutionary about confronting Catholic puritanism. The existential revolution is visible now in the work of writers like Michel Houellebecq, who have identified the new oppression as being precisely the freedoms the sixties delivered.

The fact that *Hot Press* has failed to move on is symptomatic of a condition visible more generally in Irish social and political life: the refusal to accept that the war has been won. *Hot Press* is today crippled by a shallow neurosis developed in response to the exigencies of a particular moment of conception, resulting in an often embarrassing datedness in its obsessions with sex, political correctness and socialist politics. Unless you're a leftie, lesbian, or belong to another short-listed "minority" group, you get no respect in latter-day *Hot Press*, whose ethos is defined by the fact that its star columnist is the social-ist reactionary Eamonn McCann.

Of course, part of the problem relates to a larger one concerning rock 'n' roll itself. It is now a throbbing paradox, a bloated, narcissis-tic brat cosseted by a multinational, multibillion industry. From be-hind the tinted glass it wails about the oppression of the marginalised, its primal impulse short-circuited by neurosis and fetid politics.

Just one band in the history of popular music has fulfilled the rock 'n' roll mission to absolute completion. I refer to the Plastic People of the Universe, the Prague-based band jailed by the communist regime of Czechoslovakia in the mid-1970s for "coarse indecencies" and for creating a public nuisance. Their imprisonment led directly to the formation of the revolutionary body Charter 77, which spearheaded the drive that eventually resulted in the toppling of communism in 1989. The Plastic People's music was an expression not of agitprop energies but of existential refusal. The present President of the Czech Republic, Václav Havel, in explaining the influence this music had on him and his contemporaries, spoke about its magic, sadness and long-ing for salvation. He said their trial and imprisonment represented "an attack on life itself".

The Plastic People of the Universe have never been featured in *Hot Press*. By virtue of being seen to be in opposition to a socialist regime, albeit a savage and inhuman one, they disqualified them-selves from celebration by the high priests of the western groove.

(June 2002)

6

THE STATE OF PROGRAMMELESSNESS

WHEN WE WERE CHILDREN IN THE 1960S, having no television in the house, my sisters and I used to refer to looking out our bedroom window in the evening as "watching television". Mrs Lavin, who lived opposite, had her grandchildren come visiting in summertime, down from the North, and, before falling asleep, we would watch them having pillow fights "on television". We thought ourselves behind the times. But, watching *Celebrity Farm* last week, it occurred to me that we had been looking a half-century ahead, into the future of TV.

There are two licensed viewpoints about what is happening to television. One is the tendency to bemoan the descent from Reithian responsibility into a hip emptiness; the other, to embrace that emptiness because it is "what people want".

There's a third way. Hans Magnus Enzensberger, in his beautiful 1988 essay, "The Zero Medium: Why All Complaints about Television are Pointless", noted television's movement towards what he called "the state of programmelessness". In the beginning, he argued, a mistake had been made in imagining that this new medium would provide a platform for existing media, like theatre, film, political speeches and news bulletins. As the desires of the viewing public became clearer, it was becoming evident that television was, in a very precise sense, finding itself — discovering its own essence, free of borrowed forms.

The most urgent ambition of television is to unburden itself of content, but not even programmes like *Celebrity Farm* have yet succeeded in this.

One of the extraordinary revelations of the reality TV genre is the fascination it has divined among the public for watching people move their private selves into the open. In its early generations, television provided a platform for various kinds of public acting, in which only "drama" offered glimpses of reality, and everything seemed upside down. An actor in a TV play would simulate the behaviour of a real person, to the point of dissolving into an illusion of reality; but a politician, delivering a statement or opinion, though ostensibly real, would come across as an actor delivering lines. Reality TV reverses this paradox, restoring television to the role of unfiltered window on the world.

It's early days yet, but the future is visible. At a fairly banal level, we watched *Celebrity Farm* last week and delighted in the disjunction between, for example, what those who were turfed off the farm were saying about their banishment and the body language they could not control. At other levels, we were learning of what we seem to want from television, from life and from one another.

By Monday night, I knew George would win. Something told me that the official spin about Twink being the first casualty — that viewers didn't understand they should vote for the person they least liked, rather than their favourite — was off the mark. It became clear that the winner would be the most childlike, innocent and silliest of the celebrities, and that was always down to a tussle between Gavin and George. The moment that convinced me George would win was when he painted Tamara's nails, a perfect encapsulation of what the world would like men to be like. I had a slight question-mark over Tamara until early Friday night, when I heard the psychologist praising her adult attitude, and instantly knew she was doomed.

I wouldn't be certain this is simply about young people texting in their responses. We live in a society craving youthfulness, exuberance and more benign forms of stupidity. In the near future, the concept of *Celebrity Farm* will reveal itself as crude and rudimentary, because it

will have opened a door into something else, from where the true possibilities of television will become clearer. And soon thereafter, a half
hour of seeming banality may tell us more about what we are really
like than thirty years of *Late Late*s.

It's pointless tearing our hair out. It is as ridiculous to attack *Celebrity Farm* for lacking substance and depth as to attack the Pope for
being insufficiently Jewish. This may not just be the future of television, but the future of drama, life and everything. The insistence that
television should educate, inform and entertain — in that or any other
order — emerges as the truly banal aspect of this discussion. Broad-
casters will continue to produce programmes of cultural, educational
and informational excellence, for the edification of the public. But,
for all our desire to improve ourselves with worthy programmes and
lofty thoughts, we will grow to hanker after an Ireland whose fields
and villages would be joyous with the sounds of romping celebrities,
and whose firesides would be forums for the innocence of the ageless.

(September 2003)

7

THE SUDDEN DEATH OF
JOHNNY ROTTEN

THE TRAGEDY OF YOUTH ICONS is they must hang around after their moments of glory, sporting faces they no longer own, with leftover lives to kill.

For anyone to whom those opening chords of "Pretty Vacant" still mean something, Johnny Rotten on *I'm a Celebrity . . . Get Me Out of Here*, was going to be a moment of truth. It just couldn't mean what, on the face of it, it seemed to: that Johnny's creator, John Lydon, was past it, down on his luck, had lost his sense of irony, had turned into yet another self-promoting celeb. No, his appearance was going to be saturated with irony, a classic postmodern moment, an encore for the third millennium. He was going to show them what it had all been about.

Well, he did, even if who "they" are is unclear. Us, I suspect — though, even with those illusions still in place, there was some mystery about what Lydon meant when he said that he had "changed the world twice" and was going to do it "again".

Once, certainly, he had been at the scene of the incident. The Sex Pistols' achievement was not simply displacing Genesis and Pink Floyd. The impact of "Anarchy" and "Pretty Vacant" was that, when you heard them, you had to re-evaluate the continuity of your own life against the messages they carried about something having shifted dramatically somewhere else.

But that was then, and here, from last week, is Johnny's description of fellow celebrity, Page 3 Girl Jordan, reading like a reprise of "Pretty Vacant", though without Glen Matlock's catchy ditty: "It doesn't do anything, and if it does, it nags its way through it. It ain't funny anymore. It doesn't contribute. It's a parasite. It doesn't know how to cook, walk or talk. It's a moron. It's a bicycle pump. What does it do? It's just a pair of blow-up boobs. They're two a penny in any crap disco." His valedictory piece-to-camera, in which he told us that he couldn't "be beat", warned of the likely fate of cultural rebels unless they keep their mouths shut.

Let's not be naïve. Punk was, in essence, a tabloid creation. Malcolm McLaren, a man with a tabloid soul, said: "The media was our helper and our lover, and that, in effect, was the Sex Pistols' success . . . to control our media is to have the power of government, God, or both."

I can see why, a generation on, Lydon might have liked the idea of sending Rotten into the jungle. Reality television is the latest phase in the cartooning of society. To begin, a celebrity was somebody famous, whose life became fair game for public voyeurism. In phase two, the celebrity was reinvented as cartoon figure, whose life was a fictional collaboration between subject and medium. All around us now are people who are almost entirely the creations of tabloid culture: cartoons, but having the appearance of real people. Now, in the third phase, the celebrity soap opera moves to supplant fiction and turn the world, finally, into soap. Reality TV is the antithesis of what its name conveys: it presents "real" people in situations to which they respond by being as unreal as is necessary for their "survival".

The problem, in terms of the potentially revolutionary impact of his appearance, was that Rotten had not grown up. Once, he shocked by saying "shit" on TV; now he spits the c-word and everyone smiles indulgently at this terrible tousle-haired throwback. Outrage no longer outrages.

The reasons he gave for withdrawing were that he feared he was going to win and he didn't want to turn into Des O'Connor. This was half an explanation. Jordan, her alleged bimboism notwithstanding, got the other half: "Deep down, I think he didn't want to be voted out. He'd rather walk himself than someone tell him to walk."

There are no points for being snobbish about reality TV. You can participate or deride, but not both. For Lydon to place his creation in the situation was courageous to begin with, but one assumed he knew what he was doing. Instantly, the cracks began to appear and we could see that he knew shit.

Rotten had been a one-trick pony: he couldn't sing or play, he looked awful and he went a long way. But he was the creature of minds greater than his creator's, and it showed last week to painful effect. Lydon walked because of the limits of his character, unable to handle winning or losing. The Rotten we thought we remembered might have been graceful, menopausally wry, avuncular, a greying malcontent whose anger had metamorphosed into something a little subtler. But there was nothing ironic or postmodern about this. Rotten leered, spat and fumed like it was still '77, and in doing so betrayed that, even then, he'd already been little more than a cartoon. Compared to this, Des O'Connor is someone to be.

(February 2004)

8

GOD OUT OF THE MACHINE
(A DEFENCE OF *TELLYTUBBIES*)

T HE RECENT ONSLAUGHT BY RIGHT-ON international broadcasting
executives on *Tellytubbies* gave an interesting new slant on the
ambitions of those who seek to dictate what we, the people, should
consume. Instead of the usual breast-beating about the harmful nature
of violent or risqué programming, we were being told that the Tubbies
were harmful because they were too cheerful and nice. Programme-
makers, mostly from Europe and America, informed their colleagues
at the recent World Summit on Television for Children that they did
not like the Tubbies because they failed to deal with "serious children's issues". One Australian TV executive complained that the programme was "regressive for any child who has gone beyond the bab-
bling phase". *Tellytubbies*, she alleged, was "not about learning and
challenges". Other charges were that the programme was "superficial", "non-educational" and "overly commercial".

The main thrust of the objections seems to come from Scandina-
vian countries, where television companies have refused to buy in
Tellytubbies. One Norwegian producer complained about the programme on the basis that "Children are invited into an alien-looking
world with some alien-looking babies talking in baby language". This
is true, I suppose, in much the same way as *Ulysses* is a book about a
Jew walking around Dublin. But, she went on: "What is there for
them to grow towards if the characters are a copy of themselves living
in a world they will never encounter in their life?"

Having spent many hours in the company of my baby daughter as she watched the Tellytubbies in both their scheduled and videotaped incarnations, I consider myself something of an expert on this subject. And as someone who begins from a position of being deeply suspicious of television in general, and of the idea of television as surrogate babysitter in particular, I have to say that I could not agree less with the criticisms outlined above.

What kind of "children's issues" could be more interesting or important to a one-year-old than the problem of getting Laa-Laa's ball down from a tree? In the solving of such conundrums lies the secret of many future life dilemmas. But such an argument is so obvious that it hardly needs to be made. In truth, *Tellytubbies* is an immensely educational programme, whose technique is precisely that it presents the world to the child in the child's own language. It teaches children a vast amount about relationships, friendship, play, work, nature, colour, difference, sound, music, life, God, fun and creativity. I have no doubt that the BBC is telling the truth when it says that research indicates that the repetitive nature of the programme helps very young children to learn, by presenting them with "a world from the experiences of other children". But, I believe, *Tellytubbies* is much more important than that.

At the risk of a sojourn in Pseuds Corner, I would say that the appeal of *Tellytubbies* could be described as quasi-Biblical. There is a sense of mystery and wonder in it that is beautiful to behold, especially when reflected in the eyes of a small child. Tinky Winky, Laa-Laa, Dipsy and Po, far from inhabiting some "alien" world, are residents of the Garden of Eden. When you come to think of it, the green grass, trees, flowers, animals, etc. of Tubbyland are bound to offend the sensibilities of people whose only true faith is in concrete and ideology. (We have many such people around these parts as well.)

For everywhere about *Tellytubbies* is the idea of God and His creation. The baby in the sky gurgles and laughs and sees that it is good. The animals walk on, two by two. A green field becomes a lake in seconds, and four ghostly boats pass across it. One can almost hear a voice declaim, "Let the water under the sky be gathered in one place, and let dry ground appear." I would much prefer my child to be watching this than learning about the "evils of the world" some years before she needs to. It would be nice if, before she learned that the world is a terrible place, she was confronted by the basic proposition that life can be worth living. Soon enough she will be off to university to learn about what bastards men are.

One of the criticisms of *Tellytubbies* appears, at first glance, to be a technical one. One delegate complained that the idea of the TV screens in the bellies of the characters was "hard to swallow". This could only have been said by someone who has not watched the programme in the company of a child. Had she done so, she would have been struck, as I have been many times, by the element of continuity by which this device enables a range of immensely educational matters to be introduced under the spell of the Tubbies. Films are shown of children doing all manner of things, from playing in the rain to helping their daddies fix punctures, which contain a vast range of cultural and other information. But the fact that these films emerge from the tummies of the Tellytubbies causes them to hold the child's interest far longer than would otherwise be the case.

It is at first a little strange that *Tellytubbies* causes such offence to those of correct political sensibilities, for I doubt if any other programme has gone to such lengths, between Dipsy's coloured face and Tinky Winky's handbag, to give a rounded version of the PC world we inhabit.

But of course it is the God Thing that is really at the heart of the objections, the fact that *Tellytubbies* is really a religious programme, thinly disguised. When these television executives claim that the building in which the Tubbies do their thing is "alien" and "unreal", what they actually mean is that it resembles a church. Similarly, when one female executive from Warner Brothers USA complained that the "idea of a baby laughing in the sun projects a false image of the world", she was saying that it is a bad idea to teach young children that a benevolent being in their own image might reside in the sky.

God is dead, and if He knows what is good for Him He'll stay that way. *Tellytubbies*, she maintained, was "vaguely sinister", which must surely be a contradiction of her earlier point that the programme did nothing to prepare children for "the evil in the real world".

What is most interesting, however, is that none of this has been cited by those who make the programme, and who are now obliged to defend it. The creator of *Tellytubbies*, Anne Wood, defended herself on the basis that children had a right to enjoy themselves, and that television programmes for children were not intended to be an answer for the world's ills. This seems sensible. It is difficult to argue with her either when she says that it would be a great pity if we did not allow children to be joyful. "When you're very young, you live in an adult world you understand only partially. We try to present a world from their perspective because, if they're smiling they're confident and if they're confident they're reassured and if they're reassured they will feel stronger in themselves."

The fact that she neglected to mention what is surely the most striking element of *Tellytubbies* — the existence of a Higher Being with dominion over all He (or even She) surveys — is a shocking indication of the fear in television land of the consequences of breaching the orthodoxies of politically correct society. Nevertheless, the subversive and counter-revolutionary nature of *Tellytubbies* is a source of hope that the damage to the human spirit wrought in recent generations is at last beginning to find its cultural antidote.

(March 1998)

9

PROXIMITY WITHOUT INTIMACY

T HERE WAS A TIME WHEN BEING CAUGHT talking to oneself was regarded as a sign of madness. Not any more. In fact, talking to oneself is now recommended as a cure for brain damage. The solution, it appears, to the health risks posed by mobile phones is for users to use a small microphone pinned to their lapels, thus avoiding their heads being in prolonged, and possibly dangerous, contact with the receiver/transmitter. I have already encountered people walking around using these devices, and there are few so disorienting experiences in the modern streetscape. At first encounter, they are indistinguishable from lunatics.

I believe there is something deeper here for us to take a look at. If mobile phones pose a threat to our health, then maybe this is nature's way of telling us that we do not need them, or that they are damaging to us in other ways.

If one was to imagine oneself in the world before cities were invented, it would be impossible, I believe, to anticipate the effect of putting millions of people in close proximity to one another. The way cities have actually evolved would be the last thing you would guess at.

I remember, when I was in my early twenties, the experience of standing on a hot summer's day in a field at the centre of a farm in Loughglynn, County Roscommon, and reflecting on how ridiculous it seemed that, at that very same moment, there were people walking, talking, rushing, bustling on Baggot Street in Dublin. I thought of Baggot Street because I had been there several times and was on

272

reasonably intimate terms with its appearance and state of busyness. Here in the country, I was surrounded by silence. The nearest house or road was half a mile away. The only sounds were those of birds and the wind, occasionally broken by perhaps the thud of a sledgehammer on a fencing post in the far distance. There was nobody to talk to, nobody to watch. If you were to ask me, at that moment, to imagine a place in which lots of people lived, worked and sat side by side, in which humanity moved fluidly in a common space — in other words, a city — I would have drawn a picture of human communication, cooperation and intimacy. I would have imagined that the more people lived together in the same space, the greater their sense of closeness and fellow-feeling. But this notion, which would have been drawn from the wishfulness of my own isolation, would have been utter fantasy. For, as we well know, the more people live together in close proximity to one another, the farther apart they tend to grow. In truth, there is not a street or a train or a bus in London, Paris or Dublin that is in any sense less lonely than the most isolated field in County Roscommon.

There is, of course, an issue of degree. Dublin, not being as big as, for example, London, is not yet as lonesome as it might be. For this reason, it is still possible to carry out a certain amount of research with regard to the comparisons between places at different stages on the road to utter desolation. For some time now I have been trying to put my finger on the precise difference in the respective moods of a London Underground tube train and a DART train in Dublin. I have long been aware that such a distinction existed, but I had previously been unable to separate it entirely from my own sense of either location.

But now I am convinced that the difference lies in sounds. The DART still has about it a certain quality of the parish pump. People still talk to one another, and not just those who happen to be travelling together. If you stop and listen to the sound of the DART, or if the DART stops on the line and you just listen, you realise that there is something there still of the quality which I might have fondly imagined from my field in Loughglynn. London tubes, however, are almost always bereft of spontaneous human conversation. The noise of the moving tube makes this difficult to apprehend, but if, for some reason a train stops in a tunnel, there is almost always silence.

This is not to say that people do not talk on the Underground. In fact, when people travel together on the Underground, which is much less frequently than you'd expect, they seem to talk loudly and animatedly, in an almost exaggerated fashion, to one another. I can never quite make out whether they are trying to shut out the silence of their fellow passengers or simply taunting them with the notion that they, at least, still have some friends. On the DART, conversation is intimate. People do not do it for show. The quality of the sound is of a low hum, evenly spread throughout the carriage. On the Underground, the quality of the sound is of deathly silence punctuated by frantic outbursts of talk and laughter.

Sometimes, however, I have had the experience of sitting on a London tube train and suddenly finding myself transfixed by the sound of human conversation which immediately strikes me as real, warm and truly intimate. A voice, confident and clear, will pronounce some term of endearment and convey some trivial piece of information. There will be a short burst of laughter born out of genuine pleasure. But even before I look, I know that the person I am listening to is speaking on a mobile phone. At no time are people on the Underground quite so animated as when they are speaking on mobile telephones.

It is extraordinary to note the difference these have made to the manner of telephone communication. I do not mean ease of use or transportation, but rather the way in which they seemed to have finally liberated us from any pretence of privacy. Once, a public telephone was something to be whispered into while you turned your back on the crowd. Today, a mobile telephone is a way of saying: "There is more to my life than sitting on trains. I have someplace to go and someone there to wait for me."

The mobile phone is the instrument of the anonymous city. It belongs to the octopus-shaped communities which cities breed in the midst of their suffocating alienation. It is useful, of course, in maintaining contact between the individual and the small cell of friends and acquaintances which often seems to represent the totality of the life of a modern city-dweller, but in truth it is not so much an instrument of communication as an instrument of non-communication. It enables the user to impart information and greetings within his or her own network, but far, far more loudly it says to all those within eye- or earshot: "I do not care to talk to you."

It is not surprising that the mobile phone carries risks of illness and damage, for anything that to such an extent attempted to rework the fundamental nature of human contact would be bound to do so. The extent of the risk is a measure of the damage we are attempting to do without admitting to it. The mobile phone is an instrument of alienation. Far from assisting communication, it is designed to destroy it.

First we invent the city so that we can be together; then we invent the mobile telephone so that we can talk to anyone but those we are near.

(November 1999)

10

In Defence of Postman Pat

SOME READERS MAY HAVE NOTICED in recent weeks that a strange hieroglyphic has started to appear at the end of this column, in the place where sometimes it might say, for example, that "John Waters is unwell" (no news to right-thinking *Irish Times* readers) or "We apologise for the above article by Ruth Dudley Unionist, but John Waters is on holiday". This squiggle, I am told, is what is termed an "e-mail address".

But if you have sent me an e-mail and are waiting for a reply, I have to tell you that you wait in vain. I do not know how to "retrieve" (I believe this to be the correct terminology) my e-mail correspondence, nor do I want to. I have neither been asked for permission to have "my" e-mail address published, nor been told how e-mail works.

To suggest that we must all be on e-mail is a bit like saying that, because whiskey exists, we should all be drunk all the time. Again and again, we are reminded that we live in a "technological age", that we are all "citizens of cyberspace". We live, in fact, in an era of technological fetish, technological obsession, technological fascism, in which we are pummelled with the notion that it is necessary to be instantaneously available to everyone at all times, and that to wish it otherwise is evidence of backwardness. The obsession with technological communication is part of the cultural obsession with youth. It is part of the thoughtstream which dictates that everything young people say, do, believe or desire is self-evidently good. And because there is a belief that young people enjoy sitting in front of computer screens, turning themselves into zombies, this is something we are all obliged to engage in, on pain of obsolescence.

The computer culture with which we have such a latter-day preoccupation is a way for young people to separate themselves from the channels of their elders, but also a way for old fogeys to pretend to the world what they have already succeeded in selling to themselves: that just because they are as bald as plates doesn't mean they're not hip to the chip. E-mail is not about better communication, but about being thoroughly "modern".

I am told that the benefits of being "online" (you see how modern I am, in spite of everything!) include the opportunity of having more "interaction" with readers, as well as obtaining additional information and new ideas. Anyone who reads the type of letter printed about me on the letters page opposite will have a sense of how likely this is: most of these letters are no more than gratuitous personal attacks, devoid of facts or argument, written by people who have deep pathological problems with fact, ideas and freedom of expression. Does anybody seriously expect me to add to my electricity and telephone bills to receive more of the same?

As for information and ideas: no offence, but in nearly ten years of writing this column, the number of times I got an idea from a letter written by a reader could be numbered on the fingers of one hand. As for information, my house is already half-full of paper, most of which I will never read. What we need is not more information, but more sense, and I do not imagine that e-mail is conducive to sense. Maybe I'm wrong, but I suspect that, with e-mail, anybody who is disposed to have an idle thought can simply sit at a keyboard and dash off a one- or two-line rant, without placing anything of themselves on the line. E-mail is green-biro heaven.

I am not a citizen of cyberspace. I am a citizen of the Republic of Ireland. There is no earthly reason why I should be available at all times for people to inundate me with their opinions and abuse simply because they pay eighty-five pence to buy *The Irish Times*. I write a column, on a weekly basis, and submit it for publication. If people wish to read it, that's fine; if they like what they read, that's great. But if not, no problem. It is not part of my job description to make myself available as an intellectual punchbag for people who have got out of the wrong side of the bed. There is no more basis for providing readers with an e-mail address for John Waters than there would be for giving them my home telephone number or issuing a general invitation to attend for tea at my house on Saturdays at four.

There are other, more serious, objections. It tends to take a long time, with any new technological or cultural development, to see that there is a price tag attached. We're only now beginning to become aware, for example, of the potential health risk of the mobile telephone. The obsession with computers, similarly, has a vast hidden cost, not least in the creation of isolationism and alienation in a generation of youngsters strung out on the Internet, and in the numbing effect on creativity and imagination which is the inevitable consequence of such a withdrawal from the world.

What's wrong with Postman Pat? For fifty years, my father drove a mailcar, delivering mail around Roscommon, Mayo and Galway. For several years I did likewise. Many of those from whom I would be likely to receive e-mails would wish that I had stayed with it. I didn't, but I retain a high regard for the sacred nature of letter-writing, the ritual of the post, and the centrality of communication as meaningful human intercourse rather than technological fetish.

The process of letter-writing involves an investment of time and thought, which functions, almost as though so calculated, to reduce the incidence of nuisance or abusive missives. To go to the trouble of writing a letter, it is, generally speaking, necessary to care, to think, to reflect. This is not true of sending an e-mail. So if people wish to write to me, there is a time-honoured way of doing so. First you purchase an envelope and some writing paper, then you sit down and write me a letter. When you have committed your thoughts to paper to your satisfaction, you place the letter in the envelope, on the outside of which you write: Mr John Waters, Mucksavage Department, *The Irish Times*, 10–16 D'Olier Street, Dublin 2. Then it is time to go to the post office. You will find the fresh air will do you good, and in no time at all that throbbing in your left temple will have abated.

In the post office, you will, in return for a small consideration, be given a stamp, which you should stick on to the top, right-hand corner of the envelope, on the same side as the address. You should then look around for a small rectangular aperture in a wall or pillar box, into which you should place your missive. In a matter of days, I will receive your letter, and, if you are sufficiently polite and I am interested enough in what you have to say, you will receive a reply in due course. At the end of all this, it is possible that both of us will feel better.

Vote for Postman Pat.

(November 1999)

11

THE CELTIC TRINITY

THERE WAS A TIME WHEN BONO on the cover of *Time* magazine
would have sent us into paroxysms of national self-
congratulation, but now we take it in our stride, suspecting that it is
more about him than about us. The first time U2 were accorded that
not insignificant recognition, almost two decades ago, their being
dubbed "Rock's Hottest Ticket" provided their fellow citizens with an
opportunity for an orgy of reflected glorying. Now, I detect, we realise that Bono has not just outstripped the rest of the rock 'n' roll pack
and become far bigger than his own band, but has left the present
Celtic Tiger mindset behind as well. And yet there is something in his
elevation to universal saviour so related to his origins that we would
be missing something if we were not to remind ourselves of it.

The current *Time* cover story relates mainly to Bono's solo attempt to persuade world leaders to find a way of forgiving Third
World debt. The cover headline, "Can Bono Save the World?" is almost free from irony, and there is a sense that this may for the first
time be entirely justified. "Don't laugh," the cover blurb goes on, "the
globe's biggest rock star is on a mission to make a difference." Bono
has crossed into territory where no celebrity spokesman for his generation has gone before, earned considerable international respect for
himself and his motivations, and somehow managed to crack the code
of the old conundrum concerning whether rock 'n' roll can move beyond its Dionysian obsession with sex and drugs.

The irony is confined to the first line of the *Time* article: "Bono is an egomaniac." There have been efforts to suggest that his current mission is an ego-trip, but anyone who knows him knows it has more to do with his humility, a sense of personal gratitude and awe at what he has achieved in his own life, combined with a genuine grief that such things are denied to many of his fellow human beings.

There is an interesting section towards the end of Josh Tyraniel's article, which begins: "At 41, Bono says he has given up on music as a political force. He believes his work negotiating in political back rooms is more vital and effective than singing in sold-out stadiums." Tyraniel quotes W.H. Auden: "Poetry makes nothing happen", and says Bono agrees. "I'm tired of dreaming," he tells the interviewer. "I'm into doing at the moment. It's like, let's only have goals that we can go after. U2 is about the impossible. Politics is the art of the possible. They're very different, and I'm resigned to that now. . . . When you sing you make people vulnerable to change in their lives. You make yourself vulnerable to change in your life. But in the end, you've got to become the change you want to see in the world."

Three things occurred to me on reading this. The first is that Bono, with Bob Geldof, has rewritten the rock 'n' roll manifesto. It used to maintain that art and politics failed to mix only because the system had not (yet) changed enough to tune in. Now it recognises that art and politics are parallel realities, which can cross-pollinate but never intersect. Geldof recently said something to the effect that music itself is not a force for change but those who acquire influence through it can use that for good in other ways.

Bono, I believe, is nudging at a new frontier. His age hints at the ironies and the inevitability of the fact that it has taken so long to discover a formula for translating the moral clarity of youthful idealism into a new kind of political vision. Hence the second thing that occurred to me was that Bono is now a little older than John Lennon was when Mark Chapman blew the dream away. For the two decades since his death, and the best part of two more before that, Lennon's ethical stature and searching intelligence cast a moral shadow over rock 'n' roll's inability to transcend its own contradictions. What Lennon had striven for — the means of translating his artistic power into something more "practical" — Bono now stands on the point of achieving, and with this achievement comes the realisation that he has now, finally, stepped beyond the shadow of the original rock 'n' roll messiah. This presents both a moment of exhilaration and a chill of anxiety on his behalf.

And the third thing that occurred to me is that Lennon, Geldof and Bono have something else in common: they are all, in a sense, Irishmen. I'm not suggesting this makes them holier than anyone, just observing that it may be more than coincidence and might, conceivably, have to do with certain cultural memories of quite recent historical experiences of conditions that now afflict other parts of the globe. Famine, yes, but also, more recently, the experience of being strangled by debt. Up there in what B.P. Fallon might call the Mainmanland, John Winston must be looking down on the creatures of his influence with no little pride, and acknowledging that Paul Hewson has finally become his natural representative on earth. (The "Bono" business he would probably dismiss, as he did the "Dylan" business, as "bullshit".)

Lennon, Geldof, Hewson — through the searching of this Celtic Trinity, we may finally have reached a breakthrough moment of rock 'n' roll possibility, considered elusive if not unattainable since Yoko Ono broke up the Beatles.

(March 2002)

12

THE VITAL ART OF THE BEGRUDGER

IF PROOF WERE NEED THAT BEGRUDGERY is dead, we need look no
further than the existence of *VIP* magazine. One wonders what the
hero of the opening chapter of Breandán Ó hEithir's *The Begrudger's
Guide to Irish Politics* would have made of this latest addition to the
Irish literary tradition, that doughty Cork blacksmith who, on the day
after the signing of the Anglo-Irish Treaty in 1921, riposted to his
parish priest's assurance that "We're going to have our own gentry
now", with a spirited "We will in our arse have our own gentry".
Well, now we have the next worst thing: our own *Hello!* magazine.

But one does not wish to be unfair to *Hello!*. *VIP* has none of the
rich literary resonance, none of the exhilarating sense of tradition,
none of the inspired touch of the esoteric, none of the thirst for deeper
meaning, none of the refined taste for ancient civilisation, none of the
profound sense of knowingness and irony, and none of the subtle commitment to the metaphysical which are (comparatively speaking) so
much the hallmarks of *Hello!* magazine. *VIP* is a magazine full of
photographs of people famous for having their photographs taken. It
features Irish "personalities" and "celebrities" — at home, at play, in
the company of beautiful wives/husbands/cars and houses, at charitable functions like the recent "Media Ball in aid of Kosovo". (Judging
from the *VIP* spread, not a single Kosovar showed up, which just goes
to show that you're wasting your time trying to help these people.)

VIP is the Celtic Tiger in full-blown form, a testament to the sorry
pass at which we have now arrived. If the boys in the GPO on Easter

Monday 1916 could only have had a premonition of a *VIP* cover,
Irish history would have taken an entirely different direction. They
would, I suspect, have gone straight home to their beds.

The title, I imagine, stands for "Vacuity in Perpetuity", or perhaps
"Vanity in Public". Whatever it stands for, *VIP* is a publication utterly
bereft of redeeming features. No, I tell a lie: the fact that no Irish person contributed as much as a single original idea to this magazine
must surely be to our credit — even the colour codes on the cover are
ripped off from *Hello!*. This might be described as the publishing
equivalent of the showband, except that this would represent a gross
defamation of such comparatively startling creative colossi as Samba
and the Philosophers, Magic and the Magic Band and Hugo Duncan
and the Tall Men.

There was a time when a publication like *VIP* would have become
one of the richest jokes in the culture, but now it is seen only as a
mark of our "sophistication", its promoters feted as courageous entre-
preneurs, not to mention creative geniuses. Is there none among us
now fit to emit a snort of derision when it is so badly needed? Oh
where, where are they now, those dark moustachioed men who once
could be relied upon to toss a well-turned jeer at such endeavours?
What would we not give now for what J.J. Lee called a "cosmic dis-
placement of bilious resentment", with which to give utterance to
what surely must be our deepest feelings about *VIP* magazine?

The Celtic Tiger has brought the final extinction of the increasingly
lesser-spotted begrudger. Ever since the precursor boom of the Lemass
era, the begrudger had been getting a bad press. For the kind of mediocrity represented by *VIP* magazine to prosper in the land, it was essential that the begrudger's heart be stilled forever. This was finally
achieved by a process of constant whingeing by the mediocrities about
the extent of the resentment which greeted their every achievement,
resulting in the creation of a kind of phantom notion which bore no re-
semblance to the reality of actually existing begrudgery. Most of the
time, save for the occasional slightly curled lip, nobody was taking the
blindest bit of notice of such people or their activities. (I noticed the

same tendency in interviews by the promoters of *VIP* magazine, who lamented the fact that their endeavours were being "resented" in the Irish media. In truth, there is nowhere near a sufficiency of resentment of these people and their endeavours — almost nobody "out there" knows who they are, and few could care less — and most other media people appear to think them very fine fellows indeed.)

As a result of several decades of anti-begrudger propaganda, we tend to identify begrudgery purely with negativity, envy, jealousy and spite. In fact, there may, in the modern world, be a profoundly re-demptive quality to this much-maligned disposition. A couple of years ago, Dr Oliver James, a British clinical psychologist, suggested that perhaps the principal difference between the 1990s and the 1950s is the fact that most or all of us now "know" far, far more people than we would have known a generation ago, and thus have a ready fund of "successful" celebrity archetypes with whom to compare ourselves negatively. (See "The Divine Right to Perfect Happiness", pages 86–88.) This creates chemical imbalances which attack our self-esteem, spawning envy, depression, addiction and other disorders.

It is, in short, the green-eyed monster as pathological condition, and at its heart in modern Britain is the spectre of *Hello!* magazine, the forum in which the unattainable "achievement", "celebrity" and "glamour" of the famous is flaunted before the general public. *Hello!* and *VIP* are part of a culture which sells to the addicted public the means to feed its own self-abasing masochistic envy by presenting a regular diet of photographs of and information about people whose lifestyles no normal person can possibly hope to emulate.

Begrudgery, which, as Joe Lee outlined in *Ireland 1912–1985, Politics and Society*, is a defence mechanism born of the need to maintain a sense of status and dignity in a society with scarce re-sources, may be the only known antidote to this condition. This is why it is a mistake to confuse begrudgery with simple envy or jeal-ousy: a begrudger does not envy the target of his rancid passion; he tears him down, dismisses him and consigns him to oblivion. In the begrudger's denunciation lurks also an annunciation of pride and self-satisfaction which nullifies any danger of succumbing to true envy.

Begrudgery is therefore a form of what Oliver James calls "discounting", which is to say a device to minimise the demoralising effects of the relative success or attractiveness of others. If upward social comparisons are not to result in a depressing sense of inadequacy, James wrote in *Britain on the Couch*, we need to remain mindful of ways in which the object of the negative comparison has been more privileged compared to ourselves, or alternatively disadvantaged in ways we are not. The art of the begrudger in remembering the celebrated and successful when they hadn't a pot to piss in becomes, therefore, a device for the preservation of sound mental health and the avoidance of unnecessary feelings of inferiority.

(September 1999)

13

THE SELFISHNESS OF COMPASSION

THE DEATHS THIS YEAR, WITHIN A WEEK of one another, of Diana, the Princess of Wales, and Mother Teresa, caused a degree of comment which linked the two women on account of their charitable activities. This, I believe, approached an interesting question, but failed, for the sake of what might be called charity, to actually ask it. The question is admittedly difficult to formulate. It has to do with the quality and meaning of compassion, philanthropy and altruism.

There were, to the objective eye, at least as many dissimilarities as similarities between the two women. Yes, they were both engaged in what we call charitable activity, but the manner of their engagement in such work made them, ostensibly at least, utterly different from one another.

This difference may very well have been a matter of appearances, but it existed nevertheless. In fact, it existed to such an extent as to suggest that the two women were from different eras. Diana was a creature, indeed a creation, of the media age. Her life was conducted in the public eye, and, for all the ambivalences she may have felt about it, this was an essential aspect of her persona. She was clearly someone who thought a great deal about the fact that people were watching her. Every aspect of the way she looked, dressed, how she behaved in public, was the consequence of this awareness. Her public personality, therefore, appeared to be the product of the cameras that were observing her.

Mother Teresa, on the other hand, gave the impression of someone who did not seem to be aware she was being watched. Much of
her life was as public as the Princess of Wales's, but she appeared to
make no concessions to the watching world. She didn't acknowledge
cameras. In fact, her personality suggested that she had never looked
in a mirror. She had no sense of that Diana self-awareness.

Of course, if one wanted to be cynical, one could decide that the
difference was simply to do with the quality of acting: Diana was a
bad actress, who could not sufficiently sublimate her own ego to play
the part of the global altruist; Mother Teresa was such a great actress
that she might well have been someone else playing herself.

But I don't think this is the point. I've often remarked upon the
fact that people who met Mother Teresa always reported how struck
they were by her "holiness", which I could never hear other than as an
empty cliché. But, learning of Mother Teresa's death within a week
of Diana's, I had a sudden insight into what they were saying. They
meant, I believe, not the piety that I imagined, but a sense of indifference to the watching world. We think that the similarity between
Mother Teresa and Diana is that they both "cared", but in point of
fact, what distinguished Mother Teresa not merely from Diana, but
from most of the rest of us, was that she didn't care at all. She did
what she did despite, not because of, the eyes of the watching world.

This idea is now almost extinct in the western world. The Gospel
notion of doing good deeds in secret is now virtually impossible, at
least at the political level. In a world of telethons, flag days, coffee
mornings and sponsored fasts, charity has become a matter of doing
good deeds in public.

Is this a problem? Yes, because it changes utterly the meaning and
function of charity. A superficial analysis might be that it makes it
impossible to locate an act of charity with pure motives. But this is
not quite what it means.

All charity is essentially selfish. This is not a criticism of it. The
line about it being better to give than to receive is not an empty plati-
tude: it is a straightforward statement of fact. By giving, we get back

a range of emotional and psychological benefits that cannot be purchased in any other way. There is, perhaps, no such thing as pure altruism, in the sense of an act that is entirely motivated by thoughts of others. The nature of charity, as indeed the nature of all social exchange, is essentially to do with the aspect of each one of us that is itself social, and therefore dependent on the health of the wider world. We all breathe the same air. We all, if to varying extents, take from the world and give back to it. The quality of what we receive, therefore, is dependent on the quality of what is provided by the collective effort. Other than through various forms of psychosis, we cannot continue to receive from the world while failing to give back, without experiencing negative feelings like guilt, alienation and shame. Charity is a way of mitigating these feelings in ourselves. If you want to put the issue in an economic perspective, charity is the means by which we buy back peace of mind, by which we square the moral circle and allow ourselves to live in a world which outrages us metaphysically by virtue of its manifest inhumanity and our own individual inability, as citizens of the world, to rectify this.

If I give a pound to a beggar in the street, I walk on with an increased sense of moral superiority and well-being. I am better able to walk into a shop and buy an expensive book, CD or item of clothing. I have, for the moment, a clear conscience. This places the transaction between myself and the beggar in a different light to what conventional wisdom would have it be. Our self-serving culture perceives the incident as an act of pure philanthropy: one party who contributes nothing in receipt of a hand-out from another, who has no obligation to give. In a certain narrow, legalistic sense, this characterisation is accurate. But if we take into account the existential, psychological and emotional levels of human interaction, the transaction is much more interesting. By giving the beggar a pound I am, in fact, buying from him a degree of peace of mind. A beggar may be part of what we call the flotsam and jetsam of society, but, standing on the footpath, he is actually a highly sophisticated functionary in our economic life. He might as well be carrying a box of objects called "Guiltrelievers". In fact, this is precisely the function of the stickers and other badges that charities give to benefactors on flag days. Except, as we shall see, they don't quite work as they should.

The price of guilt-relief is not fixed, despite being regulated by market forces. Even for a comparatively wealthy person, a pound given to a beggar can buy a great deal of conscience-quieting. In fact, the wilful blindness of our society to the two-way nature of such transactions allows us all to get away much more lightly than is good for us. That pound, which is still a significant sum of money to give away "for nothing", might, spent in this way, purchase a lot more serenity, self-satisfaction and ease than, for example, twenty pounds spent on alcohol. It is possible also that the effect would last much longer, and would not have comparably bothersome after-effects. If our economy was correctly adjusted, the degree of relief obtainable through charitable donations would be commensurate with the cost of other forms of conscience-deadening, and we would therefore feel the need to give as much money to beggars as we spend on, for example, drugs and drink.

The problem is that, for all the immediate sense of relief and smugness, charity doesn't really work for the giver any better than drink. Because the motive is suspect — and especially so when the donation is made publicly and ostentatiously — it doesn't really purchase the correct commodity. We can fool our heads, but not our guts. The hole in the psyche gets bigger and bigger, and what we withhold from the beggar must be spent a hundredfold in filling it.

And so, the quality of the product we purchase from the beggar is entirely dependent on the nature of our own motivation. It's not a question of selfishness, because the entire exercise is selfish at some level. It is a question of how we understand our own needs. If we give money for show, what we purchase from the beggar is not relief of conscience, but public admiration. For the pound I throw ostentatiously into the upturned cap, I get the admiration of a passing nun, but not peace of mind. The sticker I buy from the woman with the collection tin allows me to walk around for the day with the air of someone who cares, but I cannot at the same time expect it to still my conscience.

There is nothing wrong with charity for show, and it is arguably better than the absence of charity, but if that is what I buy, my conscience remains unsatisfied. My guilt goes on eating away at my insides.

The injunction to "do good works in secret" is a strategy not for philanthropy but for self-fulfilment. And if the modern mass media consciousness makes this more difficult, it is likely that the level of guilt we are all carrying around is growing and growing. This is, I believe, a critical change, perhaps one of the most significant but invisible effects of modern media. It is still, of course, possible to slip money into an envelope and send it to the St Vincent de Paul, but our culture makes it much easier to do good works that have ulterior motives and are therefore less satisfying to the human soul. At a global level, in particular, it is increasingly difficult for those who volunteer to organise and administer the operation of charity to do so without elements of ego, careerism and self-advancement creeping in.

Perhaps the only way forward in a media world is the attitude taken by Bob Geldof: it doesn't matter why you do it, so long as you do it. I once asked him what he had to say to those who raised political questions about the efficacy of charity, and he replied: "I say, 'Fuck up and gimme a pound.'" The problem is that while this may work for the receiver, it does not work for the giver, or at least it allows the giver off the hook in a manner ultimately harmful to himself.

To put all this another way: perhaps the reason Mother Teresa did not have an eating disorder was that she didn't care whether or not there was anyone watching. But then again, how do we know that?

(December 1997)

14

THE EVIL OF WHEEL-CLAMPING

FEW EVENTS IN RECENT HISTORY HAVE illustrated the supine, defeated state of the Irish public as comprehensively as the introduction of wheel-clamping in Dublin. The public response to this outrage has been characterised by casual submissiveness and an almost sadomasochistic fascination with the clamping device itself. Those who operate this monstrous insult to public liberty have been informing us, courtesy of the media, that the public's response has been "generally very good". Most people have been understanding, we are told, of the necessity to "free up" the capital's traffic system. Those who have fallen victim to this appalling abuse of their rights have been philosophical, and have taken their medicine with polite resignation.

What has happened to us, a once-proud people? Judging from the almost total absence of protest at this outrage, it is possible to believe that, if the authorities decree that illegal parking be punishable by the administration of fifty lashes on the spot, the car drivers of Dublin would be queuing up with their trousers down. Whenever I see a clamped car, I am filled with empathy and compassion for the victim, not simply on account of the inconvenience which has been visited upon them but on account of the public humiliation which this practice bestows. I long for our beaten people to rise to their feet against this alien scourge.

For let us be absolutely clear. The introduction of wheel-clamping in Dublin has nothing at all — repeat, nothing at all — to do with easing traffic congestion. It has to do, and only to do, with extracting even more money from motorists, who already pay through the nose, ears, eyes and other orifices for the privilege of owning cars. A leaflet distributed to Dublin households by Dublin Corporation, as part of its highly successful public relations campaign to justify the importation of this outrageous practice, describes wheel-clamping as a "traffic-management measure" and claims that "illegal parking restricts traffic movement and causes congestion". Even if this were always true, which it is not, it would not amount to a justification of the introduction of wheel-clamping. Illegally parked cars which restrict traffic movement and cause congestion are not the kind of illegally parked cars which are being clamped under this new, inhuman regime. If traffic congestion is to be avoided, such vehicles have to be towed away. To clamp them where they stood would be absurd. Wheel-clamping, therefore, is not a "traffic-management measure"; it is a form of extortion.

The reason there has been no public outcry against such barbarism is because car-owners have been browbeaten into believing that they are a class of neo-criminals who poison the atmosphere, endanger public safety and block the roads. That they have been persuaded to believe this, while simultaneously being forced to pay for these self-same roads, is an awesome feat of public indoctrination. That car drivers have been persuaded that traffic chaos in Dublin and else-where is the result of their selfishness, their lack of public spirit, is one of the great wonders of the modern world.

Car drivers, especially those who drive in the capital city, now have no expectations other than to be treated as criminals. And the people we have allowed to tell us this are the very same people who, for several decades now, have refused to provide any semblance of an alternative.

To avoid running foul of my excellent colleague Frank McDonald, I should say at this point that I am all in favour of the abolition of the motor car. I agree that the concept of an unrestricted entitlement to a private form of transport, individual to every citizen, is rapidly approaching the status of absurdity. I agree that issues of traffic gridlock, pollution and public safety make the private motor car a difficult thing to defend. I would greatly welcome the arrival of some alternative, which would make it unnecessary for me to spend up to twenty per cent of my income on keeping a car on the road.

But Irish people have no choice. There is no other way for most of us to get around. And among the many shocking aspects of this clamping business for those of us who believe in public transport is that, whenever we have put forward arguments about the need for investment in trains, buses and so forth, we have been ignored or shouted down by the very same authorities which now add insult to injury by shackling the wheels of our regrettably indispensable motor cars.

Most of us attempt, where possible, to park legally, and to pay the appropriate tolls. But sometimes it is not possible to be perfectly precise about coming back to one's car on time. Nor is it always possible to have the correct change for the parking meter. Now, it appears, those of us who fall short of perfect adherence to the letter of the law are to have our lives disrupted for several hours, while we pay over an extortionate fee and wait to have our sole means of transport returned to us. What about people who have urgent business, deadlines or children to be collected from school? Tough, is what Dublin Corporation tells the citizens who pay its salaries.

There are some parking offences which clearly merit a stiff penalty. Blocking a bus lane might be one such; parking in a disabled parking bay would certainly be another. But most so-called parking offences are minor matters of overstaying at meters or short-term stopping at loading bays. For such offences, the penalty of wheel-clamping is utterly disproportionate.

Wheel-clamping, of course, like so much else of our public policy, is an idea imported from Britain — imitation being the most noticeable talent of those who run our public affairs. It would never, of course, occur to such people to look at the broader context in which such ideas are implemented in more civilised societies, or to steal also the ideas which make wheel-clamping in, say, London, vaguely just. Wheel-clamping has been in force in London for many years, but in the context of a public transport system that actually works. There is virtually no place in London where one is more than ten minutes' walk from an Underground station, a system rendering any area of a vast metropolis reachable within an hour. In Dublin, there is, for most people, no alternative to bringing a car into the city. Most of us would prefer not to have to do so, but we have no choice. It is unnecessary to point out that public transport in Dublin is a disgrace, and yet I have not heard this reality cited as an argument against wheel-clamping. Visitors to our capital city stare at me in disbelief when I tell them that, in fact, there is no rail link between Dublin city centre and Dublin airport, a neglect which has led to half of north Dublin being turned into a car park and made the process of parking a car at the airport more time-consuming than the air journey between Dublin and London.

The previous system of parking tickets was at least redeemed by some elements of humanity. Traffic wardens were usually vaguely human, and could be appealed to on that basis. Moreover, they had systems, which could be cracked. Once you figured out how a particular warden operated, it was possible to lengthen the odds on obtaining a penalty by various stratagems which are now, sadly, about to become obsolete. Under the old system, you sometimes won and sometimes lost, but generally speaking the system was fair, reasonable and flexible. Now, there is no prospect of escape. The clamping system is inhuman not merely in its consequences; it is so also in its demeanour, in its imperviousness to human intervention. What has always been a blood sport has now become the equivalent of hare coursing.

If an Englishman's home is his castle, an Irishman's car is his chariot, his indispensable ally in moving about this benighted land. The very same authorities which recently introduced wheel-clamping have for decades stonewalled attempts to provide an underground or light rail system for Dublin. The same people who have wined and dined and winked and nodded with lobbyists for the road and motor industries, now lecture us about our dependency on the motor car.

Truly, we are a broken people. If we had an ounce of spirit left, we would be calling upon the criminal classes to introduce a cheap, user-friendly device for declamping vehicles, a project which is surely not beyond their ingenuity.

My own car has not yet been clamped, but I expect it is just a matter of time. I suspect, however, that, when it happens, I too will hot-foot down to the "Parking Shop", with £65 of my hard-earned money clutched in my hand, to politely ask for the return of my right to make my way about my own country without let or hindrance. I am tempted to proclaim that the sorry bunch of clampers who would seek to immobilise my trusty chariot had better also arm themselves with a straitjacket, just in case I happen to catch them in the act, but I know this would just be macho posturing. The sad fact is that I, too, have given up.

(August 1998)

15

I WILL ARISE AND GO NOW

F OR MANY YEARS, MY COLLEAGUES at *The Irish Times* have been
seeking to elevate the minds of the Irish public, to instil some
sense of enlightenment and civilisation and to gently correct any tendency towards slumbering sentimentality, backwardness or wrong-
headedness. I, and indeed they, had thought these tuitions were being
received with application and diligence by the public, or at least the
section of it that reads this newspaper. Indeed, several of these tutors,
in their end-of-millennium reports, pronounced themselves very
pleased with the progress being made by the Irish people: we had left
behind us not merely our attachment to nationalistic sentiment and
Catholic superstition, but also our links with agriculture and the land,
family values and the Irish language. We were therefore, it seemed
clear, ready to take our place among the nations . . . that is among the
partners of Europe, and thus were well adapted for the next stage of
our education.

Now, I regret to say, there is some evidence that things are not as
they appeared. I refer to the publication in *The Irish Times*'s Weekend
section on the last day of the old millennium of the results of a survey
conducted jointly by *The Irish Times* and *Poetry Ireland* of the Top
100 poems by Irish poets of all time. The result must be a source of
dismay to all those who thought we had left behind the foolishness of
the past.

The first thing that strikes you is that most of the list of the favourite poets are rednecks and mucksavages who have neither once

offered an apology for their origins nor made a firm purpose of amendment. At least one of these poets, a Mr Padraic Pearse, who has no less than five entries (with a bullet?) in the Top 100, was a noted revolutionary of distinctly nationalist sentiment. Anyone who had been paying proper attention to the instruction provided by this news-paper would know that Mr Pearse was a bloodthirsty bigot, a mis-guided romantic and a mediocre poet whose deeds and writings are best consigned to the dustbin of history.

Worse still, many of the poems are concerned not with the need for progress, secularism and a stable currency, but with the inedible, and unedifying, scenery of Rural Ireland. One poem, for instance is called "Digging". Another is called "The Lost Heifer". Another is entitled "Spraying the Potatoes". Yet another is called "Blackberry-picking". Many of the poems are littered with references to cattle, larks, berries, trout, clay and suchlike. Have the readers of this news-paper failed to grasp that Rural Ireland has been abolished by Order of the Editor? And where, in the immortal words of Eoghan Harris, are our poems about briquettes?

A full ten per cent of poems are in Irish, the language in which, as readers of An Irishman's Diary will know, we are wont to express our more primitive forms of tribal identity. Several refer in uncritical terms to the Irish struggle for independence, as though the Workers' Party had never existed, still less worked long and hard at the fine art of deep-entryism. Two poems are about mothers, but both present women in stereotyped mould, and only three poems by women make the Top 100. Can this really be a survey of the preferences of *Irish Times* readers? Yes, that's what it says in the blurb. We really must do better.

But the greatest source of concern is the number one poem, "The Lake Isle of Innisfree" by William Butler Yeats. It begins:

> I will arise and go now, and go to Innisfree,
> And a small cabin build there, of clay and wattles made:
> Nine bean-rows will I have there, a hive for the honey-bee,
> And live alone in the bee-loud glade.

To what does this poem amount but a hankering after the same vision as expounded in Mr de Valera's much-criticised "Dream Speech"? In fact, by comparison with the scenario outlined in this first stanza, Mr de Valera's "cosy homesteads" sound positively luxurious. For the poet — and it appears many of the poetry-loving readers of this newspaper — aspires to living a self-sustaining lifestyle in a hut constructed of sticks and mud, with no utilities and no concern for the visual impact on the surrounding landscape. I note also that, in the context of a proposal to build in an area of high amenity value, there is no mention of planning permission. Has Frank McDonald laboured in vain? Should not the Flood Tribunal be made aware of the implications of all this? Moreover, does the poet propose to pay tax? He makes no mention of it.

He goes on, skilfully evading the issue,

> And I shall have some peace there, for peace comes dropping slow,
> Dropping from the veils of the morning to where the cricket sings;
> There midnight's all a glimmer, and noon a purple glow,
> And evening full of the linnet's wings.

Here we observe the familiar stubborn attachment to concerns of a rustic nature, coupled with an unpatriotic desire to avoid participation in the economy. Perhaps the poet is seeking tax reliefs to lure him back to the lathe. I trust the Editor will move quickly to condemn such thinking.

If this list is an accurate reflection of the tastes of *Irish Times* readers, and if the content of these poems has any significance at all, it is clear that most of the work of my colleagues in this newspaper in recent decades has been entirely in vain. It is as if Mary Robinson had never been heard of, as though the *Irish Times* editorials of the past decade and more had been e-mailed into a black hole in the public consciousness, to be accessed or reclaimed only by those who are already enlightened. Dick, Fintan, Nuala, Kevin, Frank, Vincent, Kathy, Conor, Paul, Garret, Medb, Maev, Maeve and Maev-Ann have toiled in vain in their valiant efforts to lure the Irish people out of a pious attachment to sub-modernity, tradition and arable land.

But there may be a more prosaic explanation. I believe that what the Poetry Top 100 illustrates is that most of the alleged readers of this newspaper are not readers at all, but purchase *The Irish Times* purely as an accessory to enable them to move undetected in polite society. It appears that, all this time, those hundreds of thousands of people whom our advertising department zealously, and in good faith, has presented to potential advertisers as "readers" are in fact no such thing.

My solution is radical but simple. All would-be purchasers of *The Irish Times* should henceforth have to undergo a small informal test at the newsagents each morning to ascertain whether they are actually reading the newspaper rather than simply seeking to exploit its cachet so as to fraudulently participate in civilised society. Postmen, with special training, could be empowered to carry out spot-checks on those who get their paper in the post. Failure would result in the mandatory suspension of subscriptions. A month or two of having to carry around the *Irish Independent* would bring persistent transgressors to heel.

(January 2000)